Race,
Gender, and
Health

SAGE SERIES ON
RACE AND ETHNIC RELATIONS

Series Editor:
JOHN H. STANFIELD II
University of California at Davis

This series is designed for scholars working in creative theoretical areas related to race and ethnic relations. The series will publish books and collections of original articles that critically assess and expand upon race and ethnic relations issues from American and comparative points of view.

SERIES EDITORIAL BOARD

Volumes in this series include

Race, Gender, and Health

Marcia Bayne-Smith

Editor

Sage Series on Race and Ethnic Relations

v o l u m e   15

SAGE Publications
International Educational and Professional Publisher
Thousand Oaks   London   New Delhi

For information address:

SAGE Publications, Inc.
2455 Teller Road
Thousand Oaks, California 91320
E-mail: order@sagepub.com

SAGE Publications Ltd.
6 Bonhill Street
London EC2A 4PU
United Kingdom

SAGE Publications India Pvt. Ltd.
M-32 Market
Greater Kailash I
New Delhi 110 048 India

Printed in the United States of America

Library of Congress Cataloging-in-Publication Data

Bayne-Smith, Marcia.
    Race, gender, and health/ Marcia Bayne-Smith.
        p. cm.—(Sage series on race and ethnic relations: v. 15)
    Includes bibliographical references and index.
    ISBN 0-8039-5504-9 (cloth: alk. paper).—ISBN 0-8039-5505-7
(pbk.: alk. paper)
    1. Minority women—Health and hygiene—United States. 2. Minority
women—Medical care—United States. 3. Minority women—United
States—Social conditions. 4. Women—Health and hygiene—United
States—Sociology aspects. I. Title. II. Series.
    RA564.86.B38   1995
    362.1'07'693—dc20   95-35483

96 97 98 99 10 9 8 7 6 5 4 3 2 1

This book is printed on acid-free paper.

Sage Production Editor: Diana E. Axelsen
Sage Typesetter: Danielle Dillahunt

To my sister,
Carlene Anita Bayne:
To your health!

Contents

Series Editor's Introduction

Health issues confronting women of color have rarely been discussed in social science literature in a comprehensive fashion. This volume was commissioned to offer thoughtful reviews and critiques of studies that explore the health status and needs of major populations of women of color in the United States. Under the able editorship and authorship of Marcia Bayne-Smith, this volume is an invaluable resource for scholars, students, and policymakers interested not only in the health issues of particular women of color populations but also in comparative analyses that reveal a number of important similarities women of color experience in health matters because of their racialized gendered oppression in the United States.

John H. Stanfield II
Series Editor

Foreword

This respected group of authors, researchers, and professionals, through an exhaustive bibliographic literature search, have presented in *Race, Gender, and Health* a well-written study of the current physical and mental health status of women of color in the United States. The health concerns of women of color and the disparities in their health status are presented within a rich context of social, cultural, economic, and environmental dimensions. The book provides a comprehensive overview of the health status of minority females in the United States that covers four important minority groups: African American women, Latino women, Asian/Pacific Islander women, and Native American women. It is important to note, however, that the ethnic identity of each group affects the health of these women in different ways and that the health care status of each group must be considered with respect to its global dimensions. Dr. Bayne-Smith and her associates have presented and explained material in a well organized and extensively referenced scholarly work that will serve as an excellent resource tool not only for students but for all health care professionals.

In their discussion of the health care status of Latino women, the authors give background demographics and socioeconomic characteristics of Latinas and describe health concerns within the larger context of health, social needs, and Hispanic/Latino culture.

Asian/Pacific Islander women are discussed by two A/PA women who are well-known and respected for their long-term advocacy work in the A/PA community. The available information on health issues of A/PA women is reviewed with an emphasis on the need for national data on Asian and Pacific Islanders that could enhance our understanding of the diversity among the women in this highly heterogeneous group. One theme that is clearly presented in this chapter is the need to conduct longterm, comparative epideminological studies that will provide information on the effects of acculturation on health behavior and health status outcomes in A/PA communities. The authors explore the issue of domestic violence among immigrant and refugee A/PA families, including the impact of the frustration that A/PA males experience as they attempt to establish themselves in a new country and to find ways to support their families.

In their own traditions, Native American women and Alaskan Native women who were sick were believed to be out of balance and not in harmony with their own cultures. The authors present a persuasive argument that no other ethnic group in the United States has been so profoundly shaped, guided, or misguided by Federal laws and policies. Over the centuries, the factors of poverty, unemployment, and living in single-parent homes have taken their toll on NAW/ANW women, who continue to experience health risks and problems far greater than those of women in the majority culture. According to the authors, the great disparity today in health care per capita expenditures for NAW/AUW women and for research on many of the diseases killing them and their families are related to their lifestyles. Economics, politics, culture, and lifestyle are all presented as factors having a negative impact on the well-being and health of this population.

The disparities and excess morbidity and mortality in the health status of African American women is presented in the context of its relationship to the socioeconomic status of African Americans in the United States today.

The authors of *Race, Gender, and Health* present a thoughtful and provocative discussion on redefining health in the 21st century, including an analysis of health care reform as juxtaposed to social and welfare reform. Strategies for improving the quality of care provided to minority women are detailed. The material presented is carefully and skillfully analyzed, and it makes an excellent reference document. The evidence presented in this text and the magnitude of the problem at hand indicates that now is the time to take action to improve the health status not only of women of color but of society as a whole.

Audrey F. Manley, MD, MPH

Preface

This is a book about the influence of race and gender on the health status of African American, American Indian and Alaska Native, Asian/Pacific Islander American (A/PIA), and Latino women in the United States. In this book, social, political, and economic class are defined within the context of race and gender. Then, the book looks at how these three factors determine, among other things, the environmental conditions of living, the level and quality of education, and the strength of sociocultural norms that govern gender roles, all of which affect health status.

The first chapter deals with the hypothesis that two major societal influences—race and gender—are the primary determinants of the health status of women of color in the United States. The power of race and gender to regulate social class and how this, in turn, affects health status is examined. It is important to recognize that, though dominant, the major effects of race and gender are not alone in creating poor health among women of color. To that end, the first chapter provides the theoretical and conceptual framework that demonstrates how the combined effects of race and gender influence health status among four different groups of non-white women.

A variety of social structural factors at any given moment in time can prevail on the development of social policy. In that regard, the amount of social control present in social policies is inevitably tied to the political and economic mood of the times in which the policy is designed. No less powerful a factor is the influence of culture. Culturally conditioned health beliefs and behaviors are scrutinized, with special attention paid to cultural norms that influence gender roles and health-seeking behavior. With this in mind, social trends related to labor force participation are explored in terms of the connections among work, family structure, health insurance, culture, and women's health. Finally, the Western medical model is evaluated with respect to its ability to meet the needs of people who are culturally different from the mainstream.

The next four chapters are devoted to four different groups of nonwhite women: African American, American Indian and Alaska Native, Asian/Pacific Islander American (A/PIA), and Latino women. In each instance, the chapter deals with the health and mental health status of the specific group of women in question, pointing out the influences of race, gender, class, and culture. The common, strongly reiterated themes of the contributing authors are found in their awareness of two distinct phenomena: (a) The poor health status of women in their group is the result of structural conditions in U.S. society, and (b) the Western medical model of health services delivery has not been effective in meeting the health care needs of women from their racial and ethnic groups.

The major thesis in the opening chapter is that the health status of nonwhite women suffered during this century as a result of the institutionalization of the Western medical model of service delivery, with its inherent qualities of racism and sexism and its insistent, singular focus on the treatment of disease. This is not to say that this model has always served white women well. Women's health as a medical specialty is underresearched, and women in general are underserved. Despite the fact that the major consumers of health care in this country are women, their health status and concerns show that the health care industry has not invested the same resources in their care as it has done for men because it does not view women's health with the same urgency and respect as the health of men. As a result, huge gaps in the medical knowledge base can be attributed to sexism on the part of the major players in the health care industry and to their narrow biomedical approach to health.

By contrast, in the other cultures discussed in this book, health status is given a more complete definition. In the information presented by contributing authors, all of whom are female members of the groups they write about, the objective is to provide the reader with a greater sense of the continuity of life stages and the need for congruity among the many aspects of well-being. Moreover, the presentation of health beliefs and practices of other cultures is intended to create a perspective within which the passages and transitions of the life span are more clearly understood.

The term *health care industry* encompasses the complex conglomerate of commerce and trade that operates under the aegis of the Western medical model of health service delivery. The health industry derives its income from the sale of medical goods, services, and technology prescribed by physicians. This term *health care industry* is not used here in any pejorative sense, nor is it intended to influence the reader's judgment in a negative way. The facts surrounding health care services are simply these: (a) It is the largest service industry in the United States, with more money spent on health care than in all other industrialized democracies, and (b) groups and subgroups have been historically underserved both by this industry and the underlying assumptions that govern the way services are delivered. Despite the fact that the industry has been incrementally transforming itself for the last 15 years, the likelihood exists, given the direction of these changes, that women of color will continue to be underserved.

Consequently, it is argued in the final chapter that the current shift in the shape of U.S. health services toward "managed competition" may serve to contain costs, but cost containment will come at the expense of the health of people of color. Under managed competition, it is expected that fewer health care services will be provided to women of color than in the past. Moreover, the private regulation of American health care continues to be based on the Western medical model, with its narrow definitions of health. In each chapter that follows, the authors provide sorely needed revised definitions of health that acknowledge the contributions of the Western model and build on it. Their definitions emphasize that health is more than just the absence of disease and infirmity and encompasses a state of complete physical and mental well-being. In the United States, the disease/illness dichotomy has yet to be effectively resolved.

It is time for the development of new paradigms that will lead to the delivery of sensitive, culturally appropriate health services, not only for women of color, but for everyone. That is the challenge for students, providers, health care professionals, and health policymakers for years to come.

Acknowledgments

The assembly of information on the various racial and ethnic groups of women discussed herein could not have been undertaken without the dedication of many wonderful people who came together with a single-mindedness of vision. The driving mission for all associated with this work was to contribute in some measure, however modest, to improving the neglected health status of women of color.

I would like to thank John Stanfield II for inviting me to participate in his Sage Series on Race and Ethnic Relations. I am equally thankful to the contributing authors who worked tenaciously on submission and, when necessary, on revision of drafts. Many colleagues facilitated the completion of this project. I must especially thank Dorothy Helly and all the members with whom I had the pleasure of taking the seminar "Balancing the Curriculum for Race and Gender" at Hunter College, City University of New York, during the 1994-95 academic year for their recommendations and suggestions. I also appreciate the input of Walter Stafford, as well as anonymous reviewers throughout the life of the project. I am especially grateful to my students for their encouragement and to my family and friends for their nurturing patience and comforting understanding.

I am especially indebted to Deborah Ann Beete, who served as my research assistant, for her meticulous preparation of charts and tables for this endeavor and for her clerical support during preparation of the manuscript. My sincere appreciation to Linda Poderski for her precise, quality copy-editing skills and to the staff at Sage for their help along the many stages of this project. Finally, I want to acknowledge my colleagues at Queens College for providing a supportive environment in which to work.

1

Health and Women of Color: A Contextual Overview

Marcia Bayne-Smith

I believe that an effort is being made by the medical profession to make sure that care is sensitive to gender. However, I see the gender issue as much less of a problem than the issue of race and class when (white, male) doctors deal with patients who are different than they are. The dramatic increase of women in medical schools, which is an outgrowth of the women's movement, is a beginning attempt to address the issue of gender. There is no current effort to draw the same attention to race and class.

Peter Frank,
Personal communication, April 14, 1995[1]

The health status of women of color in the United States has been determined to a large extent by the powerful abilities of race and gender to define as well as institutionalize who has access to resources, how much and what kind of resources are available to certain groups, and the manner in which those resources are provided. Race- and gender-based restrictions in education, employment, and housing, to name a few, have had deleterious impacts on the quality of life for some segments of the population and on the very chances of survival for others. In the area of health, more than in any other sphere of life, the structural restrictions of race and gender become linked to life and death.

Exploration of the health of women of color must begin with a fundamental question: What is the current health and mental health status of women of color in the United States? With the exception of reproductive issues, that question is difficult to answer for a whole host of reasons, not the least of which is the fact that research on women's health in general has been largely an ignored area (Haug, 1991; Silberner, 1990). Essentially, the only medication women use that has been appropriately researched is the birth control pill, because Congress mandated studies on "the pill."[2] Until recently, research on gender-blind conditions, such as heart disease and cancer, traditionally relied only on men as study participants. Therefore, when women are prescribed highly toxic medications on the basis of research done solely on men, women are, in essence, placed in jeopardy by the medical establishment (Schroeder, 1992).

As a result of strategic, bipartisan political pressure spearheaded by the Congressional Caucus on Women's Issues, the National Institutes of Health (NIH) were encouraged in 1987 to correct this practice of conducting male-only studies, a practice that is unfair to half the citizens of the United States. At that time, NIH instituted a policy whereby funding for research on any health issue that affected both men and women was contingent on the inclusion of women and minorities as study participants. In 1990, a follow-up study of the effectiveness of that policy was conducted by the General Accounting Office (GAO). The disturbing results indicated that NIH had not fully implemented its own policy (Schroeder, 1992, p. 1). Only since 1991 has NIH fully enforced its 1987 policy that requires all grantees to include women and minorities as study participants.

With respect to the question on the health and mental health status of women of color, the most hopeful development to date has been the establishment in 1990 of the Office of Women's Health Research (OWHR) at NIH. That office is also an outgrowth of the efforts of the Congressional Caucus on Women's Issues, cochaired by Representative Patricia Schroeder. OWHR's budget for 1993 was $10.5 million, representing a tenfold increase since 1990. Roughly half of OWHR's budget, about $5.4 million, goes to direct research, and of those research grants currently funded, about 36% or $1.8 million have gone to women researchers.

Even though research on women's health in general has begun to move into the mainstream, there continues to be grossly inadequate information about the health and mental health status of women of color. Despite the progress made by the OWHR, problems remain, particularly in the area of the inclusion of minority women. OWHR designed a multimillion-dollar Women's Health Initiative, which began in 1993 and is being jointly run within ten institutes at NIH. This research will focus on the leading causes of death and disease in postmenopausal women. Research data will be collected at 15 centers around the country that have been selected to participate in the trial. NIH's study design has designated certain centers to recruit minority populations. Dr. Alice Dan, Professor of Women's Studies at the University of Illinois at Chicago, thinks that study populations should be representative of their natural constituency. To accomplish this goal, recruitment of minority women should reflect their percentage in the population where studies are being conducted. Although recruitment of minority women is an issue of concern, it is not the only point at which efforts should be made to ensure that this research includes health issues of women of color.

Dan suggests that if OWHR has serious intentions of including women of color in its study populations, several important steps must be taken. First, OWHR must invite qualified women of color to become principal investigators. Second, OWHR must establish some of the sites for the Women's Health Initiative in communities of color. Third, community residents must be involved in planning the project.[3] As of this writing, OWHR does not appear to be making any great strides on any of these steps. Therefore, at the end of this initiative, the likelihood is great that multimillion-dollar clinical trials on women's health will have taken place and U.S. researchers will still have gaps in their knowledge base about the health issues of women of color.

What is known in the United States about health and mental health issues that affect women of color must be extrapolated, in part, from the fact that the health status of African Americans, American Indians and Alaska Natives, Asian/Pacific Islander Americans, and Latinos, as non-white groups, has been identified as being disproportionately worse than the mainstream in almost every area of measurement. For example, infant mortality, which is widely accepted as a reliable indicator of the health status of any group, serves as a clear illustration of the poor health of racial subgroups. Although the overall infant neonatal and postneonatal mortality rates are declining in the United States, postneonatal mortality rates especially among black and American Indian infants are not improving (see Figure 1.1).

Infant mortality rates for American Indian and Alaska Natives and for Puerto Ricans have been seriously underestimated in the past and therefore are now being monitored more closely by special studies (National Center for Health Statistics [NCHS], 1993). Nevertheless, improvement of minority health status continues to be minimal, at best.

The 21st century will be here in a few short years, by which time the United States government hopes to have achieved its goals to improve the overall health status of the population in general. Within this effort is a

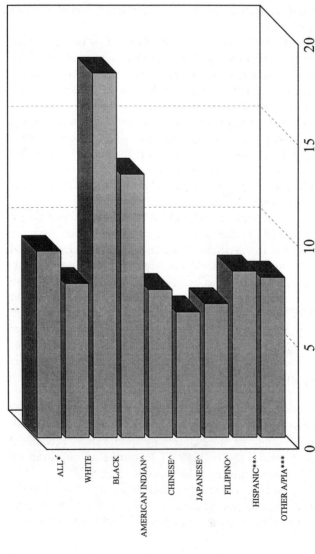

Figure 1.1. Death Among Infants Under 1 Year of Age per 1,000 Live Births, by Race and Ethnicity, 1990

SOURCE: National Center for Health Statistics (1993).

*Includes all races not shown.

**Hispanic persons may be of any race.

***A/PIA refers to Asian/Pacific Islander American persons.

^Data based on 1987.

widely publicized initiative that emphasizes specific goals to correct the racial imbalance of poor health for the subgroups of African Americans, American Indians and Alaska Natives, Asian/Pacific Islander Americans (A/PIAs), and Latinos in particular (National Center for Health Statistics, 1993). Much of this book discusses the current health/mental health status of women from these four racial groups. On the basis of information in succeeding chapters, there is reason to believe that, despite the ongoing efforts outlined above, the health status of these women continues to be negatively influenced by the effects of their race, gender, and the Western medical model of health service delivery employed throughout the United States.

RACE, CLASS, AND HEALTH

The role of race in determining the health status of Americans was made clear 10 years ago when Margaret M. Heckler, then Secretary of the U.S. Department of Health and Human Services, released the now famous *Report of the Secretary's Task Force on Black and Minority Health* (U.S. DHHS, 1985). The summary of that multivolume work, published in 1985, said that the health status for minorities in the United States was disproportionately lower than that of whites. Since that time, an entire body of literature has been produced, both government documents and independent scientific studies, on the race-based differences in health status among the U.S. population (Bayne-Smith & Mason, 1995; Hunter, Freirichs, Webber, & Berenson, 1979; James, 1984; U.S. DHHS, 1991).

This inordinate amount of documentation begs the question, Why is the health of nonwhites so disproportionately worse than that of whites? The more pertinent question appears to be, What is it exactly about race that accounts for health differences (Manton, Patrick, & Johnson, 1987)? Byrd and Clayton (1993) point out that, in response to these questions, some studies analyze health deficits in blacks by employing an approach in which they downplay the importance of race. Others resort to the game of "blame the victim" by claiming that blacks and other minorities experience poor health and premature death because of their pathological behavior. Essentially, the argument used is that minorities choose to smoke, drink alcohol heavily, consume the wrong food, engage in unprotected promiscuous sex, engage in violent behavior, and do not exercise (Melby, Goldflies, Hyner, & Lyle, 1989).[4]

In many ways, this argument is reflective of the history of U.S. health care policy toward minority populations. It is reminiscent of justifications used to defend health care policies that denied health care to blacks during a period of time when racism was sanctioned by law throughout a majority of states in the Union. In the latter part of the 19th century and the early decades of the 20th century, the prevailing sentiment toward blacks among educated whites was that of the Darwinian notion of survival of the fittest. Within that view, the black race was dying out. Therefore, any commitment to medical care for them would be a waste of resources (Jones, 1981, pp. 19-29).

After a hiatus during the 1960s and 1970s, the blame-the-victim argument resurfaced as the primary assumption on which the Reagan/Bush health policies rested (Brown, 1978; Mondragon, 1993). Blame-the-victim policies assume that individuals alone can control their health destiny without consideration of their economic capacity to do so or the availability and accessibility of health services. Moreover, the same conservative administrations that espoused "do-it-yourself health care" also lent their full political support to the alcohol and tobacco industries, whose corporate budgets for advertising are exceeded only by their budgets for lobbying. These industries target blacks and other people of color to be recipients of sophisticated, sometimes subliminal but always malevolent, advertising campaigns. These industries then camouflage the damage they do to the health of people of color with limited programs of giving that in no way strike a balance between the profits from sales in communities of color and healthy community improvement projects. The chicanery of those corporations, of conservative administrations, and of the legislation and policies they enact in support of those corporations is surpassed only by the major black publications that carry these advertisements and by the fact that very few leaders and health professionals in communities of color have organized any form of opposition to these industries (Thomas, 1992, p. 341).

Any serious attempt to answer the questions of how and why such disproportionate race-based health differences exist must begin with an examination of the stratification system at work in U.S. society. Adequate documentation exists that, in the United States, stratification and inequality are essentially inequality by race and ethnic origin, and these racial divisions often have, to a large degree, economic class divisions at their

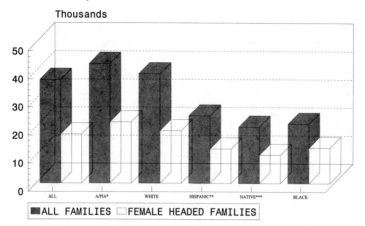

Figure 1.2. Median Family Income in Dollars, by Race and Hispanic Origin, 1992: For All Families Within Selected Population Groups and for Female-Headed Households, No Husband Present, Within the Same Selected Groups

SOURCE: U.S. Bureau of the Census (1994).
*Asian/Pacific Islander American.
**Persons of Hispanic origin may be of any race.

base (Hacker, 1992; Inhaber & Carroll, 1992, p. 111; Kerbo, 1991). Income data from the census of 1990 indicate a huge gap between the white and nonwhite populations in terms of income from both earnings (wages, salaries) and wealth (e.g., real estate, investment payments, trust funds, bonds, corporate stocks). Tax laws in the United States favor the wealthy and very wealthy by providing sufficient loopholes in the tax code that allow large amounts of income to be sheltered from taxes or not reported outright. Separate from tax laws are immigration laws that favor the entry of people who are able to bring in $1 million or more and who are willing to invest those large sums of money in U.S. businesses. This favoritism means that any assessment of the distribution of wealth is likely to be inaccurate. Figure 1.2 is a comparison of median family income for blacks, American Indian and Alaska Natives, Asian/Pacific Islander Americans (A/PIAs), Hispanics, and whites, and median family income for female householders, no husband present, for the same five population groups.

The figure indicates that although the median family income for A/PIAs was approximately $3,500 higher than for whites in 1992, both of those groups are at the high end of income distribution; Native Americans and blacks are at the low end, with less than $700.00 difference in their median incomes. As expected, female-headed households with no husband present fared much worse across the board for all women, regardless of race or ethnicity. Here again, A/PIA and white female householders had greater income than black, Hispanic, and Native American female householders. And A/PIA female householders, just as A/PIA families, earned more (approximately $2,500) than white female householders.

The slightly higher earnings of the A/PIA population requires some clarification. Prior to 1990, the self-petitioning provision of U.S. immigration law required the self-petitioner to prove to the U.S. embassy in his or her country the legal possession of $25,000 that would be used to establish a business on entry into the United States. In the mid-1980s, the $25,000 requirement was increased to $1 million and was then written into the 1990 Immigration Reform Act. The $1 million requirement for self-petitioners is an attempt on the part of the United States to pull in millionaires from around the world, especially from Hong Kong. Around 1990, concern was raised in worldwide economic circles about the approaching 1999 deadline when Hong Kong is scheduled to revert to mainland China. The concern focused on China's plans for Hong Kong. Especially worrisome was the possibility that China would nationalize the many independent business operations in Hong Kong that were part of the global economy. Wealthy Asian businesses began to establish operations in other countries, such as Argentina and Australia. Through new self-petitioner requirements, the United States attracted and facilitated the entry of wealthy Asians and their investments in U.S. real estate and other business ventures.

In addition to the entry of a millionaire class, A/PIA income is slightly higher because Asian immigrants have included those who are college bound, middle class, and from the professional classes, as well as those who come from an entrepreneurial base. Census data indicate that 37% of A/PIAs hold bachelor's degrees or higher, and they have the highest representation among nonwhites in the managerial, professional, technical, and administrative occupations; 31% are in managerial and professional specialty occupations; and 33% are in the technical, sales, and administrative support strata of the workforce. Furthermore, professionals and entrepreneurs have been willing to come into the United States, work at the bottom of some segment of the economy, such as green grocers, for as much as 10 years or more, and then plunge off into their own businesses, usually with an increase in their income.

The uneven distribution of economic resources along racial lines is even more boldly demonstrated when the focus shifts from income to poverty. Figure 1.3 provides a comparative distribution of poverty rates by race. The highest rates of poverty are clearly concentrated among Native American peoples and blacks, although Hispanics, too, have highter rates of poverty than whites.

Whatever theories of stratification one chooses to employ—functional, power conflict, or otherwise—it must be recognized that, in any money-driven economy, the people on the bottom of the stratification hierarchy will experience some level of material deprivation. The unequal distribution of income from earnings and wealth creates inequality of access to everything, from basic necessities such as food and shelter to life-sustaining resources such as education and health care. For example, McBarnette (n.d.) states that health care financing in the United States has traditionally been based on retail sales of private insurance; such a basis is unfair because it benefits primarily whites, who are more likely to be upper and middle income. Therefore, far too many nonwhites are financially incapable of purchasing health insurance privately out-of-pocket or of obtaining it as part of a job-related benefits package because of employment in low-paying jobs in small corporations. Census data support McBarnette's claim (see Figure 1.4) that 78.7% of whites are covered by private insurance, compared with only 54% of blacks and 51% of Hispanics.

Although Hispanics and blacks are seen as 3 to 4 times more likely to use government insurance than whites, it is disturbing that almost one third (29%) of Hispanics in the United States have neither private nor government insurance of any kind. The Indian Health Service is estimated to provide health care services for approximately 68% of the Native population, but there is no accurate information about how many of the remaining 32% of Native Americans have private health insurance or are simply uninsured. In effect, by relegating large numbers of those who are nonwhite to the bottom of the socioeconomic hierarchy, where access to health insurance and therefore health care is diminished, race is a major contributing factor to their poverty and to the negative health status of minority groups.

Systems theory provides a useful framework for studying the effects of material deprivation on people of color because it brings their lives, including their health status, into focus. From a systems perspective, stratification by race and the deprivations that result are seen to limit the capacity of nonwhites to function not only within the economic structure but also within the remaining structures and institutions of the society. Given the

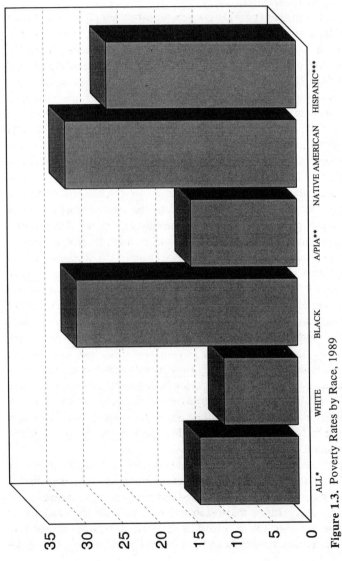

Figure 1.3. Poverty Rates by Race, 1989

SOURCE: U.S. Bureau of the Census (1993).

*Includes all races.

**A/PIA refers to Asian/Pacific Islander Americans.

***Hispanic persons may be of any race.

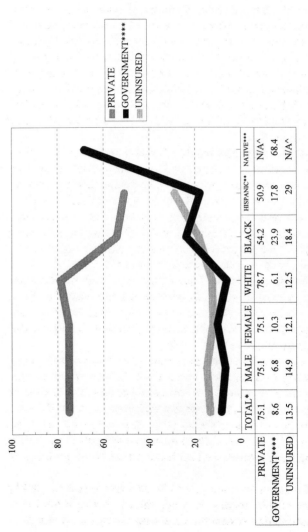

Figure 1.4. Status of Health Insurance Coverage, by Sex and Race, 1991

	TOTAL*	MALE	FEMALE	WHITE	BLACK	HISPANIC**	NATIVE***
PRIVATE	75.1	75.1	75.1	78.7	54.2	50.9	N/A^
GOVERNMENT****	8.6	6.8	10.3	6.1	23.9	17.8	68.4
UNINSURED	13.5	14.9	12.1	12.5	18.4	29	N/A^

PRIVATE

GOVERNMENT****

UNINSURED

SOURCES: U.S. Bureau of the Census (1993); U.S. Indian Health Service (1993)
*Includes other races not shown separately.

**Persons of Hispanic origin may be of any race.

***NATIVE refers to Native American-American Indian and Alaska Native persons.

****Government health insurance includes Medicare, Medicaid, military plans, and the U.S. Indian Health Service.

^ Reliable data unavailable.

historical ability of independently wealthy individuals to influence the political climate and national agenda, it appears unequivocal that economic power determines political power in U.S. society. When race contributes to a lack of economic power for people of color, it also renders them politically impotent and, therefore, doubly incapable of securing access to resources either through their own economic resources or through the political process.

The health status of people of color, therefore, provides a good illustration of how systemic deprivations are played out. Economic power and political power are crucial components of a person's ability to secure quality health care in the United States for several reasons. First, gaining access to high-quality health care is expensive because it is the most lucrative service industry in the United States. In her international study, Graig (1993, p. 16) reported that health care expenditures in the United States were in excess of $800 billion in 1992 and were projected to pass the $1 trillion mark in 1994.

Second, because the health care industry is such a profitable institution, the entire system is extremely politicized. Given the already established connection between economics and politics, no health facility, however small, whether in the most remote rural area or in a completely economically depressed and abandoned inner-city neighborhood, is ever established without intense and interminable political maneuvering among elected officials, health policymakers, community leaders, and the many interested parties to what can become a deep pocket of revenue.

Third, when health care services are being developed for the poor, rarely are the very people who will become the consumers of these services ever present at those planning sessions or at high-level negotiations. They usually do not possess the political or economic wherewithal that would gain them entrée to those circles.

Fourth, only occasionally do the poor manage to become sufficiently organized politically to make their presence felt. Without the economic power of the mainstream, groups that are nonwhite and middle class or poor have to mobilize their members so that their strength in numbers can force elected officials to seriously consider or feel compelled to respect and respond to their health needs. These economic and political inequalities compound on various levels the health and mental health problems of people of color.

The problem for people of color in the United States is complicated by the very structure of U.S. society, in which there is both a centrality of money and a stratification system driven essentially by race and money.

Inequality, however, cannot be envisioned solely in terms of income level and what that income can purchase. That view is too narrow. Negative health status does not involve only deprivations created by lack of income. Distribution of income itself is based on race. The lack of income for nonwhite people creates a more damaging and dangerous deprivation of other valuable resources and commodities. For example, studies have shown a link between political power and improved health status in black communities (Dye & Renick, 1981; LaViest, 1992). Another study, in which level of education was used as a measure of social class, confirmed that health status tends to be better for the more educated (Auster, Leveson, & Sarachek, 1972; see also Knapp & Knapp, 1972). In fact, the inadequate education available in most poor communities is probably the cruelest of all deprivations visited on people of color.

In the United States, education, even medical education, is largely supported by public dollars. But the beneficiaries are primarily those from the upper and, to a lesser degree, middle class. Not only do upper-class people attend the best schools in the country, but it is also at these schools that the transfer occurs, from one generation to the next, of elite positions in corporations, corporate wealth, and upper-class consciousness and cohesion (Useem & Miller, 1977). This situation is clearly unjust because it gives the upper classes control of the nation's resources. There is very little opportunity to address this problem and to actively recruit capable and competent members of the poor and working classes into medical schools because of a long-standing unwillingness in the United States to address issues of class. And so this system of unequal benefits continues to accrue to the upper, and somewhat to the middle, classes while many Americans hypocritically insist in public that there are no class divisions in the United States, that all are equal, and that the playing field is level. Privately, when members of the more privileged classes invite the poor and nonwhite into their circles, the question the latter sometimes ask is, "But can you get here from there?"[5]

Deprivations of political power and effective education are costly to any group, but it can be argued that the most destructive and egregious form of deprivation is a lack of group respect. Within a systems theory perspective, the groups that suffer profound economic and political deprivation in U.S. society must also experience serious difficulties in other domains of the social structure. The most obvious sphere is social. In a system of stratification by race, people of color face the more insidiously uneven distribution of such vital social resources as positive valuation, which leads to high self-confidence and self-esteem. So effective are social systems in the practice of negentropy that a more surreptitious consensus is also at work among everyone in the system, including those who suffer as a result of this agreement. Within that consensus, it is acceptable to unevenly distribute—on the basis of socioeconomic status, ergo race—the most valued of social resources: group respect (Miller, 1993).

Is there ever any question, in the periodic media coverage (usually during local, state, and national elections) about welfare reform, government programs and entitlements, crime, joblessness, and so forth, that the people being discussed are black or Hispanic? Within that thinking and without consideration of class differences or the many intervening and confounding variables that exist for various subpopulations of any racial group, a universal accord has been reached in U.S. society that, currently, Asians as a group are the model minority of choice, whereas a black male college professor continues to have difficulty getting a taxicab in New York City.[6] When any racial or ethnic minority group is deprived by the dominant culture of economic, political, or social resources such as respect and positive images, self-worth, and value, it becomes extremely difficult for the members of that group to function optimally in a social system, especially one as highly competitive as in the United States.

A more cogent argument must be made, therefore, regarding negative health behaviors and lifestyles, individual responsibility, and negative health status among members of the minority population. Any health-related "nihilistic" behavior is, in many respects, a response to the recalcitrant racism in the United States that often subjects the members of racial minorities to a "lived experience of coping with a life of horrifying meaninglessness, hopelessness and most important, lovelessness" (West, 1993, p. 14).[7] The history of persistent racism in the United States has bequeathed to the majority of people of color a legacy of intangible kinds of poverty conditions, such as feelings of powerlessness and ineffectiveness.

When these intangibles are combined with the more obvious conditions of poverty, such as poor housing, inadequate education, poor health, unemployment, and minimal opportunity, they render the lives of many people of color aimless and trivialized in a high-tech, market-driven society. Economic and political influences not only are inseparable but also are requisites for success and access to resources. In that vein, mainstream people have engaged in the intergenerational transfer of wealth, influence, and social status, which results in access to resources. As a result of race, people of color have been handing down to subsequent generations the genetic code for skin color and, by virtue of that skin color, an inheritance of poverty and many other effects of race, including the kinds of tangible and intangible deprivations that are part of the societal response to race in America. The connection between race and poverty is by no means unique to the United States. It is a global condition. World systems theory describes most European nations, in terms of the ordinal international stratification of nations within the world economic system, as *core* (upper-class) countries or, at the very least, *semi-core* (middle-class) countries (Borg, 1992). The vast majority of nonwhite nations, however, are poor and so have been relegated to low-class positions referred to as *periphery* or *semi-periphery*. According to world systems theory, a nation's position is related to the occupational hierarchies indigenous to it within the world economy (Borg, 1992, p. 277; Wallerstein, 1989). In this regard, the nonwhite nations of the world, with few exceptions, have had lengthy histories of dependent economic relationships, first with European colonizer nations and, in more recent history, with the United States, in a greater degree than to any other industrialized nation.

The connection between poverty and negative health status is also not new. Research has consistently shown that health status is unquestionably correlated with socioeconomic status (Navarro, 1991; Wallace, 1990); this correlation has been well established not only in the United States (Aday, 1993; Fein, 1986) but in other countries as well. In a paper on poverty and poor health in Britain, it was shown that the spores released from fungi growing on the damp, poorly ventilated walls of London slum housing settled on the chests of children and adults and led to respiratory infections and other disease (Townsend, 1991). In Australia, the risks of coronary heart disease have been shown to be inversely related to social status (Sawyer, Coonan, Worsley, & Leitch, 1980). What is different and new, and therefore must be addressed head-on, is the connection between race and negative health status that exists in the United States.

Race in the United States accounts for health differences because race is a pervasive issue that affects every area of life. For example, it would seem that the better one's health insurance coverage, the greater one's access to quality health care. That logic has not always been applicable. A study conducted at Queens College, City University of New York (CUNY), determined that, for the first time, black income surpassed white income in the middle-class borough of Queens in New York City, especially among foreign-born blacks. The study indicated that, despite the gains in black income, racial segregation endures, with race being a greater barrier to integration than class. This study, based on 1990 census data, also found that, when controlling for income, poor blacks and rich blacks in New York City are segregated from whites at about the same level. In other words, class made no difference for blacks because, among households with family incomes of $100,000 or more, 9 of 10 blacks continue to live in segregated communities. It appears, then, that race alone is responsible for continued segregation (Beveridge & D'Amico, 1994).

The CUNY study is significant to this discussion in that the health care industry is not different from any other institutions or structures in U.S. society in terms of their reaction to race. As a result, most inner-city nonwhite communities, irrespective of the income level of the community, tend to qualify as federal- and state-designated, medically underserved, and health manpower shortage areas because most doctors do not want to establish practices in those neighborhoods. Here again, race, by contributing to segregated communities, contributes to the lack of health care services in socially invisible communities of color, even when they are middle class.

The CUNY study also brings to mind a serious debate heard with increasing frequency in black intellectual and policy circles, as well as whenever black folk come together and ponder the plight of how best to help those blacks who have been left behind. That debate centers around the fact that, for many blacks, integration, a major quest of the civil rights movement, is no longer a goal. In fact, many questions exist about the extent to which blacks have been hurt by the instrumental goal of integration. As a black middle class emerged, they were encouraged whenever possible, under what is now viewed as the "old" thinking, to move to integrated neighborhoods. Such a move is now perceived as creating a perilous deprivation, to the younger and/or less fortunate blacks in their community, of the motivating influence of someone familiar and well-known and therefore capable of providing a discernible blueprint that others could follow to achieve success.

An even more pernicious problem exists with the goal of "integration" in many parts of the country. The noxious reality that has become clear since the 1960s, to at least two generations of blacks, is that when middle-class blacks move into an "integrated" community, white flight quickly occurs and the "integrated" community rapidly become a community of color. In response, many middle-class blacks, especially in New York City, no longer opt for integrated housing. When their economic situation allows, they make a conscious and deliberate choice to move into middle-class communities of color.

Race provides the connecting thread to the negative health status of the four groups of women discussed in this book. Whether these women are poor or middle class, the unavailability of health services to them appears connected to race. Poor nonwhite women do not have access to health care because of a lack of money. Middle-class women of color also do not have access to health care because they live in segregated communities where there is a lack of services. Of course, middle-class women of color are more likely to gain access to decent health care outside their communities if they have health insurance. The problems for poor women of color are clearly worse. Government programs such as Medicaid, Medicare, and the Indian Health Service, available to the indigent, have not always translated into access to sensitive and appropriate health care (Graham, 1989).

This common unifying theme of race and its ripple effect on economic, political, social, and cultural conditions of people of color influence the health status of the women described in the following chapters. The negative effects of race not withstanding, each author includes optimistic themes of future programs, expectations of positive outcomes that can result from ongoing changes in health care delivery in the United States, and evidence of small, incremental improvements in the health of the women of their group.

A BRIEF HISTORY OF
HEALTH CARE SERVICES
FOR WOMEN OF COLOR

In addition to race, gender has played a significant role in determining a person's position in U.S. society and, by extension, a person's health status. Women's health problems have been linked for centuries almost exclusively to their function as bearers of children, so to talk about a historical perspective of health care services for women of color is to talk about their childbearing experiences. As Beardsley (1990) explains, however, the fertility of black women placed them at a disadvantage insofar as it was used in the early part of this century to deny them better maternal and obstetrical care. If care were provided, it had been argued, black fertility would eventually outbreed the "superior" race. In other words, the fertility of black women that was welcomed during slavery was now, in the context of their freedom, viewed as a threat. From the 17th to the 19th centuries, slaveholders used women slaves as breeders; these women were encouraged to have frequent births in much the same way as with livestock (White, 1987). Women slaves gave birth to their children, assisted by midwives who were themselves slaves and whose skill at midwifery was relied on by both black and white women (Holmes, 1986). In the 18th century, birth practices changed for upper-class white women as male physicians started to attend births. In fact, so complete was the advance and impact of the Western medical model on upper-class white women that, by the end of the 19th century, doctors had successfully campaigned against the practice of midwifery on the grounds that pregnancy was a disease and demanded the care of a doctor (Ehrenreich & English, 1973, p. 21). By the 1920s, childbirth for middle- and upper-class white women moved increasingly from the home into hospitals (Bogdan, 1990). On the contrary, throughout most of the 19th century, women of color delivered their babies in or near their homes with help from midwives, family, and friends. Black women gave birth in their slave quarters, attended by midwives. For some American Indian women, childbirth took place in an isolated shelter area where they were assisted by their mothers, mothers-in-law, and midwives (Axtell, 1981, pp. 28-29).

For the first half of the 20th century, women of color continued to deliver their babies at home, attended by midwives. Although it is believed that many women of color wanted to maintain this traditional way of childbirth, it is also known that the majority of them could not afford the services of an obstetrician. The spiritual comfort, cultural ceremonies, and good intentions of the midwife notwithstanding, they simply could not avail themselves of technological backup when needed to handle problematic births. A 1920s Texas survey of black and Mexican American women who used midwives or *parteras* found that many of the new mothers were concerned about the level of skills of their midwives, in the event of problem deliveries (Litoff, 1986). Economics and tradition aside, for those women of color in the early part of this century who wanted or needed better technology because of a high-risk pregnancy or birth, the overt racism of that day would not have allowed them into a hospital. Suffice it to say, then, that prenatal and obstetrical care for women of color who wanted or needed these services was unavailable because of racism.

It has been documented by researchers and historians that neglect based on racism accounted for the disproportionate deaths of women of color, compared with white women, during the early decades of this century (Beardsley, 1987; Bousfield, 1934). After the scientific methods of the Western medical model had been institutionalized, many diseases were brought under control. Beardsley indicates that, between 1900 and 1940, black women continued to die from tuberculosis (TB), diabetes, cardiovascular disease, renal disease, and cancer in numbers that were 4 to 5 times higher than for white women. Moreover, the level of neglect and lack of medical care is best evidenced by the fact that, as late as 1940, "unknown causes" ranked as the leading cause of death, ahead of cancer, among black women, particularly in the South (Beardsley, 1987, pp. 522-523; 1990, pp. 124-125).

The Great Depression of the 1930s, for all its intense hardships, ushered in New Deal legislation such as Social Security and Maternal and Infant Care Services, later known as Maternal-Child Health Services. These programs provided the framework at the federal level for subsequent legislation such Medicare and Medicaid. Maternal-Child Health Services, initially segregated, finally made health care services available to women of color (Beardsley, 1990, pp. 134-135). As a result of civil rights legislation in the 1950s and 1960s, hospitals and other health services were then integrated. However, legislation could not and did not eliminate the racism that leads to poverty, hunger (Kotz, 1969), toxic environments, poor housing, unemployment, lack of health insurance, and all the many other contributing factors to poor health for women of color.

WORK, WELFARE, AND THE HEALTH OF WOMEN OF COLOR

Several sociohistorical events occurred between 1960 and 1990 that, when taken together, can be seen to affect the health status of women of color. As the civil rights and feminist movements gained momentum, in the 1950s and 1960s, respectively, they were accompanied by changes in the U.S. social structure. As Howard (1992) explains, African American families that emerged from the Great Depression and World War II sufficiently developed and economically strong were ready to take advantage of the new and increased opportunities and to obtain job training, higher education, access to white-collar jobs, and increased upward mobility, creating, in effect, a small but solid nonwhite middle class. The interesting phenomenon is that, for the majority of people of color unable to capitalize on the civil rights movement, the reverse happened: Their socioeconomic position actually worsened. Part of the problem here for people of color in the United States may be that the civil rights movement was not inclusive. Unquestionably, it opened the door for minorities to make social, political, and economic advancement, but it was exclusionary in that the focus of the movement was primarily on the problems of blacks, without consideration for the similar problems faced, for example, by Native Americans and other disenfranchised groups. Imagine the power of a civil rights movement designed to rectify injustice and deprivation suffered by all who are marginalized.

Nevertheless, research indicates that immediately following the 1964 civil rights legislation a noticeable increase occurred, as early as 1965, in joblessness among low-skilled black males (Wilson, 1987). Analogous to the problem of black males was an equally dramatic social force that began in the mid-1960s and involved the entry of large numbers of white women into the workforce. A suspicion raised by this phenomenon is whether the success of the feminist movement and the progress of white women in the workplace came at the expense of men and women of color in that a redistribution of income has occurred from people of color to white women, thus consolidating income earnings and wealth among upper- and middle-class whites. Ehrenreich (1995), in arguing for affirmative action, appears to confirm this suspicion by indicating that, in terms of numbers, white women benefit most from affirmative action, and because they usually marry white men, it stands to reason that white men, in terms of numbers, also benefit substantially.

Prior to the onset of the feminist movement, large numbers of black women had always worked; however, they have not made the same progress in the workplace as white women. It is therefore not far-fetched to appreciate, following Ehrenreich's argument, that the occupational hierarchy of corporate America, which is almost exclusively white and male, could consciously and deliberately hold back the progress of competent women of color not only to make way for white women but also as an expression of the same racial discrimination directed at men of color. This vitriolic refusal of U.S. society to confront enduring racism in the workplace and in other areas of society rendered the feminist movement insignificant for many women of color (Giddings, 1984).

At the time these changes were occurring in the United States as a result of the civil rights and feminist movements, the Hart-Cellar Immigration Act of 1965 became law. It superseded the conservative 1952 McCarren-Walter Immigration Act, which gave preference to immigrants from European countries on the basis of assimilability—that is, the assumed easier integration of persons from countries with historical, racial, and cultural ties to the United States (Bryce-Laporte, 1977, 1979; Department of City Planning, New York City, 1992). In contrast to the earlier McCarren-Walter Act, as Figure 1.5 shows, the Hart-Cellar Act served to balance the previous immigrant flow from predominantly European countries that

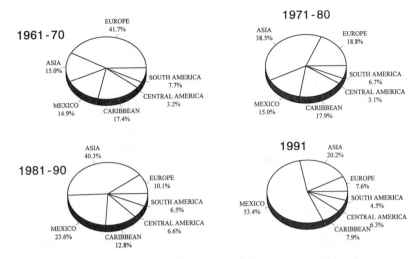

Figure 1.5. Immigration to the United States From Selected Regions, 1960-1991

SOURCE: U.S. Bureau of the Census (1993).

occurred prior to 1965. In effect, Hart-Cellar allowed for a dramatic increase in immigrants primarily from Asia, the Caribbean, and Latin America.

In the decades following Hart-Cellar, from 1970 to 1990, the surge in immigrants of color from nonwhite regions was so drastic that, according to U.S. census data, by 1990 only 10% of immigrants to the United States came from Europe and by 1991 the percentage of European immigrants had fallen to 7%. These percentages might be modified if there was a way to take into account the numbers of illegal immigrants from European nations such as Ireland and Italy in the urban underground economies of large metropolitan areas such as Boston and New York City.

Large numbers of Asians, Hispanic/Latinos, and people of African ancestry initially moved into the urban areas of the United States. These new immigrants, however, had been preceded by another migration of people of color. At first, they came in large numbers, but by the late 1960 and 1970s, a slower, less numerous migration of Southern blacks to the Northern metropolitan areas persisted. They, too, were in search of better job opportunities in the Northern cities. The migrants and immigrants of color who flocked to the Northern and coastal urban, metropolitan areas came seeking low-skilled manufacturing/factory jobs that had been available to minorities in the 1950s and early 1960s. At the time this mass movement was occurring, the United States had already begun its transformation from a primary reliance on manufacturing to an information and service economy. Research has demonstrated that this shift in economic activity was taking place at the same time as a transfer in location of the new activities (Wilson, 1987, pp. 100-103). This meant that although low-skilled manufacturing jobs began to decrease, a parallel increase was taking place in the flow of foreign and native-born, nonwhite, low-skilled laborers into the inner city. Accompanying those two events was a concurrent white flight from the inner city to the suburbs, where some of the low-skilled jobs had also moved as part of the planned relocation and refocus of many large corporations. Those plans included a move by multinational corporations of their manufacturing base out of the United States and away from unionized labor to developing nations where the multinationals were assured of a wider profit margin because of the availability of a cheap source of labor.

The structural transition that began in the U.S. economy after World War II was complete by the mid-1970s. A major consequence has been a profound reconfiguration of occupational and class divisions by race and gender among the U.S. population. As low-skilled manufacturing and factory jobs disappeared from the newly restructured economy, clerical and low-authority white- and blue-collar positions opened up. These positions, however, required new skills that demanded, at the very least, a higher than average level of literacy or, in many instances, a minimal level of computer literacy that dictated the need for formal training beyond high school. The civil rights and feminist movements served as a launching pad for white women and a small number of people of color to acquire formal education beyond high school. In fact, higher education for men of color increased from the mid-1960s. When the opportunities came, qualified white and black women often moved into the positions of lower authority in the new economy.[8] It was easier to make opportunities available to women of color because they were viewed as less threatening than men of color (Sokoloff, 1992).

The casualties of this entire confluence of social forces, U.S. economic policies, changing immigration laws, and historical events have been disproportionately affecting people of color. At this writing, corporate downsizing and a sputtering U.S. economy have yielded a loss of white- and blue-collar jobs for all races during the early 1990s. Nevertheless, as Figure 1.6 shows, the 1992 unemployment rates for male and female blacks, Mexicans, and Puerto Ricans were almost twice as high for whites for

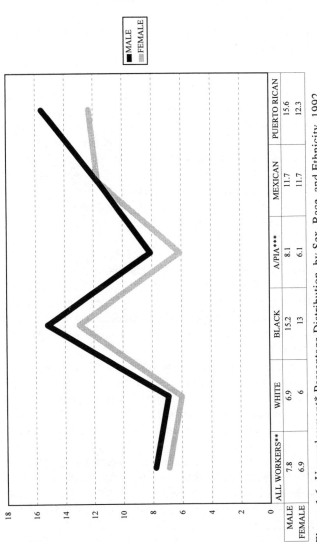

	ALL WORKERS**	WHITE	BLACK	A/PIA***	MEXICAN	PUERTO RICAN
MALE	7.8	6.9	15.2	8.1	11.7	15.6
FEMALE	6.9	6	13	6.1	11.7	12.3

■ MALE
▨ FEMALE

Figure 1.6. Unemployment* Percentage Distribution, by Sex, Race, and Ethnicity, 1992

SOURCE: U.S. Bureau of the Census (1992, 1993).

NOTE: Unemployment data on Native Americans are reported at 30% overall but do not include breakdowns for male and female.

* For population 16 years and older.

** Includes other races not separately shown.

*** A/PIA refers to Asian/Pacific Islander Americans and data from March 1991.

both sexes; there is no reason to suspect that will change in the foreseeable future.

The immobilization of millions of people at the bottom of U.S. society affects all citizens occasionally through crime and theft. The full brunt of the problems faced by poor people of color, however, is borne by the negative health and mental health status of women of color who function as keepers of families.

One of the more difficult health and mental health issues for women of color surrounds gender politics and family formation. In a 1987 study, it was demonstrated that the combined forces of high rates of joblessness, mortality, and incarceration among black men create "a shrunken pool of marriageable black males," and thereby a rise in female-headed homes (Wilson, 1987, p. 57). Although that study focused only on blacks at the time, the problems it addressed, such as the rise in the rates of out-of-wedlock births, female-headed households, and the level of poverty, are now clearly problems for various groups of nonwhite peoples. Figure 1.7 indicates that out-of-wedlock births, concentrated among women of color in the United States, are highest for the four groups of American women addressed in the following chapters: blacks, American Indians and Alaska Natives, Puerto Ricans as a subgroup of Latinos, and Hawaiians as a subgroup of Asian/Pacific Islanders.

These are the same four groups of people of color identified by the U.S. government as early as 1985 as minority groups whose health status was disproportionately worse than those of whites (NCHS, 1993; U.S. DHHS, 1985). In the four chapters that follow, it will be demonstrated that the economic, social, political, emotional, and environmental problems found in many communities of color are not divorced from the negative health and mental health status of women of color.

As the dominant culture—through structural economic changes, patriarchy, racism, sexism, and social and political disrespect—has treated the lives and efforts of men and women of color as meaningless, there has been a deleterious impact on the health status of all people of color. The hue and cry over out-of-wedlock births among women of color, then, seems hypocritical. In fact, the suspicion in some quarters is that the rise in births to women of color constitutes the fundamental concern for the dominant culture. The rising birthrate is seen as even more disturbing because of the realization that the white male elites from advanced capitalist nations held one third of the world (710 million human beings) under colonial rule prior to World War II but no longer do so (Stafford, in press).

Some developed nations have made deliberate choices not to focus on illegitimacy because, in many respects, this is an irrelevant concern. The

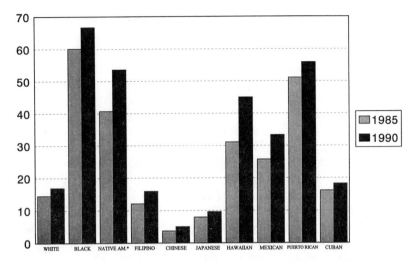

Figure 1.7. Out-of-Wedlock Live Births, by Race and Ethnicity, 1985 and 1990
SOURCE: U.S. Bureau of the Census (1993).

British, for example, chose to focus instead on health care services and social supports for female-headed families (Graig, 1993). The wisdom of that approach for the United States lies in the fact that U.S. social policy has contributed to keeping families apart. Those policies force mothers, much more frequently than not, to take on the full responsibility of caring for their families; and when they cannot, grandmothers have increasingly been called on to assume the duties of child rearing. Clearly, then, social policy must be designed to provide women as keepers of families the supports necessary to carry out those tasks.[9]

A larger issue, then, is the insistence by the mainstream culture that women of color conform to what the dominant group has defined as proper or appropriate types of partnerships for the creation of family and child-rearing structures. Women of color are very aware of the hard-won right to control reproduction. But as Bennet (1987) explains, despite the stress of pressure from mainstream society where marriage is considered the proper partnership, many black women are cognizant that marriage is not a realistic option for them. It has been estimated that 30% to 40% of black and Latino males are in jail or otherwise involved with the criminal justice system (e.g., on parole/probation), another 20% prefer same-sex relationships, and another 20% date outside their race, leaving only 20% of black

and Latino males available. Faced with a small pool of available men for
one-on-one relationships, some women choose to exercise what Hacker
(1992, p. 70) refers to as their personal "right to reproduce."

In fairness to so many women of color who are raising children without
a partner, it is important to mention here that although out-of-wedlock
births add to the number of mother-only homes, not all of them must be
viewed as depleting U.S. coffers. The number of women of color who head
self-sufficient families is small, however; they are estimated to be only
15% of the mother-only families of color. In his research on single
mothers, Hacker (1992) pointed out that, among black and Latino single
mothers, somewhat more than half, or about 55%, were receiving Aid to
Families with Dependent Children (AFDC) in 1990.

Out-of-wedlock births constitute the more serious health and mental
health problems for women of color—in some instances, for several
generations—in terms of teen pregnancy. It is estimated that half of all
teenage girls between the ages of 15 and 19 in the United States have
engaged in sexual intercourse at least once. By age 19, three quarters of
unmarried teenage girls are sexually active. Approximately 1 million girls
under age 20 become pregnant each year in the United States, and about
half of them give birth. Almost 60% of families who receive AFDC are
headed by women who were teens when they had their first child (National
Commission on Children, 1992, p. 224).

Some points of clarification must be made, lest the wrong impression
be given. First, the concern here is not with marriage for every young
woman of color, pregnant or not, as an end goal in and of itself. The major
concern must be about opportunities for teenage girls and women of color,
in a society that practices gendered racism, for personal growth and
development. The whole point of the 1994 Population Conference in
Cairo, Egypt, was that when societies empower women by providing
effective education, job training, and career advancement opportunities,
women will opt to postpone childbearing, have fewer children, and seek
to achieve financial independence (Shepard, 1994).

Second, teenagers are not having babies as a result of parthenogenesis
or cloning. In fact, many girls under age 16 become pregnant by men older
than 25. Health policymakers, legislators, and the clergy, who are overwhelmingly male, have not exhibited the same level of concern over adult
male abusive behavior toward young girls as they have over the pregnancies of teenage girls. This stance is immoral on their part, especially
because long-term negative health and mental health effects as a result of
out-of-wedlock births influence not only women of color but their children as well. Without income support from a partner and without social

support from a strong family, the teen mother of color usually forfeits her own growth and development, has difficulty with stability in child rearing, and she and her children are, with rare exception, in for very tough treatment from society. This is the same society that insists on penalizing only women and their children for an act they do not perform alone but, more often that not, perform with men who are older, should know better, and, in any event, should be held accountable.

Although some teen mothers and their children have gone on to be successful, research indicates that unwed teenage mothers and their children in the United States are usually relegated to the bottom of the stratification hierarchy, doomed to (a) a longer stay on AFDC, (b) inadequate educational and career opportunities, (c) lower-paying jobs, (d) longer periods of unemployment, (e) unstable relationships, and most serious of all, (f) a negative health status for themselves and their children. It has been shown that the children of teenagers are more likely to be of low birth weight, to lack immunizations, to suffer from malnutrition, and to be of generally poor health (Bayne-Smith, 1994; Hayes, 1987).

The mental, physical, and emotional stresses of raising children without a partner are difficult issues for older, better-educated, economically self-sufficient women to handle. These stressors are almost impossible for the average teenager to cope with. It is conceivable, therefore, that teen pregnancy presents a problematic health/mental health issue for several generations of women of color because of the precedent it sets to be repeated in succeeding generations: Most out-of-wedlock births occur in mother-only families (Committee for Economic Development, 1987).

The entire arena of gender politics and family formation, usually an emotional minefield under the best of conditions, becomes fraught with intense problems for people of color. Racism, sexism, and faulty social policy contribute to disruptions in family formation and then further penalize people of color by not providing assistance to families whose structures are different and therefore perceived as aberrant. Together, gendered racism and bad policy have waged an aggressive assault on the health, mental health, and general well-being of women of color.

THE INFLUENCE OF CULTURE
ON THE HEALTH OF WOMEN OF COLOR

When gender is considered within race, any analysis of the health status of women must take into account the cultural norms that exist in every group. These norms and the gendered behaviors that flow from them become distorted by racial issues. These distortions influence the relationship between women of color and society and, as such, have direct impact on the health and mental health of women of color.

Culture is the repository of all rituals, symbols, images, and other mechanisms that any group of people use to interpret, assign meaning to, and develop a sense of what the world is all about. Culture is the means by which people receive, organize, rationalize, situate, and understand themselves and their particular experiences in the world. Much of what culture says, people learn early in life (Saleeby, 1994), beginning in infancy. Cultural learning occurs through the telling of stories, narratives, interpretations, and myths that both transfer the meanings of any culture from one generation to another and reinforce the meanings for the adults. As a result, much of the meaning in people's lives grows out of their relationships or lack thereof, starting with their parents and others of their culture, which is to say that meaning, depending on its context, symbolic nature, and origin, can inspire or oppress (Saleeby, 1994, p. 357).

The difficulty most people experience is that culturally conditioned behaviors, responses, and ways of interacting become at the most profound levels the total framework out of which they not only operate but also interpret and judge the behavior of others. That framework, rather than serve as a reference point, becomes "truth" (Rosaldo, 1989). The caveat that must be issued here, then, is that many rituals, symbols, images, and mechanisms are available for people to choose from to create a world for themselves that has meaning. Because there are so many truths, no one culture has a controlling share of the truth. Instead, each culture has its own interpretations and cultural truths. Unless one knows the interpretations that a specific culture gives to the world, it is not possible to know the people from that culture. Nevertheless, most people go through life not even remotely aware that many of the truths they "know" have been culturally conditioned. It is not inconceivable, then, that some people experience tremendous difficulty when they encounter cultures other than their own and learn that their truths have absolutely no meaning to someone from a different culture. Because most people never develop an objective awareness of their cultural perceptions, they tend to insist on interpreting the actions and behaviors of people not of their culture by their own meaning system; this interpretation can often grossly misinterpret the lives of people from cultures or subcultures that differ from one's own (Hall, 1991).

Cultural hubris and myopia on the part of the mainstream erects major health and mental health barriers for most women of color in their efforts to secure health care. The health belief systems and worldviews of African American, American Indian and Alaska Native, Asian and Pacific Islander American, and Latino women are very different from those of the Western-trained physician in a variety of ways. First, within the culturally conditioned health belief systems of most of the women discussed in this book, there is no clear-cut separation between physical, mental, emotional, and spiritual pain. Consider the predicament of the Western physician whose Latina patient presents with physical symptoms for her emotional or spiritual pain or vice versa. Second, the health-seeking behavior of many non-Western people does not involve a direct path from illness to physician services. Instead, the initial health-seeking behavior in many cultures in response to any type of illness is an attempt at self-management. If this effort fails, it is then followed by other treatments suggested by family and trusted friends. The next step would involve the services of an alternative or folk healer. Western medicine is often used in many cultures only as a last resort.

In the United States, most people of color are marginalized groups in terms of their relationship to the dominant culture of the mainstream. The process by which the dominant culture marginalizes those who are different is first to render their individual or collective meaning and culture nonexistent. If the group insists on "remembering" its culture, then the dominant group simply proclaims that culture to be negative and seeks constantly to reinforce that negativity through the mainstream media. This situation creates great difficulty for people of color with regard to the development of positive self-worth.

As a matter of survival, then, people of color, unlike mainstream people, must develop a capacity for dual understanding of both the dominant view of how the world sees them and their own views. To that end, many health and mental health problems of women of color go unrecognized partially because mainstream professionals are often unable to relate in any meaningful way to the cultural norms of people of color and partially because people of color do not trust the mainstream enough to share the extent of their problems. Whether out of the need to protect individual and community survival on the part of those who are culturally different or as a result of lack of awareness and sensitivity to other truths on the part of the mainstream health system, the health and mental health problems of women of color go largely unreported.

The meanings and interpretations of the cultural stories that shape the culturally prescribed gender roles for women of color also present them with serious health and mental health problems. And the prescriptions are continuously refilled through the interactions that take place in relationships within the culture. The problem here is that, in a majority of instances, the cultural stories and relationships are examples of distorted and invalidated gender roles redefined by the dominant culture within the context of the hegemonic dialogue. These cultural distortions and redefinitions accomplished through negative media messages and an insidiously deceptive and misconstrued recording of history diminish people's self-esteem, their sense of what their possibilities are, their interactions, and their relationships.

For example, most cultures do not openly condone violence against women. But cultural distortions can lead to physical and emotional suffering for women of color. It is demonstrated in the following chapters that some gender and community norms encourage women of color to be understanding of abhorrent male behavior in order to avoid racial reprisals against their group. These cultural norms allow male violence against women to be blamed on everything from alcohol to hunger to frustrations about joblessness and other effects of racism. The cultural stories told in some nonwhite cultures about relationships between men and women describe some men as "evil when he's hungry," "ornery when he don't have no money," "that wasn't really him, it was the rum talking," or "he'll slap you if you give him too much back talk." Even for some women of color who are self-sufficient, these stories reinforce the role they are expected to play in their relationships with men. Because issues of race contribute to the economic, social, and political powerlessness of the group, cultural stories are distorted. As a result, these stories help create narrow roles for women that are designed to make them supportive of men but that at the same time are physically and emotionally injurious to the health and mental health of women of color.

Yet, the most damaging cultural effect for women of color relates to their sexual lives. Among the four groups of women discussed in subsequent chapters, especially those from the lower socioeconomic strata, sociocultural norms govern gender roles especially in the area of male-female interactions and communication about sexual behavior. In the national study *Women and HIV Prevention: Unintended Effects* (Davis, Brown, Alegria, Bayne-Smith, & Smith, 1993), communication about sexual behavior between African American and Caribbean American (black and Hispanic) couples was examined. It was found that, among women from cultures in which the accepted view is that men, by virtue of nothing other than their gender, are dominant, this perception detracts power from women in general and in their sexual relationships in particular (Davis, Brown, Alegria, Bayne-Smith, & Smith, 1993). In these cultures, the subject of sex is not easily open to discussion by most women. This lack of control in their sexual relationships precludes any opportunity for women to negotiate condom use as a means to control their fertility and to prevent disease (Mays & Cochran, 1988). Although control of their fertility is certainly essential for women to be able to take advantage of educational and career opportunities, the equal if not larger concern in these times must be with disease prevention. Herein lies the greatest cultural contradiction some women of color face.

Many Latino, Asian, and African American men resist the use of condoms in cultures that accept as a given that men will have extramarital affairs but that immediately set in motion punitive social sanctions against women for unfaithful behavior. When men from these cultures engage in several sexual relationships with different women at the same time, their behavior is both encouraged and endorsed by peers as vital to the development of male identity. As a result, the cultural consequence most damaging to the health and mental health of women of color can be found in the most recent statistics on AIDS/HIV in the United States. New cases of AIDS reported to the Centers for Disease Control and Prevention in 1992 showed a 9.8% increase for women, compared with a 2.5% increase for men; also, for the first time, more women were infected through heterosexual contact with HIV-infected men than were infected through intravenous drug use (American Health Consultants, 1993b; Kelley & Holman, 1993). The most disturbing aspect of this new wave of cases in the United States is the disproportionate explosion of the virus among black (52%) and Latino (20%) women (American Health Consultants, 1993a; World Health Organization [WHO], 1992, 1993). Research on heterosexual transmission of HIV/AIDS indicates that the rate of male-to-female transmission is 12 times higher than the female-to-male transmission rate (Padian et al., 1994).

Clearly, the cultural constraints exerted on some women of color are major contributors to their morbidity and mortality. But it does not end with young women. These cultural norms have the ability to oppress several generations of women. When young women become victims of HIV/AIDS, an increased burden then falls to older women who then have the responsibilities of caring for HIV+ or healthy grandchildren when their parents become too ill to provide child care and of rearing the children left behind. The phenomenon of an increasing number of grandmothers raising children is part of the findings of a study on the status of the black family in New York City. This study is based on 1990 census data that indicated (a) 36% of black households in New York City with children were headed by persons 45 years or older who were caring for children not their own and (b) almost a quarter of all households with children (21%) were headed by black women 45 years and older without a spouse (Stafford, 1994a).

WOMEN OF COLOR AND THE HEALTH CARE INDUSTRY

The health status of any group of women is surrounded by complex issues. It must be argued that nonwhite women in the United States are faced with an even greater array of complexity. The health status of women of color historically has been determined by issues of race, class, and culture, all of which have economic, political, and social implications. In addition, the health status of women of color has been affected by the structure of the very health care industry that would serve them. The term *health care industry* for purposes of this discussion is defined as the complex conglomerate of commerce and trade that operates under the aegis of the Western medical model of health service delivery and that derives its income from the sale of medical goods, services, and technology, most of which are prescribed by physicians. Graig (1993) writes that this industry consumed 12.1% of U.S. gross domestic product in 1990, surpassing all other industrialized nations.

The focus here is not on the vastness of this economic enterprise, but rather on its structural impact on the health status of women of color. This must be analyzed from four dimensions:[10]

1. Structure of the health care industry
2. Operation of the structure of health care
3. Bases of the structure of health care
4. Consequences of the structure of health care

Structure of the Health Care Industry

The health care industry provides direct hands-on health care, as well as various and sundry indirect health-related services. These services range from acute tertiary-level care to research and wellness programs.

An industry this vast has many interest groups. Currently, the power elite of the health care industry are concentrated among four main divisions: doctors and the schools that train them, health insurance, pharmaceuticals, and hospitals. Each of these divisions or branches has an internal power structure that operates at the national level, as well as locally—for example, the American Medical Association (AMA), the nationwide professional organization of physicians, which has varied levels of power (state, city, borough).

As an interest group, physicians probably employ the best paid, best organized lobbying effort on Capitol Hill, with local effort also exerted at the state and municipal levels, to protect the interests of physicians. For example, by 1985, Medicare's total payments for physician services had escalated to almost a quarter (23.6%) of total Medicare spending, up from 21.4% in 1975. Despite carefully designed plans, the Reagan administration was incapable of moving ahead with physician reimbursement reform in the mid-1980s because of organized pressure from physician opposition (Williams & Torrens, 1988, p. 366).

Women of color are well represented in the staffing of all four branches of the industry. They are found in abundance in the kitchens and housekeeping staffs of hospitals and nursing homes. As one moves up the occupational hierarchy of the health care industry, their numbers drastically diminish. The health care industry has allowed a few women of color to achieve some middle management positions, but the upper echelons of the four divisions of the health care industry continue to be closed to them as career options. The top of all four main branches of the industry remains a predominantly white male bastion of authority. Weaver and Garrett (1982), in their examination of racism and sexism in the health care industry, charge that although admissions of women and minorities to medical schools have increased, they are not found in large numbers in the high-paying specialties. Neither are they found in professional decision-making positions. The health care industry as an institution in U.S. society is unquestionably structured along race, gender, and class lines.

Operation of the Structure of Health Care

David Reisman's thesis in *The Lonely Crowd* (1950) that various interest groups in U.S. society are activated to protect any impingement on issues of central interest to their group is well suited to analysis of the health care industry. Within that context, health care policy in the United States has not been set by broad coalitions of groups with a focus on the operation of the entire industry and the needs of the citizenry. Instead, health care policy in the United States, as with most domestic policy, has been established and implemented incrementally, on the basis of windows of opportunity and the readiness of interest groups to move their agendas forward. For the most part, the exercise of power in health care policy making in the United States has varied, depending on the issue at stake and the groups most heavily invested in the stakes of that issue. For example, if the issue is the development of a plan to have government serve as the source of a single payor system in order to ensure universal coverage and more egalitarian access, then the insurance companies and their lobbyists step in to change that thinking. If the issue is physician fiscal penalty, then physicians and the AMA implement a strategy to prevent those policies from being enacted. These interest group politics of the health care industry appear on the surface to operate from a fragmented mode.

It can be argued, however, that unlike other major areas of the U.S. economic structure, the four divisions of the health care industry are a cohesive unit in that the entire industry does not obey the usual laws of supply and demand, in which demand or need comes first and then creates increased supply. The health care industry grew as fast as it did by operating the most manipulative of economies, in which customers are steered by their physicians toward a newly created supply of technology, drugs, and surgical and other procedures and services. Physicians are probably the only other professionals besides lawyers with what is sometimes viewed as the greatest amount of "expertise" power in U.S. society. As such, they are in a unique position to steer the less informed masses toward a newly created medical device by intoning its ability to better diagnose, ease pain, improve functioning, prolong life, or make the difference between life and death, even if other means are available or the device is not capable of achieving any of these promises. From that vantage point, it is not hard to convince patients that they cannot, must not ever, be without this new supply going forward. In effect, the power of this industry is best evidenced by its ability to create a demand where none existed before.

Bases of the Structure of Health Care

At the base of the American health care industry is the European-influenced, Western biomedical model of health service delivery. Power tends to be patterned according to the structure of interests in a society (Kornhauser, 1967, p. 637). The interests of the health care industry coincide and coalesce around the scientific methods of the biomedical model and its technology.

For most of the 20th century, the power of the health care industry has been consolidated in medical doctors, in medical schools, and in the access only doctors can provide to medications, to the technology available in hospitals, and to other medical devices (Ehrenreich & English, 1973, pp. 75-82). That white male physicians have held on to the power of this industry for so long is no surprise. Apart from the financial rewards and the economic, social, and political power that it generates, this industry is also very firmly entrenched in and anchored by the philosophical views and belief systems of the dominant U.S. culture. The more powerful mainstream members of U.S. society and indeed the world have had a shared interest in a specific worldview for more than 300 years. That view is based on the mechanistic, linear, reductionism espoused by René Descartes, William Harvey, and Isaac Newton, among other 17th-century contributors to the scientific revolution and its Age of Enlightenment (Capra, 1982). Often referred to as Cartesian thinking, or scientific thought, this view is not the exclusive domain of white males; they only appropriated it as such and from that position marginalized all other approaches by rendering them nonessential.

In this view, there is a total separation of mind from body, and a particular analytical method of reasoning is employed. Cartesian reductionism says that all physical matter, including the human anatomy, can best be understood by reducing it to its component parts (Foss & Rothenberg, 1987). This form of thinking resulted in the biomedical model of the 19th century, still in place today. Essentially, the biomedical model is concerned with only four concepts: the patient, the disease, the diagnosis, and the treatment (Foss & Rothenberg, 1987). Medical training based on this model of reductionist, linear thinking prepares physicians to discount the feelings and emotions of their patients and to dismiss any inclusion of the effects of social, economic, political, environmental, and cultural forces from their diagnosis and treatment recommendations. Cartesian thinking, representative of the worldview of the dominant culture, is at the heart of the biomedical model and permeates the health care industry and indeed the entire mainstream U.S. Anglo society. The ubiquity of the medical model in U.S. society is such that the "medical model" has been appropriated by several other nonmedical disciplines.

The pervasiveness of the medical model, together with the historical exclusion of women in general and women of color in particular from the centers of power of this industry, has resulted in a lack of trust in Western medicine and negligible use patterns for people of color. By their refusal to expand the biomedical model to a more comprehensive paradigm suitable for health service delivery in a multicultural society, mainstream providers are unable to address the disproportionately worse health status of people of color.

Consequences of the Structure of Health Care

The technological advancements of the biomedical model must be duly credited with extraordinary life-saving success in the course of the 20th century. This very legacy, however, is part of medicine's undoing. First, the cost of that technology has created a fiscal crisis in medicine in the United States that prevents large segments of the population who do not have health insurance from gaining access to any of that technology. Second, the manipulation of an interminable demand for the most recent technology in health care services in the United States has in many ways created runaway expenditures. Third, the technology has also led to an ever-widening chasm between physicians and patients. Physicians, in keeping with their biomedical training, must reduce the patient and his or her symptoms, through the diagnostic process, to a translated mechanical language that will segment the body part or biological system where the disease is located and where treatment must be concentrated (Engel, 1977).

Finally, and probably most significant, is the fact that as a result of an insistence on the biomedical model, Western-trained professionals have been taught to recognize only disease. Completely excluded from their education has been any ability to recognize the more important culturally conditioned concepts of illness and wellness and how to treat either of these (Kleinman, Eisenberg, & Good, 1978). For example, menopause, which many cultures view in the same way as the onset of menstruation—as a transitional passage—has been medicalized into a "hormonal deficiency disease" for which estrogen replacement therapy (ERT) is the treatment (Lock, 1994; McCrea, 1983). In essence, then, even though the Western medical model has been employed for all these years, if menopause were stripped of its disease properties, doctors and researchers would still be unable to offer any advice other than what menopausal women have been able to obtain from family, friends, cultural norms, or Sheehy (1992).

CONCLUSION

In the chapters that follow, the authors discuss the health and mental health difficulties endured by the women of their group. They also talk about their strengths and their optimism for improving their condition. It is important to note that the women of each group discuss not only the biological conditions that plague them but also the social, economic, environmental, psychological, cultural, and family conditions as these also affect health status. It appears that, for many non-Western peoples, there are many more dimensions to "health" than what traditional bio-medicine seems willing to take into consideration. It also seems clear that many non-Western peoples of color continue to practice culturally condi-tioned health-related behaviors that are very different from those of the mainstream.

It is time, therefore, to redefine health as more than the absence of disease. The forces of race and gender clearly determine the economic, social, political, and environmental components of class status that shape health status. Good health as a product is the result of many different kinds of investments that include housing, education, exercise, proper diet, self-esteem, healthy lifestyles, social supports, and acceptable health care services. The complexities of the health and mental health status of women of color demand that any redefinition of health also include cultural, behavioral, ecological, migration, and population factors. Inclu-sion of these additional dimensions into the biological model will not be easily accomplished. The hegemony of the biomedical model over the vast health care industry is found in the reliance of the industry on this model in order to operate and to protect its financial interests. In turn, the entire industry cooperates in the practice of negentropy to sustain and validate the biomedical model.

The impact of race and gender on the health and mental health of women of color is described in the next four chapters. The authors provide the most recent information on the health and mental health status of African American, American Indian and Alaska Native, Asian/Pacific Islander American, and Latino women. This material examines the major biologi-cal complaints suffered by women of color. It also discusses the social, economic, cultural, and environmental dimensions of their health status. Although this discussion is in no way exhaustive, we hope it contributes to an expanded perspective of traditional biomedicine, one that is better suited to meet the health and mental health needs of all Americans, including women of color.

NOTES

1. Comments made by Dr. Peter Frank to the editor, Marcia Bayne-Smith, during a telephone interview on April 14, 1995. Dr. Frank is coauthor of a study comparing the competence of male and female doctors in taking care of women. The results of that study indicated that women who used female doctors were more likely to have had a Pap test in the last 3 years and a mammogram at some point in their lives.

2. Comments made by Dr. Florence Haseltine, of the National Institute of Child Health and Human Development, at the Conference on Women's Health Research, Jacobs Institute of Women's Health, 1993.

3. Comments made by Dr. Alice Dan at the Conference on Women's Health Research, sponsored by the Jacobs Institute of Women's Health, Summer, 1993.

4. For an explanation on why and how we blame the poor, see Kerbo, H. R. (1991). *Social stratification and inequality: Class conflict in historical and comparative perspective* (2nd ed.). New York: McGraw-Hill, p. 314.

5. This question was put to editor Bayne-Smith after she was provided with clear travel directions to a country club on Long Island's North Shore, where she was making a presentation to the board of directors of the organization she worked for.

6. Cornel West, in his book *Race Matters,* talks about standing on the corner of 60th Street and Park Avenue in New York City, where 10 taxi cabs refused to pick him up. He finally gave up and took the subway.

7. An examination of the nihilism that increasingly pervades black communities is found in West (1993).

8. A discussion on women and work is found in Muller (1990). See also Goldin (1989).

9. For a discussion on the rise of grandmothers caring for their grandchildren because parents are jobless, incarcerated, or dead, see Stafford (1994b).

10. For a discussion on analysis of power in society, see Kornhauser (1967).

REFERENCES

Aday, L. (1993). *At risk in America: The health and health care needs of vulnerable populations in the United States.* San Francisco: Jossey-Bass.

American Health Consultants. (1993a, September). Black women with AIDS lack access to treatment. *AIDS Alert, 8,* pp. 145-146.

American Health Consultants. (1993b, September). Women and AIDS: Brief overview. *AIDS Alert, 8,* pp. 131-132.

Auster, R., Leveson, I., & Sarachek, D. (1972). The production of health: An exploratory study. In V. Fuchs (Ed.), *Essays in the economics of health and medical care* (pp. 135-138). New York: National Bureau of Economic Research.

Axtell, J. (1981). *The Indian peoples of Eastern America: A documentary history of the sexes.* New York: Oxford University Press.

Bayne-Smith, M. A. (1994). Teen incentives program: Evaluation of a health promotion model for adolescent pregnancy prevention. *Journal of Health Education, 25*(1), 24-29.

Bayne-Smith, M. A., & Mason, M. A. (1995, July/August). Developmental disability services to Caribbean Americans in New York City. *Journal of Community Practice: Organizing, Planning, Development and Change, 2*(1).

Beardsley, E. H. (1987). *A history of neglect: Health care for blacks and mill workers in the twentieth-century South.* Knoxville: University of Tennessee Press.

Beardsley, E. H. (1990). Race as a factor in health. In R. Apple (Ed.), *Women, health, and medicine in America: A historical handbook.* New York: Garland.

Bennet, M. B. H. (1987). Afro-American women, poverty, and mental health [Social essay]. In *Women and Health, 12*(3-4), (Special double issue on Women, Health, and Poverty), 213-228.

Beveridge, A., & D'Amico, J. (1994). *An analysis of black and white income in Queens, N.Y.* Unpublished manuscript, Queens College, City University of New York.

Bogdan, J. C. (1990). Childbirth in America. In R. Apple (Ed.), *Women, health, and medicine in America: A historical handbook* (pp. 101-120). New York: Garland.

Borg, M. J. (1992). Conflict management in the modern world system. *Sociological Forum, 7,* 261-282.

Bousfield, M. O. (1934). Reaching the Negro community. *American Journal of Public Health, 24,* 209-215.

Brown, J. (1978). *The politics of health care.* Cambridge, MA: Ballinger.

Bryce-Laporte, R. S. (1977, September/October). The new immigrant wave. *Society* [Special edition].

Bryce-Laporte, R. S. (1979). New York City and the new Caribbean immigration: A contextual statement. *International Migration Review, 13*(2), 214-234.

Byrd, W. M., & Clayton, L. A. (1993). The African-American cancer crisis: Part II. A prescription. *Journal of Health Care for the Poor and Underserved, 4*(2), 102-116.

Capra, F. (1982). *The turning point: Science, society, and the rising culture.* New York: Simon & Schuster.

Committee for Economic Development. (1987). *Children in need.* Washington, DC: Author.

Davis, D., Brown, P., Alegria, M., Bayne-Smith, M., & Smith, V. (1993, December). *Women and HIV/AIDS prevention efforts: Unintended effects.* Final report of a national research project funded by the Centers for Disease Control and Prevention, Grant #U50/CCU304522-04.

Department of City Planning, New York City. (1992, June). The newest New Yorkers: An analysis of immigration into New York City during the 1980s. New York City: Author.

Dye, T. R., & Renick, J. (1981). Political power and city jobs: Determinants of minority employment. *Social Science Quarterly, 62,* 475-486.

Ehrenreich, B. (1995, March 13). Planet of the white guys [Essay]. *Time,* p. 114.

Ehrenreich, B., & English, D. (1973). *Complaints and disorders: The sexual politics of sickness.* New York: Feminist Press at the City University of New York.

Engel, G. L. (1977). The need for a new medical model: A challenge for biomedicine. *Science, 196,* 129-136.

Fein, R. (1986). *Medical care, medical costs: The search for a health insurance policy.* Cambridge, MA: Harvard University Press.

Foss, L., & Rothenberg, K. (1987). *The second medical revolution: From biomedicine to infomedicine.* Boston: New Science Library-Shambhala.

Giddings, P. (1984). *When and where I enter.* New York: William Morrow.

Goldin, C. (1989). *An economic history of American women and their families* (National Bureau of Economic Research Monograph). New York: Oxford University Press.

Graham, Y. (1989). Maternal and child health profile of the Caribbean population in New York City. In V. J. Clarke & E. Riviere (Eds.), *Establishing new lives: Selected readings on Caribbean immigrants in New York City* (pp. 110-149). New York: Medgar Evers College-CUNY, Caribbean Research Center.

Graig, L. (1993). *Health of nations: An international perspective on U.S. health care reform* (2nd ed.). Washington, DC: Government Printing Office.

Hacker, A. (1992). *Two nations: Black and white, separate, hostile, unequal.* New York: Ballantine.

Hall, E. T. (1991). *Beyond culture.* New York: Anchor-Doubleday.

Haug, M. R. (1991). Health care and gender. *Contemporary Sociology: An International Journal of Reviews, 20*(4), 621-622.

Hayes, C. (1987). *Risking the future.* Washington, DC: National Science Academy.

Holmes, L. J. (1986). African American midwives in the South. In P. S. Eakins (Ed.), *The American way of birth* (pp. 273-291). Philadelphia: Temple University Press.

Howard, J. P. (1992, March). *Doing what it takes to make schools and communities drug free.* Keynote address to the Conference on Making Schools and Communities Drug Free, Chicago.

Hunter, S. M., Freirichs, R. R., Webber, L. S., & Berenson, G. S. (1979). Social status and cardiovascular disease risk factor variables in children: The Bogalusa Heart Study. *Journal of Chronic Disease, 32,* 441-449.

Inhaber, H., & Carroll, S. (1992). *How rich is too rich? Income and wealth in America.* New York: Praeger.

James, S. A. (1984). Socioeconomic influences on coronary heart disease in black populations. *American Heart Journal, 108,* 669-672.

Jones, J. (1981). *Bad blood: The Tuskegee syphilis experiment.* New York: Free Press.

Kelley, P. J., & Holman, S. (1993, March). The new face of AIDS. *American Journal of Nursing, 93,* 26-35.

Kerbo, H. R. (1991). *Social stratification and inequality: Class conflict in historical and comparative perspective* (2nd ed.). New York: McGraw-Hill.

Kleinman, A., Eisenberg, L., & Good, B. (1978). Culture, illness, and care. *Annals of Internal Medicine, 88,* 251-258.

Knapp, D. A., & Knapp, D. E. (1972). Decision-making and self medication: Preliminary findings. *American Journal of Hospital Pharmacy, 29*(12), 1004-1012.

Kornhauser, W. (1967). Power elite or veto groups. In P. I. Rose (Ed.), *The study of society: An integrated anthology* (pp. 633-646). New York: Random House.

Kotz, N. (1969). *Let them eat promises.* Englewood Cliffs, NJ: Prentice Hall.

LaViest, T. A. (1992). Political empowerment and health status of African Americans. *American Journal of Sociology, 97,* 1080-1095.

Litoff, J. (1986). *The American midwife debate: Sourcebook on modern origins.* Westport, CT: Greenwood.

Lock, M. (1994). Menopause in cultural context. *Experimental Gerontology, 29*(3-4), 307-317.

Manton, K. G., Patrick, C. H., & Johnson, K. W. (1987). Health differentials between blacks and whites: Recent trends in mortality and morbidity. *Milbank Quarterly, 65,*(1), 129-199.

Mays, V. M., & Cochran, S. D. (1988). Issues in the perception of AIDS risk and risk education activities by black and Hispanic/Latino women. *American Psychologist, 43,* 949-957.

McBarnette, L. (n.d.). *Women, poverty, and health: The insidious cycle of dependency.* Unpublished paper.

McCrea, F. B. (1983). The politics of menopause: The discovery of a deficiency disease. *Social Problems, 31,* 111-123.

Melby, C. L., Goldflies, D. G., Hyner, G. C., & Lyle, R. M. (1989). Relation between vegetarian/nonvegetarian diets and blood pressure in black and white adults. *American Journal of Public Health, 79*(9), 1283.

Miller, S. M. (1993, Spring). The politics of respect. *Social Policy,* pp. 44-51.

Mondragon, D. (1993). No more "Let them eat admonitions": The Clinton administration's emerging approach to minority health [Guest editorial]. *Journal of Health Care for the Poor and Underserved, 4*(2), 77-82.

Muller, C. (1990). *Health care and gender.* New York: Russel Sage.

National Center for Health Statistics (NCHS). (1993). *Healthy people 2000: Review, 1992.* Hyattsville, MD: U.S. Public Health Service.

National Commission on Children. (1992). *Beyond rhetoric: A new American agenda for children and families.* Washington, DC: Government Printing Office.

Navarro, V. (1991). Race or class or race and class: Growing mortality differentials in the United States. *International Journal of Health Services, 21*(2), 229-235.

Padian, N., Marquis, L., Francis, D. P., Anderson, R. E., Rutherford, G. W., O'Malley, P. M., & Winkelstein, W. (1987). Male to female transmission of human immunodeficiency virus. *Journal of the American Medical Association, 259,* 788-790.

Reisman, D. (1950) *The lonely crowd.* New Haven, CT: Yale University Press.

Rosaldo, R. (1989). *Culture and truth: The remaking of social analysis.* Boston: Beacon.

Saleeby, D. (1994). Culture, theory, and narrative: The intersection of meanings in practice. *Social Work: Journal of the National Association of Social Workers, 39*(4), 351-359.

Sawyer, T., Coonan, W., Worsley, A., & Leitch, D. (1980). Sex, social status, and ethnic origin in relation to coronary heart disease risk factors in Adelaide school children. *Medical Journal of Australia, 2,* 331-334.

Schroeder, P. (1992). *Women's health: A focus for the 1990s* (Vol. 12, No. 1). Washington, DC: Jacobs Institute of Women's Health.

Sheehy, G. (1992). *The silent passage: Menopause.* New York: Random House.

Shepard, R. F. (1994, December 31). Nafis Sadik: World leader of the year. *Earth Times,* p. 12.

Silberner, J. (1990, September 24). Health: Another gender gap: A crackdown on research bias against women would produce change. *U.S. News & World Report,* p. 54.

Sokoloff, N. (1992). Black women, double advantage. In *Black women and white women in the professions* (pp. 93-112). New York: Routledge.

Stafford, W. (1994a, February). *A preliminary profile of a vibrant community: New York City's black family.* Research report presented at the Black Family Summit, Columbia University, New York.

Stafford, W. (1994b). *Principal findings of a preliminary profile of a vibrant community.* From a research study on New York City's black family, sponsored by the office of Ruth Messinger, Borough President of Manhattan.

Stafford, W. (in press). If there's a post modernism, is there a post racism? In B. Bowser (Ed)., *Impacts of racism on white Americans.* Thousand Oaks, CA: Sage.

Thomas, S. B. (1992). The health of the black community in the 21st century: A futuristic perspective. In R. L. Braithwaite & S. Taylor (Eds.), *Health issues in the black community* (pp. 338-349). San Francisco: Jossey-Bass.

Townsend, P. (1991, April). *Income inequality, poverty, and ill health: The British case.* Paper presented at a seminar on Deprivation and Health at Queens College, City University of New York.

U.S. Bureau of the Census. (1992, March). The Asian Pacific Islander population in the United States, March 1991 and 1990. *Current population reports* (Series P20-459). Washington, DC: Government Printing Office.

U.S. Bureau of the Census. (1993). *Statistical abstract of the United States.* Washington, DC: Author.

U.S. Bureau of the Census. (1994). *Statistical abstract of the United States.* Washington, DC: Author.

U.S. Department of Health and Human Services (U.S. DHHS). (1985). *Report of the secretary's task force on black and minority health.* Washington, DC: Government Printing Office.

U.S. Department of Health and Human Services (U.S. DHHS). (1991). *Healthy people 2000: National health promotion and disease prevention objectives.* Washington, DC: Government Printing Office.

Useem, M., & Miller, S. M. (1977). The upper class in higher education. *Social Policy, 7*(4), 28-31.

U.S. Indian Health Service. (1993). *Trends in Indian health.* Washington, DC: U.S. DHHS.

Wallace, S. P. (1990). Race versus class in the health care of African American elderly. *Social Problems, 37*(4), 517.

Wallerstein, I. (1989). *The modern world system: Vol. 3. The second era of great expansion of the capitalist world economy, 1730—1940s.* New York: Academic Press.

Weaver, J. L., & Garrett, S. D. (1982). Sexism and racism in the American health care industry: A comparative analysis. In E. Fee (Ed.), *Women and health: The politics of sex and medicine* (pp. 79-104). New York: Baywood.

West, C. (1993). *Race matters.* Boston: Beacon.

White, D. G. (1987). *"Aren't I a Woman?" Female slaves in the plantation South.* New York: Norton.

Williams, S. J., & Torrens, P. R. (1988). *Introduction to health services.* Albany, NY: Delmar.

Wilson, W. J. (1987). *The truly disadvantaged: The inner city, the underclass, and public policy.* Chicago: University of Chicago Press.

World Health Organization (WHO). (1992, January 20). Statistics: Reported AIDS cases rose to 115,681 by end of 1991. *AIDS Weekly,* p. 91.

World Health Organization (WHO). (1993, November 8). Statistics: AIDS toll hits 339,250 with influx from expanded definition. *AIDS Weekly,* pp. 2-4.

2

African American Women

Lorna Scott McBarnette

Despite the dramatic social changes that have occurred during the past three decades, adult women, irrespective of race, ethnicity, and age, are more likely than men to be poor. The construct of socioeconomic status is used frequently and convincingly to identify and describe the position of certain groups within the larger society. This construct is critically important in any discussion of the health status of African American women because it is derived from the notion of a stratification of people from lower to higher in terms of access to power, prestige, and property. These abstract terms are generally expressed by using measures of education, occupation, and income (Hale, 1992). On each of these measures, African Americans rank lower than whites despite the fact that, as a group, substantial gains in education have been made during the past 20 years. African Americans lag in terms of median years of education and in the proportion finishing high school and college. Patterns of income and occupation echo these differences in education. In 1987, the median household income of whites was 1.6 times that of African Americans, and among those who were employed, half as many African Americans as whites held managerial or professional positions, whereas nearly three times as many worked in service jobs (Hale, 1992, p. 8).

Closely related to socioeconomic status is the concept of poverty, or having a family income below the federally designated poverty level—a measure that varies with family size and is calculated in terms of dollars needed to purchase food (O'Hare, 1985). In 1987, approximately 9.1% of white families and 31.8% of African American families were living below this poverty threshold, and female-headed families were particularly likely to be living in poverty. The U.S. Bureau of the Census reported that 29.5% of white families were female-headed, compared with 54.8% of African American families (U.S. Bureau of the Census, 1988).

In 1987, more then 82.5% of African Americans lived in metropolitan areas, compared with 75.6% of whites. The exodus of middle-income families during the 1970s and 1980s resulted in a concentration of poor people in many central cities. At the same time, jobs in the central cities decreased as they followed population movement. The resulting diminution in the tax base available to fund public services, including health, affected African Americans disproportionately (Kasarda, 1988).

National surveys over the years have provided ample evidence of a connection between health status and poverty and socioeconomic status, demonstrating lower health status among low-income, low-status groups. The poor health status of African American women, collectively, is viewed by many as a direct result of poverty, racism, and a lack of access to power and prestige. Women as a class have undergone remarkable adjustments in their self-perception and traditional attitudes toward money, marriage, family life, and structure. These rather profound attitudinal changes have positive implications for their self-esteem, potential for autonomy, and improved socioeconomic status. Simultaneously, countervailing trends result primarily from the absence of social arrangements designed to help them achieve an improved quality of life.

Because of the pluralistic nature of U.S. society, social changes do not necessarily affect all segments uniformly. Social and individual behaviors are affected by historical, cultural, and social value systems, as well as by the prevailing societal attitudes concerning race, gender, and ethnicity. In the case of African American women, the results of racism and sexism intersect to create a double whammy. Both are motivated by similar economic, social, and psychological forces and arise from the struggles for black civil rights and for women's rights. For U.S. society to grant even an inch in either struggle would mean that the prevailing power structure would have to cede economic as well as political privileges. According to one popular writer, society has slowed the progress of African American women in order to expiate itself from blame for the plight of African American men who have yet to achieve their full places in American society (Giddings, 1984).

The disparities in health status between African American women and white women have been acknowledged by other researchers, and because of the burden of illness among African Americans, there is some interest in improving health consumer patterns in their communities. To achieve any level of improvement, policymakers must arrive at an understanding and a convincing explanation of the underlying belief systems that prompt behaviors in seeking and using health care and improved health status.

Among African American women in particular, their marked degree of cultural diversity is worthy of note and brief discussion. The black women now described as African American come from several specific cultural experiences that are different in terms of language, learned behavior, beliefs, and values. They come from the African continent, from the English-, French-, Dutch-, Portuguese-, and Spanish-speaking nations of the Caribbean, and from the Americas, including the urban and rural areas of the United States. They mingle and live together in neighborhoods in the United States; because of their commonality of black skin and features, society regards them all as African Americans and aggregates their health and social problems as though they all share the same backgrounds, family structure, and belief systems. Unfortunately, this type of analysis, though relatively easy to do and report in the context of health policy and health status indicators, masks issues of cultural diversity, illness behavior, and preferences among these women. Society observes only their black skins and relative poverty. Those who would analyze and proffer potential solutions do so for the "average African American woman" and can never understand why these remedies fail.

Health care for women of color in the United States is seriously wanting. Irrespective of the measures of health status, access to services, and use of services, a serious and inappropriate gap exists between African American and white women. The strategies for improving this situation must include sociological and anthropological perspectives that will assist people in understanding the behaviors of these women of the African diaspora. The reasons for the underuse of health services among African American women, despite the fact that they bear a heavier burden of disease, are complex and represent an intersection among economic, cultural, and historical factors, including increasing poverty, limited access to health insurance, and a health belief system that is not entirely steeped in the biomedical model. Furthermore, the persistent poverty among African American women suggests that they will be at the bottom of the ladder in terms of chronic illnesses and disabilities; data from the National Health Interview Survey indicate a positive correlation between income and health status. This relationship between low health status and poverty is insidious and cyclical and presents almost a chicken-and-egg situation regarding causation.

The variation in culture and historical background among African American women is significant because a relationship exists among health practices, beliefs, and outcomes, and these combine to influence behavior. Knowledge of these alternative belief systems that prompt behavior is essential in order to implement programs that effectively reach all African American women.

Many African American women enter the United States as immigrants—documented or undocumented. Most are documented immigrants who travel in search of work, sometimes leaving spouses and children behind. As they slowly reunite their families, they are temporarily forced into becoming heads of households or single parents when their children arrive. Many of these women occupy entry-level jobs in small companies that do not provide health insurance and health services. For undocumented immigrant women, the fear of discovery makes their lives secretive and isolated. In general, immigrants entering the United States without family support systems are likely to resist interactions with the public health system.

It is important to note, in the context of this discussion of immigration, that 43.0% of working-age noncitizens of the United States were uninsured in 1993, compared with 10.4% of nonelderly citizens. This variation in uninsured rates among citizens versus noncitizens may be, in part, because a higher proportion of noncitizens than citizens had family incomes of less that $30,000 and worked in small firms; both factors are associated with lower rates of insurance coverage. According to the Employee Benefit Research Institute (EBRI), citizenship is a factor affecting the likelihood that an individual will not have health insurance coverage, and in six states a higher proportion of the total uninsured population were noncitizens than in the 6.4% for the nation as a whole: California (37.8%), New York (26.6%), Florida (21.7%), New Jersey (20.8%), Illinois (19.9%), and Texas (17.8%) (EBRI, 1995).

Setting the causation aside temporarily, African Americans are poorer than whites, and African American women are poorer than white women and white men. The relationship among socioeconomic status, poverty, and health has been well documented over time. Contemporary researchers have made yet another connection among women, poverty, and ill health. Perales and Young (1988) described the injurious health consequences of impoverishment among women as a pressing but neglected issue; McBarnette (1988), in examining the relationship between poverty and reproductive status, attributed the differentials between African American and white women to the absence of financial and other resources. The relationship between regular and continuous health and medical care and improved health status has been widely acknowledged, yet many women in the United States, including a disproportionate number of African American women, do not have easy access to the health care system. This is so because the chief mechanism by which health care costs are funded is through the purchase of health insurance or the availability of public insurance coverage based on financial eligibility criteria. Gaps in insurance coverage and the unavailability of provider resources in many poor communities restrict access to services for a growing segment of the population, and women are vulnerable because of the structure of insurance coverage and certain demographic factors.

In this chapter, I focus on the health status of African American women and identify some social factors that contribute to the differentials. Furthermore, in the concluding section, I identify the public policy issues related to the dilemmas of African American women in the context of their health status.

AFRICAN AMERICAN WOMEN AND SOCIETY

The health of black Americans is influenced by their generally low socio-economic status as well as the cultural environments of their communities. (Leigh, 1992, p. 1)

The National Health and Nutrition Examination Surveys (NHANES) found that more than half of African American women in the 18 to 25 age-group in a 1979 survey reported they live in a state of psychological distress (National Center for Health Statistics [NCHS], 1979). These women rated their level of distress higher than did white women of the same age who were diagnosed with mental disorder. Byllye Avery (1992), on the basis of this finding, posited, "An examination of the context of our lives becomes essential in determining the etiology of illness and appropriate health promotion strategies" (pp. 35-36). Other researchers have explored the disparities in health status, as well as the growing differences in death rates among racial and socioeconomic groups. Navarro (as cited in Pappas, 1994) wrote, "Disparities in health status between Blacks and Whites are best understood in terms of the groups' underlying

living circumstances." He continued, "Race is often used as a proxy for
social class; we know that the poorer education, lower income, and lower
occupational standing of Blacks have important effects on the survival of
both adults and children" (pp. 892-893). In one significant study, the
racial differences in death rates were eliminated after an adjustment for
income, marital status, and household size. When these socioeconomic
factors were controlled in cause-specific mortality, African Americans
were at lower risk than whites for death from respiratory disease, accidents, and suicide; they were at equal risk for cancer and circulatory
diseases; and they were at higher risk for infectious diseases, homicide,
and diabetes.

Low socioeconomic status and the accompanying poverty constitute a
vicious cycle from which escape is difficult, at best. The Social Security
Administration's definition of poverty, which was determined in the early
1960s and updated only by the annual Consumer Price Index since that
time, continues to serve as the basis for public assistance eligibility,
excluding most marginal families and individuals who truly need assistance, albeit temporarily. In 1984, approximately 14.4% of the population—34 million persons—lived in poverty, 67% in households with
incomes under 75% of the poverty level and 38% with incomes under 50%
of the poverty level. The rates for women living in poverty were consistently higher then for men in the late 1980s. In almost every category, women
fared worse, according to a 1990 U.S. Bureau of the Census report. The major
determinant of women's poverty appears to be household composition and
status. Women who are heads of households are nearly 5 times more likely
to be poor than men who are heads of households. During the past 30
years, the share of people living in female-headed households has doubled, rising from 18% to 35%. This group, coupled with the sizeable
number of poor married women, comprises a preponderant number of
women living in poverty.

African Americans are sociodemographically distinct from the white
population. On average, they are younger and are more often female and
unmarried. African American communities are disproportionately concentrated in central cities or Southern states. Endemic racism and classism
in the United States have relegated many women to low-paying jobs or to
no jobs at all. Avery (1992) argued that it is important to examine the lives
of women who are surviving on lower incomes because their lives and
health suffer most in the United States. The same inhibiting factors have
led to significantly reduced educational opportunities for women, and
sexism has played a major role in robbing women of self-esteem. Thus,

in examining the health status of African American women, the focus must continue to include analyses of sexism, racism, and classism, as well as other contributory factors, such as structural unemployment and illiteracy.

National studies during the past three decades have found ample evidence of the connection between ill health and poverty, persistently reporting lower health status on a variety of indicators among low-income groups. Sixty percent of children from poor families have one or more chronic diseases, and the incidence of all forms of cancer is inversely related to income (Dorn & Cutler, 1959). Heart disease and diabetes are more prevalent among the poor (Ellis, 1958). Infant mortality rises as income decreases, and for the poor, the risk of dying under age 25 is 4 times the national average (U.S. Department of Health, Education, and Welfare, 1973).

As the general health of the U.S. population improves, studies continue to find significant gaps in health status between African Americans and whites. The 14-year life span gap between African Americans and whites has narrowed, but white Americans still live, on average, 5 ½ years longer than African Americans. And although other important indicators have improved somewhat, African Americans are still less likely to receive the same quality and types of health and medical care or to experience the same outcomes as whites.

The case of the disproportionate impoverishment of women has been established widely, as well as the likelihood of being poor if one is an African American. Impoverishment relegates the poor to living in substandard housing in lifestyles that are detrimental to their health and well-being. Impoverishment is also tantamount to being denied access to health care and medical services on a regular basis. The *Report of the Secretary's Task Force on Black and Minority Health* in 1985 noted that income and education are major influences affecting health status and that lack of income and education must be recognized as risk factors for disease and death in Blacks (U.S. DHHS, 1985)

HEALTH STATUS

Sixty thousand more African Americans than white Americans die each year as a result of cancer, cardiovascular disease, chemical dependency, cirrhosis of the liver, diabetes, homicide, and accidents. African American women are 4 times more likely to die in childbirth, and their children are 3 times more likely to die within the first year of life than white children.

Of particular relevance to African American women are lack of access to regular prenatal care, poor nutritional status (high salt intake and limited ingestion of dairy products because of lactose intolerance), inability to afford vitamin and mineral supplements, and obesity. This cycle of deprivation begins in childhood because poor children are less likely to be insured; 80% of these children are afflicted with one or more untreated conditions, according to the Children's Defense Fund (1986). Poor nutrition and poor health during childhood can negatively affect development and increase the probability of learning disorders and developmental disabilities. During childhood and adolescence, untreated visual and hearing disabilities and dental and mental health problems can contribute to poor academic performance and poor school attendance.

The seminal *Report of the Secretary's Task Force on Black and Minority Health* (U.S. DHHS, 1985) demonstrated unequivocally that African Americans and other minorities suffer excess morbidity and mortality from preventable conditions directly related to social inequities. Although most illnesses are not gender specific, certain problems affect women more frequently than men and thereby contribute to higher morbidity rates among women. Some disorders are also unique to women, more prevalent or serious in women than in men, or require different intervention strategies.

Cancer Morbidity and Mortality

Cancer is a leading cause of death in the United States and is a significant burden in terms of morbidity, years of life lost, and economic and emotional costs. This burden is disproportionately borne by African Americans, who have the highest age-adjusted cancer incidence and mortality rates of any population group in the United States. For many types of cancers, mortality rates among African Americans are increasing, in contrast with the trend among whites. In a 1991 report, trends in cancer incidence, mortality, and survival point to increasing disparities between African Americans and whites (Baquet, Harm, Gibbs, & Greenwald, 1991).

Cancer is the leading cause of death in women aged 35 to 54. Most cancer deaths are attributed to breast cancer, followed by cancer of the lung, colon, rectum, ovary, uterus, and esophagus. The American Cancer Society confirms that the incidence of cancer is proportionately higher for African Americans than for whites and that the death rate from cancer is also higher. For example, although the incidence of cervical cancer has dropped for both African American and white women in the past 14 years, the incidence in African American women is still double that of white women. According to Avery (1992),

> Conventional medical wisdom about cervical cancer has tended to focus on women and their sexual behavior, suggesting that their promiscuity is the cause. More recent studies have suggested that it may be males who are transmitting viruses and other organisms to women and that their promiscuity may be the source of infection in monogamous women. (p. 47)

Samuelson, Speers, Ferguson, and Bennett (1994) examined racial differences in cervical cancer mortality in Chicago and found that age-adjusted mortality in blacks—10.0 per 100,000 population—was twice the rate found in whites—4.6 per 100,000 population. Age-specific rates also showed significant excess mortality among blacks. After stratification by a group-level-defined poverty indicator, the racial differential in age-adjusted rates remained significant. The authors observed that, in addition to disparities in screening practices, the race differential in cervical cancer mortality can also be viewed as a function of the less favorable survival experience seen among blacks. Black women not only are less likely to be diagnosed with localized cervical lesions but also are less likely than whites to survive at the same stage of diagnosis.

Endometrial cancer is the third most common cancer among U.S. women. The 5-year survival rate for this type of cancer is 34% for white women and 35% for African American women. The National Center for Health Statistics (1990) reported that 29 of every 100,000 deaths among African American women were due to breast cancer in 1980.

Although fewer African American women than white women get breast cancer, the survival rate is lower: 64% versus 76%. In attempting to explain this apparent increased vulnerability—to separate issues of poverty from those of race—researchers are beginning to examine the social, environmental, and nutritional factors, beginning in childhood, that may lead to a weakened immune system in many African American women (Avery, 1992). Studies in the United States have reported that African American women have higher fatality rates than white women after a diagnosis of breast cancer and are more likely to be diagnosed with late-stage cancers. Coates, Bransfield, and Wesley (1992) attempted to evaluate these racial differences by looking at the length of time from symptom recognition to initial medical consultation. They concluded that the small difference in length of time from symptom recognition to medical consultation is unlikely to account for the large racial differences in survival rates and in stage of disease.

Mortality rates for lung cancer among African American women are twice as high as for nonminority women, and this difference has been attributed to lifestyle factors, such as smoking (National Cancer Institute, 1989). Lung cancer in women entering the 65 to 74 age-group has supplanted breast cancer as the leading cause of death from cancer among U.S. women.

In a study on nutrition and cancer Hargreaves, Baquet, and Gamshadzahi (1989) concluded that about 35% of all cancers may be associated with nutritional causes. The study questioned whether the poorer dietary and nutritional status of African Americans may be associated with their higher incidence of mortality from certain cancers, compared with whites. Researchers found that African Americans eat more nitrates and animal foods and not enough fiber in relation to protein, fats, and carbohydrates. African Americans have poorer nutritional status with respect to getting enough thiamine, riboflavin, vitamins A and C, and iron, and females are obese, whereas many males are underweight. These findings are in agreement with hypotheses regarding the interactions between diet and cancer.

Because certain chemicals and other agents in the environment are carcinogenic—solvents, dyes, heavy metals, pesticides, and herbicides, all of which can be found in the workplace—a new concern has arisen regarding employment of African Americans in less skilled jobs, where exposures to hazardous substances tend to be greater, (Baquet & Gibbs, 1992; Schulte, Ringen, Hemstreet, et al, 1992).

Disorders of the
Female Reproductive System

U.S. women make more than 20 million visits each year to physicians for disorders of the reproductive system, excluding diseases of the breast. Many of these disorders are serious, such as pelvic inflammatory disease, which can lead to infertility and death. Problems deriving from sexually transmissible diseases, such as gonorrhea and herpes, have serious effects on women because of the resultant higher risk of infertility and cancer. Pregnant women with sexually transmissible diseases face the additional risk of passing the disease on to their offspring. In the United States, 5% of sexually active women carry *Chlamydia trachomatis* organisms in the uterine cervix. Infants born to these women run a 60% to 70% risk of contracting the infection at birth. Chlamydia is the most common cause of neonatal eye infection and leads to an estimated 74,000 cases of inclusion conjunctivitis each year. Afebrile interstitial pneumonia in infants under 3 months of age is caused most frequently by chlamydia.

Numerous disorders in African American women are associated with the menstrual cycle. These disorders are as diverse as amenorrhea, iron deficiency anemia, premenstrual problems, and problems associated with premature cessation of the menses, which requires treatment with drugs that inhibit production early in the cycle of prostaglandin to relieve symptoms of dysmenorrhea. Although the causes of premenstrual syndrome are unclear, many posit that hormonal imbalances, nutritional and chemical deficiencies, and neurobiological dysfunction—all treatable conditions—are associated with premenstrual problems. Nearly 20% of menopausal women have symptoms that are severe enough to require medical attention, yet many poor African American women find difficulty in obtaining this type of non-emergency treatment.

In other areas, too, African American women are negatively affected. Nationally, the rate of births to adolescents has declined, whereas births to women over age 30 have increased. In African American communities, more than 500,000 infants are born each year to women under 20 years of age. Teenage pregnancy, which is associated with high infant mortality and other serious lifestyle problems, has become a national concern. Because pregnancy in teenagers can be risky to the health of both mother and infant, reproductive health services providers and facilities are critical to the survival of the African American female. In her work with teenaged African American women, Bayne-Smith (1994) designed interventions that demonstrated how early pregnancy affects the education of the adolescent mother, her ability to prepare for an occupation, and the loss of income opportunities for life.

Dramatic improvements have occurred in the health of mothers and children, in part because of better service delivery systems, improvements in the availability of financial resources, and advances in prenatal and perinatal care as a result of biomedical and behavioral research.

The U.S. maternal death rate dropped from 36.9% per 100,000 live births to 7.7% per 100,000 live births between 1961 and 1990. The rates among African Americans, however, remain higher and are of significant concern. A 1990 study found that maternal-age-specific neonatal mortality risk differs by race, with the risk for women in their mid-20s low for whites but not African Americans, probably partially because of worsening health for African Americans, relative to white women (Geronimous & Bound, 1990). Ectopic pregnancies are related to pelvic inflammatory disease and sexually transmissible diseases, both of which occur more often among poor women. The number of reported ectopic pregnancies tripled between 1970 and 1980, and the rate among total pregnancies doubled. As a result, ectopic pregnancies are the leading cause of death of the mother during the first 3 months of pregnancy and the leading cause of death among African American women of childbearing age (McBarnette, 1988).

Yet another contributor to maternal deaths is cesarean childbirth, the incidence of which has increased. Maternal morbidity among women having cesarean sections is 12 times more than for those having vaginal childbirth. In a study of maternal deaths, Seifert and Dos Martin (1986) found that embolism, hypertensive disease, and obstetrical hemorrhage led the list of causes of death in pregnancies not ending in live births. They reported that black women in the United States were 3 times more likely to die in childbirth because of living conditions and inadequate access to prenatal care.

Only 61% of African American women receive prenatal care in the first trimester of pregnancy (U.S. DHHS, 1990). In 1986, 18 of every 1,000 African American babies born died in the first year of life, and 12.5% of all births to African American women were of low birth weight. These rates were almost double the rates for whites, a 40-year pattern. Petitti, Coleman, Binsacca, and Allen (1990), in a study of 766 black women and 462 white women who gave birth in Alameda County, California, in 1987, explored potentially modifiable factors associated with the start of prenatal care, as well as the groups in which it was most likely to be late. Variables related to insurance coverage and financial status showed the greatest difference between early and late attenders at prenatal care in both groups. At virtually every level of almost every variable studied, black women were less likely than white women to begin prenatal care in the first trimester. The findings suggest that some differences in the timing of prenatal care may be a result of "lack of awareness and failure to pay attention to signs of early pregnancy" (p. 5). The authors concluded that although addressing insurance coverage and financial status is critical to the solution of the problem, attention should be paid to internal factors, such as depression and denial, as modifiers of the earliness of seeking prenatal care. Emanuel, Hale, and Berg (1989), in attempting to explain the dramatic excess of low birth weight and infant deaths among black babies as compared with white babies, found that the differences were not completely explained by differences either in sociodemographic factors or in prenatal care patterns. The study suggests that part of the explanation resides in characteristics of the mothers' own intrauterine and childhood environments that interfere with their optimal growth and development and that become manifest later in suboptimal reproductive outcome. Conditions in the adult environment under which pregnancies occur also appear to interfere with fetal development. The authors concluded,

> This evidence points to the need for programs to care for children as they grow and develop and for women before and during their pregnancies. Research should be encouraged which may help to elucidate the biological mechanisms by which intrauterine, childhood, and adult environments of one generation translate into health hazards for the next generation. (Emanuel et al., 1989, p. 303)

These data suggest that African Americans constitute an almost entirely separate class of people in the United States (Avery, 1992, p. 40). The issue of infant mortality in the African American communities needs to be more clearly linked to women's health, nutritional status, and the high rates of both intended and unintended pregnancies among young unmarried African American women.

Family planning services have not always been easily available to poor African American women, again because of the inability to pay for these services. Kirkman-Liff and Kronenfeld (1994) found that insurance coverage was an important factor for access to family planning services. They used Arizona survey data from 1984 to 1989 to examine the importance of insurance coverage in accessing family planning services and reported that, after family planning coverage was included by 1989, low-income women were 2.3 times more likely to receive services in 1989 than in 1984.

AIDS

The human immunodeficiency virus (HIV) causes acquired immune deficiency syndrome (AIDS). Viral infection, however, is only one element in a complex set of problems commonly referred to as the AIDS epidemic. The spread of infection, and consequently AIDS, is the product of human behaviors enacted in social contexts. Both the behaviors and the circumstances in which they occur are conditioned and shaped by culture and larger social structures. Since AIDS was first recognized, there has been growing appreciation and understanding of the role played by people who engage in same-gender sex (men with men), by people who inject illicit drugs (intravenous drug users), and by the role of sexual and other exchanges of bodily fluids in fostering the spread of infection. Regardless of the source of the particular infection, women have been materially affected by the AIDS epidemic. They have lost spouses and significant others to the epidemic, and they serve in many instances as primary caregivers to other persons with AIDS. They are themselves infected by bisexual partners and by partners who are intravenous drug users, or they infect themselves and eventually their children by sharing drug-injecting equipment.

At present, AIDS has no cure, and the treatments approved for palliation, prolongation of life, and generally keeping a patient functional are expensive and beyond the reach of many. Furthermore, the American response to the AIDS epidemic has targeted primarily men who have sex with men. In 1992, there was an alarming absence of women in trials that tested new drugs for introduction into the HIV treatment marketplace. As a result, the understanding of women's biological and other needs relative to AIDS is just beginning to grow.

AIDS has disproportionately affected African American communities. In 1986, African Americans accounted for 22% of total deaths while constituting only 12% of the total population; 11% of reported deaths were caused by heterosexual contact with drug-using partners. Women, especially African American and Latino, are the fastest growing group at risk for HIV infection: 52% of female AIDS cases are listed as black, non-Hispanic; 20.5% are Hispanic; and 26.5% are white, non-Hispanic (Centers for Disease Control and Prevention [CDC], 1990). AIDS among children is the result of infection in their mothers, and a significant number of cases are reported annually among African American newborns and children. The number of cases among African American women is growing rapidly, and faster than any major race-gender group. AIDS is the leading cause of death among women aged 15 to 44, and each year the number of deaths increases dramatically—from 739 in 1987 to 995 in 1988. Ellerbrock, Bush, Chamberland, and Extoby (1991) reported that 6,000 infants are born to HIV-positive women each year, with 25% to 35% becoming HIV positive themselves.

Diabetes and Related Chronic Diseases

Diabetes mellitus is a fairly common, chronic systemic disease characterized by glucose intolerance or the inability of the body to properly use glucose. A person develops diabetes because his or her pancreas does not make enough insulin or stops making insulin entirely (Murphy & Elders,

1992, p. 121). In 1986, diabetes mellitus was the 7th leading cause of death in the United States and the 13th leading cause of potential life lost before age 65 (CDC, 1991). Diabetes affects African American women disproportionately. Cowie, Harris, Silverman, Johnson, and Rust (1993) found a higher prevalence of non-insulin-dependent diabetes mellitus in U.S. blacks, compared with whites. In a study of 4,379 subjects for whom non-insulin-dependent diabetes mellitus was ascertained by medical history and oral glucose tolerance test and for whom data on risk factors were available, the authors reported a 60% higher prevalence in blacks than in whites and the highest prevalence in black women. They also found an elevated risk of non-insulin-dependent diabetes in black women who were obese.

The risk associated with obesity was greatest in black women (Cowie et al., 1993). Obesity may also be a possible explanation for the higher cardiovascular disease mortality in black women, compared with white women. The National Heart, Lung, and Blood Institute Growth and Health Study was designed to assess factors associated with the development of obesity in black and white preadolescent girls and its effects on major cardiovascular disease risk factors. This 5-year cohort study of 2,379 girls aged 9 through 10 at entry reported that, in subjects 9 and 10 years old, racial differences in obesity and blood pressure were already present ("Obesity and Cardiovascular Disease," 1992).

High blood pressure is a major health problem in African American communities, affecting approximately 7.5 million persons and half of African Americans over age 50. Hypertension is the leading cause of kidney failure and hypertension-related end-stage renal disease and is a major contributor to heart disease and stroke (U.S. DHHS, 1985). Although heart disease and related circulatory conditions are leading causes of death for all Americans, African Americans are disproportionately overrepresented. Compared with African American men, however, African American women experience excessive deaths from coronary disease. Recent studies in the United States have found that women with coronary artery disease are less likely than men to undergo major diagnostic and therapeutic procedures (Ayanian & Epstein, 1991; Steingart, Packer, & Hamm, 1991).

The Secretary's Task Force on Women's Health Issues (U.S. Public Health Service, 1985) found that some chronic diseases affect women more frequently than men. For example, urinary tract infections affect one in five women during their lives, and women are 5 times more likely to develop urinary tract infections than men; and if these infections are not treated in the early stages, renal damage could occur. Lupus, gallstones, arthritis, and thyroid disorders all affect women more often than men, and according to the Task Force, African American women bear a disproportionate burden. In general, life expectancy is shorter for African American women, rates of infant and maternal mortality are higher, and the health problems of African American women are compounded by poverty, poor nutritional status, low levels of motivation and self-esteem, and adverse environmental factors.

Drug and Alcohol Use
Among African American Women

Earlier I referred to the level of stress in the lives of African American women. It is important to analyze the relationship between this stress-filled lifestyle and the mental health status of African American women. Although no alcohol, drug abuse, or mental health problems are unique to women, several are more prevalent among women than men or affect women differently. The most common of the mental disorders is depression, a treatable disease that was most often associated with dementia in old women. Untreated depression can be serious because it can lead to social isolation and withdrawal and to inattention to basic nutritional needs and sanitation, causing physical decline and confusion.

The perception is that the rates of mental illness are higher for women than men, and the literature has been consistent in showing higher rates of reported depression among women than men. African American women, according to Taylor (1992), "experience a double disadvantage in living in a society that values both whiteness and maleness, [and] they are vulnerable to mental disorders often precipitated by prejudices and discriminatory practices" (p. 27). Others have pointed out that the stereotypes and prejudices relative to low-income black women have adversely affected their self-concepts and feelings of adequacy. The combined effects of being poor, black, and female tend to create an array of health risks and problems that are physical as well as mental. The probability of receiving adequate mental health care is small because prevalent race, class, and gender biases are likely to be reflected at the institutional level, as well as in the therapeutic encounter (Olmeda & Parron, 1984). The higher rate of attempted suicide among women in comparison with men has been documented. Baker, in 1984, studied the charts of 56 African Americans aged 16 to 29, 39 female and 17 male, who attempted suicide and were admitted to the hospital. Females were younger than males and were less likely to have severe diagnoses. Of the 39 females who attempted suicide, 54% had made a prior attempt. The suicide attempts among African American women have been associated with strong feelings of hopelessness, powerlessness, and overall depression. Overall, regardless of actual success at committing suicide, the rate of suicide attempts is higher for African American women than for African American men—6 to 1, compared with 3 to 1 for whites.

African American women have been turning increasingly to the use of alcohol and other drugs, probably as a reprieve. African American women have been reported to have higher rates of heavy drinking than white women, although they comprise a higher rate of abstainers. According to the President's Commission on Mental Health (1978), alcoholism was the third leading diagnosis for admission to state and county hospitals; rates for African American and white women were 50.1 and 12.4 per 100,000, respectively.

Chasnoff, Landress, and Barrett (1990) reported on the use of illicit drugs and alcohol during pregnancy. During the study period, they screened 715 pregnant women for alcohol, opiates, cocaine and its metabolites, and cannabinoids. The overall prevalence of a positive result was 14.8%; little difference in prevalence was found among women seen at public clinics versus private offices. The frequency of a positive result was also similar among white women (15.4%) and black women (14.1%). Black women more frequently had evidence of cocaine use (7.5% vs. 1.8% for white women); white women more frequently had evidence of the use of cannabinoids (14.4% vs. 6.0% for black women). During the study period, 133 women were reported in Pinellas County, Florida, after delivery for substance abuse during pregnancy. Despite the similar rate of substance abuse among black and white women in the study, black women were reported at approximately 10 times the rate for white women, and poor women were more likely than others to be reported. The researchers concluded that the use of illicit drugs is common among pregnant women regardless of race and socioeconomic status.

Alcohol abuse is also becoming a serious problem among women, and gender plays an important role in the etiology, effects, and treatment of alcohol abuse and alcoholism. Although women as a group drink less than men as a group, the acute and chronic effects of alcohol on women are greater. Because women have more body fat, when a woman consumes the same amount of alcohol as a man of equal weight, her tissue concentrations of alcohol will be higher than his. Women who become alcohol dependent experience greater morbidity and mortality than male alcoholics. For example, women develop more extensive liver damage earlier in their drinking history and at lower levels of alcohol intake. The decrease in life expectancy is estimated to be 15 years. Black women suffer disproportionately from alcohol-related illnesses and causes of death, yet very little is known about the extent that poorer outcomes are a function of differences in drinking, the use of health services, or some combination of related factors. A 1991 study used interview data obtained from the Baltimore Epidemiologic Catchment Area Household Survey to compare racial differences in alcohol use and abuse in a sample of 2,100 women (Lillie-Blanton, MacKenzie, & Anthony, 1991). After controlling for differences in sociodemographic characteristics, black women were found to be at no greater risk than white women for heavy drinking or for suffering from alcohol abuse or dependence. Racial differences, however, were observed in heavy drinking by years of education. A similar percentage of black women and white women who had not completed high school were heavy drinkers, but black women with 12 or more years of education were less likely to be heavy drinkers than white women with comparable education. These findings raise questions about the extent to which differences in drinking contribute to the poorer alcohol-related health outcomes of black women in Baltimore. The finding that education is inversely related to heavy drinking among black women may be helpful in shaping early alcohol abuse treatment and intervention services that target black women.

Although some scientists and health professionals describe alcohol and other substance addictions as diseases, suggesting a genetic predisposition to drug and alcohol dependency, others have used the disease model to denote a manifestation of underlying psychological problems, such as depression. Whatever the cause, substance abuse may mask other medical and/or psychiatric problems and significant numbers of patients with dual diagnoses of substance abuse or addiction and psychiatric disorders. African American theorists lean more toward the notion that chemical dependency in African Americans is related to environmental influences. Some assert that the primary factors leading to substance abuse in the African American population include economic deprivation, racism, and stress (Nobles & Goddard, 1992, p. 65).

DISCUSSION

African Americans are sociodemographically distinct from the rest of the U.S. population. As a class, they are poorer than whites, less likely to graduate from high school or college, more often female and unmarried, and concentrated in central cities or Southern states. They are disproportionately represented among the poor and have not benefitted materially from public health programs designed to diminish the risks of poor pregnancy outcomes, to decrease the incidence of death from preventable diseases, or to detect and treat chronic conditions.

The major societal issues that combine to create the relatively poor health status picture presented in this chapter for African American women are (a) lack of health insurance, which controls access to health and medical services, (b) racial discrimination among providers and institutions, and (c) gender politics. African American women, according to Wattleton (1992), suffer the triple jeopardy of sexism, racism, and classism. They persistently face substandard educational and vocational opportunities; this lower quality results in economic disparity: 56% of African American women aged 15 to 44 have family incomes below the federal poverty level; and for African American females aged 15 to 19, the figure is 69% (p. 301).

Health Insurance Coverage

As noted earlier, a disproportionate number of African American women do not have access to the health care system. The chief mechanism by which health care expenditures are funded in the United States is through the purchase of health insurance or the availability of public insurance coverage based on financial eligibility criteria. Health care expenditures have increased dramatically in recent years, a trend that suggests many more people are consuming health and medical services; however, gaps in insurance coverage restrict access to services for growing numbers of the population, and African American women are especially vulnerable because of the numerous demographic factors mentioned earlier—specifically, unemployment and marginal employment. The erosion of health insurance coverage is generally linked to employer-engendered cost-containment policies, restrictive eligibility criteria for public insurance programs, and changes in the characteristics of the workforce (Tallon & Block, 1988). One critical problem is the linkage between health insurance and employment status. Today, many small firms do not provide health insurance for their employees, and people who are between jobs are extremely vulnerable in terms of their ability to access reasonably priced health insurance. The eligibility criteria for public insurance exclude many people, and even those who have public insurance lack access to certain types of services. The point is that lack of health insurance is a barrier to health services, especially preventive services, and leads to a multi-tiered system of health care based on health insurance coverage. Another problem is that people who are in poor health or who have preexisting conditions are prevented, by virtue of their health status, from qualifying for coverage under most plans. Factors associated with lack of insurance vary by current employment status. For example, employed persons with an annual household income of less than $10,000 are 3.6 times more likely to lack insurance than employed persons with a higher income (Diaz et al., 1994).

Numerous strategies have been tried at both federal and state levels to close the gaps in insurance coverage, yet the number of uninsured Americans is cause for alarm. Insurance or lack of it is a serious matter when it comes to access to health care. Weis (1992) examined differences among demographic characteristics, health status indicators, and resource use of maternity clients privately insured, insured through public entitlement funds, or uninsured. The uninsured were in their early 20s, black (44%), single (52%), living in the central city area, employed in service occupations without health care benefits, and sought prenatal care either late in the pregnancy or not at all. Compared with the privately insured, the uninsured had more lifestyle risks and shorter hospital stays with more maternal complications. Insurance coverage and prenatal care were positive predictors of birth weight. Poor women also suffer because of the structure of health insurance benefit programs. Systems of copayments and deductibles create additional problems because many forego care if they lack cash resources.

The importance of financial resources in seeking and gaining access to health and medical services should not be underestimated. A 1987 study (U.S. DHHS, 1989) showed that the use of health services is closely correlated with insurance coverage. Insured individuals in the study used physicians' services 54% more than uninsured persons; and among blacks, insured individuals received twice as many physicians' services as their uninsured counterparts. Uninsured blacks in the same study lagged behind uninsured whites in terms of the average number of visits made to a physician.

U.S. policies tend to impede benefits and social supports for poor women and families. They are particularly punitive toward poor African American women, who are held responsible for their own conditions, especially drug addiction and out-of-wedlock pregnancies. Evidence supports the notion that the most severe health problems facing African American women are caused by poverty, racism, and lack of opportunity.

Racial Discrimination
in the Health Care Delivery System

Many studies have demonstrated an association between race and use of health and medical services. Blustein (1994) examined the quality of the measures of race in hospital discharge abstract data in New York State relative to cardiac patients. Evidence suggests that the misclassification of race in hospital discharge abstract data is nondifferential; thus, racial discrepancies in access to medical services are probably even greater than those previously reported.

Black Americans receive fewer medical services than their white counterparts. During the past 30 years, persistent barriers to preventive and primary care services influenced not only the quality of life but also the patterns of illness observed among African Americans. Despite the gains associated with the Civil Rights Act of 1964; Medicaid and Medicare legislation of 1965; and Title VI of the Civil Rights Act, which prohibited racial discrimination in any institution receiving federal funds, African Americans continue to have disproportionately large numbers of premature and excess deaths, compared with whites.

On the heels of the *Black Report,* which demonstrated that, after decades of universal access to health services, health inequalities are persisting and increasing, the American Public Health Association pointed out the importance of access to medical care: a better standard of living, ensuring better nutrition, basic education, safe water, decent housing, secure employment, and adequate income (McBeath, 1991). In the absence of these prerequisites, the health status of African Americans will continue to be a major cause for concern. The impact of racism and institutional racism in the health care delivery system can be substantiated by a variety of indicators. First, the usual hours of operation are not conducive to easy access for poor women, in terms of their own working requirements, child care needs, and geography. Second, the racial and sociocultural composition of the workforce and the level of racial and cultural understandings are barriers. This last factor relates to the paucity of African Americans in the fields of medicine and health, a long-standing issue. The racial and ethnic mix of the general population is not reflected in the health workforce. For example, although African Americans make up approximately 12% of the U.S. population, less than 3% of U.S.

physicians, less than 3% of dentists, and less than 2% of biomedical scientists are of African American descent (Gunby, 1989). This absence of African American providers is critical in terms of ameliorating the mismatch between providers and consumers and of addressing the cultural needs of African Americans in the health care system.

The policies and rules that govern the health care system are also an issue. Insurance benefits programs are restrictive in terms of the types of services for which they will pay—usually Western medical interventions. African American women coming from a variety of ancestries may be more prone to use services that are more holistic and in keeping with their cultural perspectives on health services consumption. For example, some insurance policies do not provide coverage for maternal and infant care, and Medicaid fee schedules are below the standard charges, a fact that limits physicians' willingness to serve pregnant Medicaid recipients. Actually, the number of obstetricians and gynecologists who provide specialized reproductive services and who participate in Medicaid or treat uninsured women is decreasing. In 1985, 4 of 10 physicians who provided obstetrical services did not accept Medicaid beneficiaries for both financial and liability reasons (Alan Guttmacher Institute, 1985). In New York State, for instance, the maximum allowable is such that, in the marketplace, specialist care for poor women is almost unavailable. National data show that obstetricians and gynecologists have lower participation rates than all other primary care physicians, and they are less likely to accept poor patients than the majority of secondary specialists (Center for Health Economics Research, 1982). People who are not covered by insurance are exposed to health risks as well as financial risks; and African American women and Latinas account for 50% of those who became uninsured between 1977 and 1987. Recent studies demonstrate the connection between race and poverty, lack of insurance, and delayed access to care. One study surveyed five hospitals in Massachusetts and found that delays in care were reported by 16% of patients. The odds of reporting delays in care among patients who were African American, poor, and uninsured or without a regular physician were 40% to 80% greater for patients in lower socioeconomic positions.

REFERENCES

Alan Guttmacher Institute. (1985). Paying for maternity care. *Family Planning Perspectives, 17*(3), 103-111.

Avery, B. Y. (1992). The health status of black women. In R. L. Braithwaite & S. E. Taylor (Eds.), *Health issues in the black community* (pp. 35-51). San Francisco: Jossey-Bass.

Ayanian, J. Z., & Epstein, A. M. (1991). Differences in the use of procedures between women and men hospitalized for coronary heart disease. *New England Journal of Medicine, 325,* 226-230.

Baker, F. M. (1984). Black suicide attempters in 1980: A preventive focus. *General Hospital Psychiatry, 6*(2), 131-137.

Baquet, C. R., & Gibbs, T. (1992). Cancer and black Americans. In R. L. Braithwaite & S. E. Taylor (Eds.), *Health issues in the black community* (pp. 106-120). San Francisco: Jossey-Bass.

Baquet, C. R., Harm, J. W., Gibbs, T., & Greenwald, P. (1991). Socioeconomic factors and cancer incidence among blacks and whites. *Journal of the National Cancer Institute, 83*(8), 551-557.

Bayne-Smith, M. A. (1994). Teen incentive program: Evaluation of a health promotion model for adolescent pregnancy prevention. *Journal of Health Education, 25*(1), 24-29.

Blustein, J. (1994). The reliability of racial classifications in hospital discharge abstract data. *American Journal of Public Health, 84,* 1018, 1021.

Center for Health Economics Research. (1982). *Access to ob-gyn services under Medicaid, Boston, Mass.* Unpublished research report.

Centers for Disease Control and Prevention (CDC). (1990). *HIV/AIDS surveillance report.* Atlanta: Author.

Centers for Disease Control and Prevention, Division of Diabetes Translation. (1991). *Diabetes surveillance report.* Atlanta: Author.

Chasnoff, I. J., Landress, H. J., & Barrett, M. E. (1990). The prevalence of illicit drug or alcohol use during pregnancy and discrepancies in mandatory reporting in Pinellas County, Florida. *New England Journal of Medicine, 322*(17), 1202-1206.

Children's Defense Fund. (1986). *An analysis of the FY 1987 federal budget and children.* Washington, DC: Author.

Coates, R. J., Bransfield, D. D., & Wesley, M. (1992, June). Difference between black and white women with breast cancer in time from symptom recognition to medical consultation. *Journal of the National Cancer Institute, 84*(12), 938-950.

Cowie, C. C., Harris, M. I., Silverman, R. E., Johnson, E. W., & Rust, K. F. (1993). Effect of multiple risk factors on differences between blacks and whites in the prevalence of non-insulin-dependent diabetes in the United States. *American Journal of Epidemiology, 137*(7), 719-732.

Diaz, T., Chu, S. Y., Conti, L., et al. (1994). Health insurance coverage among persons with AIDS. *American Journal of Public Health, 84,* 1015-1018.

Dorn, H. F., & Cutler, S. J. (1959). *Morbidity from cancer in the U.S.* (U.S. Public Health Service Publication No. 590). Washington, DC: Government Printing Office.

Ellerbrock, T., Bush, T., Chamberland, M., & Oxtoby, M. (1991). Epidemiology of women with AIDS in the U.S., 1981-90. *Journal of the American Medical Association, 265*(22), 2971-2975.

Ellis, J. M. (1958). Socioeconomic differences in mortality from chronic diseases. In E. G. Jaco (Ed.), *Patients, physicians, and illness* (pp. 24-30). New York: Free Press.

Emanuel, I., Hale, C. B., & Berg, C. J. (1989). Poor birth outcomes of American black women: An alternative explanation. *Journal of Public Health Policy, 10, 299-308.*

Employee Benefit Research Institute (EBRI). (1995, January 25). Analysis of March 1994 current population survey. *EBRI News,* p. 1.

Geronimous, A. T., & Bound, J. (1990). Black/white differences in women's reproductive-related health status: Evidence from vital statistics. *Demography, 27*(3), 457-466.

Giddings, P. (1984). *When and where I enter: Impact of black women on race and sex in America.* New York: Bantam Books.

Gunby, P. (1989). Minority physician training: Critical for improving overall health of nation. *Journal of the American Medical Association, 261*(2), 187-189.

Hale, C. B. (1992). A demographic profile of African Americans. In R. L. Braithwaite & S. E. Taylor (Eds.), *Health issues in the black community* (pp. 6-19). San Francisco: Jossey-Bass.

Hargreaves, M. K., Baquet, C., & Gamshadzahi, A. (1989). Diet, nutritional status, and cancer risks in American blacks. *Nutrition and Cancer, 12*(1), 11-28.

Kasarda, J. D. (1988). Jobs, migration, and emerging urban mismatches. In M. G. McGeary & L. E. Lynn Jr. (Eds.), *Urban change and poverty* (pp. 148-198). Washington, DC: National Academy Press.

Kirkman-Liff, B., & Kronenfeld, J. (1994). Access to family planning services in low-income Arizona women. *American Journal of Public Health, 84,* 1010-1012.

Leigh, W. A. (1992). *A health assessment of black Americans: A fact book.* Washington, DC: Joint Center for Political and Economic Studies.

Lillie-Blanton, M., MacKenzie, E., & Anthony, J. C. (1991). Black-white differences in alcohol use by women: Baltimore survey findings. *Public Health Report, 106*(2), 124-133.

McBarnette, L. (1988). Women and poverty: Effects on reproductive status. In C. Perales & L. Young (Eds.), *Women, health, and poverty* (pp. 55-81). New York: Hawthorne.

McBeath, W. (1991). A public health vision. *American Journal of Public Health, 81*(12), 1560-1565.

Murphy, F. G., & Elders, M. J. (1992). Diabetes and the black community. In R. L. Braithwaite & S. E. Taylor (Eds.), *Health issues in the black community* (pp. 121-131). San Francisco: Jossey-Bass.

National Cancer Institute. (1989). *1991 budget estimate.* Bethesda, MD: U.S. Public Health Service.

National Center for Health Statistics (NCHS). (1979). *Health United States* (DHEW Publication No. HRA-80-1232). Hyattsville, MD: U.S. Public Health Service.

National Center for Health Statistics (NCHS). (1990). *Health United States, 1989.* Hyattsville, MD: U.S. Public Health Service.

Nobles, W. W., & Goddard, L. L. (1992). Drugs in the African American community: A clear and present danger. In R. L. Braithwaite & S. E. Taylor (Eds.), *Health issues in the black community.* San Francisco: Jossey-Bass.

Obesity and cardiovascular disease risk factors in black and white girls: The NHLBI Growth and Health Study. (1992). *American Journal of Public Health, 82*(12), 1613-1620.

O'Hare, W. P. (1985). Poverty in America: Trends and new patterns. *Population Bulletin, 40*(3), 2-43.

Olmeda, E. L., & Parron, D. L. (1984). Mental health of minority women: Some special issues. *Professional Psychology, 15,* 403-417.

Pappas, G. (1994, June). [Editorial]. *American Journal of Public Health, 84*(6), 892-893.

Perales, C., & Young, L. (Eds.). (1988). *Women, health, and poverty.* New York: Hawthorn.

Petitti, D., Coleman, C., Binsacca, D., & Allen, B. (1990, March). Early prenatal care in black and white women. *Birth, 17*(1), 5.

President's Commission on Mental Health. (1978). *Report of the task panel on minority mental health, 1978.* Washington, DC: Government Printing Office.

Report on the work of Seifert and Dos Martin (1986, August 16). U. of Michigan. *N.Y. Amsterdam News.*

Samuelson, E. J., Speers, M. A., Ferguson, R., & Bennett, C. (1994). Racial differences in cervical cancer mortality in Chicago. *American Journal of Public Health, 84,* 1007-1009.

Schulte, P., Ringen, K., & Hemstreet (1992). Risk assessment of a cohort exposed to aromatic amines: Initial results. *Journal of Occupational Medicine, 27,* 115-121.

Steingart, R. M., Packer, M., & Hamm, P. (1991). Sex differences in the management of coronary heart disease. *New England Journal of Medicine, 325*(4), 226-230.

Tallon, J., & Block, R. (1988). Changing patterns of health insurance coverage: Special concerns for women. In C. Perales & L. Young (Eds.), *Women, health, and poverty* (pp. 119-134). New York: Hawthorne.

Taylor, S. E. (1992). The mental health status of black Americans: An overview. In R. L. Braithwaite & S. E. Taylor (Eds.), *Health issues in the black community* (pp. 20-34). San Francisco: Jossey-Bass.

U.S. Bureau of the Census. (1988, March). Household and family characteristics, March 1988. *Current Population Reports* (Series P-20, No. 4377). Washington, DC: Government Printing Office.

U.S. Department of Health, Education, and Welfare (HEW). (1973). *Mortality trends: Age, color, and sex, U.S. 1950-69: National health survey, vital and health statistics* (Series 20, No. 15, pp. 1-40). Washington, DC: Government Printing Office.

U.S. Department of Health and Human Services [U.S. DHHS]. (1985). *Report of the Secretary's task force on black and minority health.* Washington, DC: Government Printing Office.

U.S. Department of Health and Human Services [U.S. DHHS]. (1989). *National medical expenditures survey.* Washington, DC: Government Printing Office.

U.S. Department of Health and Human Services [U.S. DHHS]. (1990). *Healthy people 2000: National health promotion and disease prevention objectives* (Publication No. PHS 91-50213). Washington, DC: Government Printing Office.

U.S. Public Health Service. (1985). *Report of the secretary's task force on women's health issues.* Washington, DC: Author.

Wattleton, F. (1992). Reproductive rights and the challenge for African Americans. In R. L. Braithwaite & S. E. Taylor (Eds.), *Health issues in the black community* (pp. 301-313). San Francisco: Jossey-Bass.

Weis, D. (1992). Uninsured maternity clients: A concern for quality. *American Nursing Research, 5*(2), 74-82.

3

American Indian and Alaska Native Women

Jo Ann Kauffman
Yvette K. Joseph-Fox

Estimates of the total number of American Indians living in the continental United States at the time of European contact vary from 10 million to 26 million Vogel (1970). By the late 1800s, an estimated 200,000 American Indians were still alive within the lower 48 United States (Vogel, 1970). To *decimate* literally means to destroy or kill 1 out of every 10. The destruction of American Indian tribes was far more devastating then decimation. Moreover, the loss of lives cannot be understood unless one looks also at the tremendous loss of Native cultural knowledge, which sustained Indian societies for thousands of years and was the foundation for a natural state of balance. To understand the health care and health status of Indian people—specifically, Indian women—one must begin with the notion of health itself. Contemporary Western medicine tends to define health by first defining sickness, disease, or pathology, and then defining health as the absence of these disease. Native American cultures for centuries understood health to mean simply the balance or beauty of all things physical, spiritual, emotional, and social. Sickness was seen as something out of balance, the absence of harmony.

Women represent an integral force within American Indian societies, a force for balance and harmony. Traditionally, Indian women were recognized among many tribes as the center of the extended family system, the sacred lifegivers, teachers, caregivers, herbalists, doctors, political voices, spiritual messengers, and even warriors (Niethammer, 1977). Today, those roles have become mired in the complexity of Western cultural views of women and men, extreme poverty, anomie, and a loss of the traditional ties of Native society and support systems. Indian women are searching for balance, harmony, and beauty in the face of tremendous odds (Brafford & Laine, 1992). In this chapter, we examine the health care and health status of American Indian and Alaska Native women and their struggle to attain balance and well-being.

BACKGROUND

No other ethnic group in the United States is so profoundly shaped, guided, or misguided by federal laws and policies than American Indians. This is because of the unique relationship—based on explicit provisions in the U.S. Constitution, treaties, statutes, and court decisions—that exist between Indian tribes and the federal government (Cohen, 1982). The federal relationship with and obligations to Indian people exist because of their status as members of federally recognized tribes, not their representation as a minority group. This legal political relationship is based on the cession of more than 50 million acres of land and thus sets Indian people distinctly apart from other minority groups in the United States. Indian tribes were historically dealt with as sovereign nations, and agreements were ratified between the variety of nations. This government-to-government relationship continues today. As early as 1836, tribes signed treaties with the U.S. government that included the provision of medical supplies and physician services and the promises of hospital construction for the relinquishment of millions of acres of land (Cohen, 1982). Health care for American Indians first began on a broad scale while the Bureau of Indian Affairs (BIA) was established under the U.S. War Department in 1832 in order to protect U.S. soldiers and non-Indian neighbors from becoming infected with smallpox, measles, diphtheria, malaria, and other diseases that were wreaking havoc on Indian camps at that time (Cohen, 1982). The BIA was eventually transferred to the Department of the Interior, and although there were sporadic periods of concern about the poor health conditions of Indians, the record was shameful for the next 90 years.

By 1900, the BIA employed 160 physicians to care for Indian people across the United States (Stearns & Wilson, 1993). Still, the onset of tuberculosis, trachoma, and other diseases prompted public outrage that resulted in the intervention of President Taft to urge Congressional action (Stearns & Wilson, 1993). In 1921, Congress passed the Snyder Act, mandating Congressional appropriations for "the relief of distress and conservation of health" of Indians throughout the United States.[1] An organized and meaningful health program was finally beginning to take shape.

THE INDIAN HEALTH SYSTEM TODAY

According to the 1990 U.S. census, 1.9 million Indians are identified as residing in the United States. The Indian Health Service (IHS) in the Department of Health and Human Services has identified its service population at 1.3 million, which includes members of federally recognized tribes located within established IHS service areas, patients of IHS and tribal clinics, and patients of urban Indian health clinics. According to the U.S. census, over half of the total Indian population resides off the reservation, many in urban settings. The IHS provides health care to Indian people through three major mechanisms. The first mechanism is through the IHS system directly through federal service unit clinics and federal hospitals. IHS operates 76 service units, 42 hospitals, 66 health centers, 4 school health centers, and 53 health stations. The IHS also maintains a limited budget to pay private specialists and hospitals for care provided to IHS beneficiaries on a preapproved basis. The second mechanism is through IHS contracts with Indian tribes that administer their own health care delivery system under a federal law authorizing the transfer of such responsibilities at the discretion of the tribe. Tribes operate 64 service units, 8 hospitals, 98 health centers, 3 school health centers, 59 health stations, and 172 Alaska village clinics. The third mechanism is a small program that represents less than 1% of the IHS budget: the urban Indian Health Program. The urban program funds grants and contracts to 34 nonprofit Indian organizations in urban areas to provide health education, referrals, and outpatient health care to Indians residing in urban areas. This program operates 28 health clinics and 6 referral centers. In addition to these direct services, the IHS also has environmental and public health responsibilities for tribes, including water and sewer sanitation, environmental engineering, public health nursing, health education, and outreach.

The IHS operates on annual appropriations from Congress. In 1994, the IHS operated on just under $2 billion. The per capita expenditure for

Indian beneficiaries of the IHS system is less than the per capita health expenditure for U.S. citizens. The limited budget forces IHS to ration care, so that not all services are guaranteed. The distribution of health care resources across Indian country is inequitable, with one area receiving a full range of services, another perhaps receiving very little, on the basis of historical investment in that area, geographical isolation, cost, and other factors.

Socioeconomic Conditions

The 1990 census reported that 34% of the Indian population is younger than age 15, compared with 22% of the U.S. population. The median household income of Indians living on a reservation is $19,865, compared with the U.S. median of $30,056. Thirty-five percent of Indians live below the federal poverty level, with an unemployment of rate of 21%.

The health status of American Indian and Alaska Native women is directly related to the socioeconomic conditions affecting Indian communities. Substantial evidence suggests that poverty, unemployment, and living in a single-parent home pose significant risks for the development of health problems, particularly in behavioral health areas (U.S. Congress, 1986). The Bureau of Indian Affairs Work Force data (1991) indicate that, of the 1.9 million American Indians and Alaska Natives, approximately 1 million Indian people live on reservations (the workforce represents individuals between the ages of 16 and 64). And, on average, 46%, or 239,179, of the Indian people on reservations are unemployed. The BIA data also indicate that, of 236,691 American Indians and Alaska Natives employed in Indian country, only 28% individuals, earn $7,000 a year or more. The average unemployment rates for American Indians and Alaska Natives range from 0% to 85% throughout the United States.

According to 1990 census data, 35% of Indians live below the federal poverty level, and 14% live in deep poverty, compared with 9.8% of white persons. Fifty-one percent of American Indians and Alaska Natives receive some sort of welfare payment, according to the *Population Bulletin* (1992). The *Population Bulletin* also reports that 21% of American Indian and Alaska Native households are headed by women, compared with 8% in white households, 33% in African American households, 7% in Asian American households, and 17% in Hispanic American households.

The educational achievement of American Indians and Alaska Natives in the labor force is comparable yet does not influence their employability:

36% of Indian people in the labor force have less than a high school education, compared with 37% among white people; 67% of Indian people have graduated from high school, which is the same among the white labor force; 75% of the Indian labor force has some college, compared with 73% among the white population; and 84% of American Indians and Alaska Natives have graduated from college, compared with 82% of the white labor force (*Population Bulletin,* 1992).

In 1992, testimony before the U.S. Senate Select Committee on Indian Affairs by the National Commission on American Indian, Alaska Native, and Native Hawaiian Housing reported a documented need of between 70,000 and 100,000 new or substantially rehabilitated housing units and that the need appears to be growing in Indian country.

The IHS estimated in 1991 that 186,566 housing units in their service areas are eligible for sanitation services. The IHS also reported that 20,335 Indian homes do not have potable water in the home. Of these, more than 10,000 are on the Navaho Reservation, and nearly 7,000 are in Alaska Native villages. The IHS also estimates that almost 7% of Indian homes have neither a safe water supply nor an adequate sewage system and that nearly 8% lack one or the other. In summary, the IHS estimates that 128,262 Indian housing units have no water or sewer systems or their systems are inadequate or fail to meet pollution control laws (U.S. Indian Health Service, 1991). It is not surprising that the health status of American Indians and Alaska Natives is far behind that of the general U.S. population, in part because of the environmental health hazards affecting Indian families.

The disparity in health care per capita expenditures was clarified by Judith Feder, Assistant Secretary for the Department of Health and Human Services, at a U.S. Senate Committee on Indian Affairs hearing on S. 1757, the American Health Security Act, held on January 31, 1994. Feder testified that American Indians and Alaska Natives, on average, expend $1,156 on health care per patient, compared with $3,127 per patient in the general U.S. population. Despite legislative efforts to improve the health conditions of American Indians and Alaska Natives, the overall health status of these populations remains below the national average. The IHS reported that only 15 of the 505 IHS, tribal, and urban Indian health facilities nationwide could actually provide the basic health benefits package proposed in the American Health Security Act. It is anticipated that comprehensive health care reform on a national basis will improve the availability of health care services for all Americans. The challenge remains, however, for members of Congress, the administration, and tribal governmental officials to ensure that a variety of comprehensive benefits will be equally available to American Indians and Alaska Natives. Much of the discussion specific to Native American health care reform efforts has focused on global issues affecting the entire population. The potential to improve access and the range of health care services for American Indian and Alaska Native women during the health care reform debate and in subsequent implementation efforts provides hope for the future.

Morbidity, Mortality, and Selected Causes

The federal moral and legal responsibility to provide health care to Indians and Alaska Natives evolved from the unique tribal/federal history and was later reaffirmed in federal law.[2] Data regarding the health status of American Indians and Alaska Natives were not well maintained until 1955, when the responsibility for the federal health program transferred from the BIA to the U.S. Public Health Service, where it remains today.[3] Reliable morbidity and mortality data can be tracked back to 1955. It is clear from these data that the health status of American Indian women has improved in many ways.

Maternal mortality has dramatically improved for Indian women since 1955, as it has for other women in the United States. Increased access to hospitals for complicated deliveries has had its impact. Death due to complications of childbirth was once a leading killer of Indian women. Today, it does not rank among their leading causes of death. In 1958, the maternal mortality rate for Indian women was 82.6 deaths per 100,00 live births, compared with the U.S. rate for all races of 37.6 deaths per 100,000 live births. The most recent data, from 1990-1992, reflect a rate of 8.9 Indian maternal deaths per 100,000 live births, compared with 17.9 deaths per 100,000 live births for U.S. all races (U.S. Indian Health Service, 1995). Although the overall rates have dramatically improved, the ratio of Indian rates to white rates reveals a maternal mortality rate still almost 2 times greater for Indians. Table 3.1 compares Indian maternal mortality rates (based on 3-year averages indicated by the mid-year) with the annual maternal mortality for U.S. all races and U.S. white population from 1958.

Historically, Indian mortality data have proved to be an undercount (U.S. Indian Health Service, 1993). American Indian people are among the most misidentified racial group on death certificates nationally (Duke, 1992). Indian people, although identified as Indian on birth certificates (which are filled out by the mothers), are often misidentified on death

Table 3.1 Maternal Death Rates (American Indians and Alaska Natives Within the IHS Service Area and U.S. All Races and White Populations 1958-1988)

Indian Year	All Races		Indian Ratio to:		
	U.S. Rate	White Rate	Rate	U.S.	White
1988	10.2	8.4	5.9	1.2	1.7
1987	8.5	6.6	5.1	1.3	1.7
1986	5.5	7.2	4.9	0.8	1.1
1985	4.5	7.8	5.2	0.6	0.9
1984	8.0	7.8	5.4	1.0	1.5
1983	6.9	8.0	5.9	0.9	1.2
1982	7.2	7.9	5.8	0.9	1.2
1981	5.0	8.5	6.3	0.6	0.8
1980	9.4	9.2	6.7	1.0	1.4
1979	13.1	9.6	6.4	1.4	2.0
1978	12.7	9.6	6.4	1.3	2.0
1977	8.5	11.2	7.7	0.8	1.1
1976	8.9	12.3	9.0	0.7	1.0
1975	13.0	12.8	9.1	1.0	1.4
1974	15.5	14.6	10.0	1.1	1.6
1973	27.7	15.2	10.7	1.8	2.6
1958	82.6	37.6	26.3	2.2	3.1

SOURCE: U.S. Indian Health Service (1993).

certificates (which are usually filled out by funeral directors). Indians are often classified as white, black, or Hispanic. Until all states participate in steps to improve vital events data, Indian mortality data should be considered an undercount or a conservative estimate. Given this qualification, trends in mortality data shed light on the health status of Indian women and are even more alarming given the likelihood of an undercount. Data reveal that Indian women suffer mortality rates higher than all U.S. races from deaths due to accidents, diabetes mellitus, chronic liver disease and cirrhosis, pneumonia and influenza, and tuberculosis (see Table 3.2). The leading cause of death for Indian women remains diseases of the heart. Alcoholism and alcohol abuse have been linked to 5 of the top 10 causes of death. Cirrhosis and chronic liver failure are the sixth leading cause of death for Indian women today.

Table 3.2 Leading Causes of Death by Sex in Rank Order for Indian Women
(American Indian and Alaska Natives in the IHS Service Area
1987-1989, Rate per 100,000 Population)

Cause of Death	Indian Rates		U.S. All Races	
	Male	*Female*	*Rate*	*Ratio*
Diseases of the heart	143.1	97.8	166.3	0.8
Malignant neoplasms	74.9	73.1	132.7	0.7
Accidents	133.0	43.9	35.0	2.7
Motor vehicle	72.6	26.7	19.7	2.6
Other accidents	60.4	17.2	15.3	2.7
Diabetes mellitus	19.6	26.7	10.7	2.9
Cerebrovascular diseases	24.7	24.0	29.7	0.9
Chronic liver disease/cirrhosis	25.5	21.1	9.0	3.3
Pneumonia and influenza	22.7	17.9	14.2	1.5
Perinatal conditions	—	8.4	—	—
Chronic obstructive pulmonary	13.9	8.4	19.4	0.7
Nephritis, nephrotic syndrome	—	8.3	—	—

SOURCE: U.S. Indian Health Service (1993).

The diseases killing Indian women today are lifestyle related. Mortality and morbidity data suggest that the traditional medical model approach to prevention and treatment will have little lasting impact. Indeed, to affect the health status of Indian women today, a strategy for "getting back into balance" is key. Although diseases of the heart and cancers represent leading killers of Indian women, their rates remain below that of the U.S. all-races population. Examining the causes of death that are disproportionately higher than national rates reveals a web of medical, environmental, and psychosocial challenges.

Alcoholism and Alcohol Abuse

Alcoholism and alcohol abuse remain the number one health problem facing Indian people, although patterns vary from tribe to tribe and region to region. The *Report of the Secretary's Task Force on Black and Minority Health* (U.S. DHHS, 1985) found that 5 of the top 10 leading killers of American Indian people were directly related to alcoholism or alcohol abuse. Research by May (1982) and others finds that the vast majority of Indians report to be abstainers, followed by those reporting to be heavy drinkers, and a surprisingly disproportionate few moderate or social drinkers, compared with similar data on the general population. Indian deaths from alcohol occur at younger ages, usually violently and related to risk-taking behaviors. This finding is a contrast to the image of the older chronic alcoholic and gives more credence to the hazards of rural roads, isolation, binge drinking, insufficient emergency response systems, and self-destructive impulses of the young. In fact, of all Indian deaths annually, over 35% are to persons under the age of 44, compared with 11% for U.S. all races. The two leading causes of death for Indians between ages 15 and 44 are accidents and cirrhosis of the liver (U.S. Indian Health Service, 1993).

Indian women, however, show a different, emerging alcohol abuse pattern. For many years, Indian alcoholism was considered a problem primarily with men, whereas women were seen as the stable caretakers. Contemporary researchers of American Indian alcoholism report that the two groups with the fastest growing rates of alcoholism prevalence are Indian women and Indian adolescents (Flemming & Manson, 1990). Indian women generally drink differently than Indian men. Indian men who drink tend to be heavier drinkers, compared with Indian women who drink, although tribe-specific exceptions are known (Flemming & Manson, 1990). Heath (1989) reports that rural Sioux women drink more frequently than rural Sioux men. Although the drinking behavior of Indian men results in higher rates of alcohol-related accidental deaths, homicides, and suicides, Indian women tend to move more quickly toward the development of cirrhosis of the liver. Indian women die from cirrhosis at 3 times the rate of black women and 6 times the rate of white women. According to IHS testimony before the U.S. Senate Committee on Indian Affairs on May 23, 1991, data suggest that, for 35- to 44-year-old females, the alcohol mortality rate is over 5 times that of the U.S. rate. For 45- to 54-year-old females, the mortality rate is almost 8 times as high as the U.S. rate.[4] The DHHS Secretary's Task Force in 1985 found that the rate of death for Indian women from cirrhosis was even greater than cirrhosis mortality rates for black men, Hispanic men, and white men. The IHS reported that, of all Indian deaths from cirrhosis of the liver, half are women. These data challenge old notions that alcoholism is a problem primarily of Indian men and raise public policy questions about the allocation of treatment resources and specially focused treatment programming. Nationally, the IHS operates 7 of 46 inpatient alcohol treatment facilities that specifically address the needs of women. Heath (1989) reports that only 20% of the total number of clients treated in Indian alcoholism programs are women.

Flemming and Manson (1990) suggest that Indian women abuse alcohol and other drugs because of (a) cultural disruption, (b) loss of social controls, (c) prejudice, (d) poverty, (e) role reversals, (f) peer group dynamics, (g) familial socialization, and (h) decreased self-worth and alienation. Earlier theories suggesting a genetic predisposition to alcoholism related to race have been all but abandoned. Native American communities in particular are examining the cultural and historical factors that place families and communities at risk for alcohol and other drug abuse. The traditional roles of women and men in Indian communities have been uprooted and twisted. High mortality rates combined with high birth rates result in Indian women bearing increasingly greater amounts of stress in the care of their families. Treatment workers report that Indian women are more likely to try to keep their families together even in the face of their own alcoholism. This behavior has made it difficult for Indian women to access inpatient treatment facilities, which are not normally equipped to take children. For an Indian women in need of treatment, the choice between entering inpatient care and safeguarding her children can be difficult, particularly when alcoholism is pervasive throughout the family system and there are no sober relatives to fill in for the duration of treatment. The right decision for her disease could cost her custody of her children, her connection to family, and her link to the future (Kauffman, 1992).

Pressure to do more for Indian women in need of alcohol or other drug treatment is increasing. Much of that concern has come from increased awareness of the long-term, damaging effects of prenatal alcohol use on the unborn fetus. Fetal alcohol syndrome (FAS), which can result in a constellation of physical malformations, brain damage, and other disabilities, has been identified as the leading cause of mental retardation in the United States, surpassing Down syndrome and spina bifida (Streissguth, Aase, Clarren, LaDue, & Smith, 1991). Although FAS surveillance efforts are not ideal, May (1982-1983) reports higher FAS rates in certain regions of Indian country, particularly in the northern plains states, compared with U.S. rates. IHS testimony indicates that, in some communities, the incidence rate (cases per 1,000 births per year) of FAS appears to be 2 to 5 times the general U.S. rate. Unfortunately, the wave of concern for fetal victims falls far short of understanding the complexity of the alcoholic Indian woman. Early efforts to combat FAS in some communities included passing tribal law-and-order codes requiring the incarceration of pregnant Indian women drinkers (May, 1982-1983). Although these codes offered an immediate and simple solution, they created an environment in which women will be more likely to hide their drinking, hide their pregnancies, delay or refuse prenatal care, and generally distrust the support system of the community, and, moreover, the codes are sexist in their execution. Heath (1989) points out increasing evidence that chronic male drinkers may cause teratogenic damage to the germ plasm, resulting in similar outcomes. The thrust to prevent FAS, however, remains focused on keeping women from drinking at all during pregnancy. To truly have an impact in Indian country, much more needs to be done to expand the number of treatment resources and the quality of the treatment program, so that the needs of Indian women will be met to bring about the long-term health and sobriety of Indian women, not just during their ninth months of pregnancy.

Indian women require a different treatment environment then men. In addition to the problem of children who may need to be attended to during treatment, Indian women have different treatment needs. Women who have been victimized by males in domestic abuse situations or who are child abuse survivors may not respond well to the confrontational approach of many 12-step treatment models incorporated into Indian programs, particularly if the professional counseling staff is dominated by males (Heath, 1989). One of the largest Indian alcohol treatment programs in the United States, the Thunderbird Treatment Center in Seattle, Washington, reports that over 95% of the women in treatment are also victims of child sexual abuse. A movement is under way to finally begin to blend the alcoholism treatment and mental health counseling fields so that support can also be provided for the complexity of historical traumas that emerge as a woman becomes sober. This approach is a tremendous break from the rigid rules of the past that treated claims of related mental anguish as a diversion from or denial of the underlying problem of alcoholism.

Alcoholism prevention, treatment, and recovery in American Indian communities are moving to a higher level of holistic understanding by incorporating the mental, physical, spiritual, and social needs of the individual. Alcoholism and other drug abuse, including inhalant abuse, are viewed as a means to self-medicate other problems. Recent treatment interventions that respond to the full spectrum of individual and family needs on a holistic as well as cultural basis offer new hope for the Indian woman who drowns her sorrows in alcohol and other drugs. The National Association for Native American Children of Alcoholics, which was formed in 1988, has triggered a groundswell across American Indian communities in the United States and Canada dedicated to recovery, not just from alcoholism but from the traumatic effects of cultural oppression, racism, poverty, and child abuse and neglect (Moz, 1994). This is a strategy, not just for treating or preventing alcoholism, but for getting back into balance with Native values.

Violence

Violence inflicted on Indian girls and women has been linked by activists in the field to the loss of traditional cultural values, the negative influences of Christianity and Americanization, and misuse of alcohol (Gunn-Allen, 1990). The National Coalition Against Domestic Violence estimates that every 15 seconds in the United States, a woman is beaten to the point of requiring medical assistance. Although data on the numbers of Indian women beaten are limited, other data suggest that violence remains a part of all communities. The problem of domestic violence in Indian country led Congress to pass legislation in 1990 that would provide programs for families in crisis. Unfortunately, in the years following the enactment of this initiative, no funds have been provided to begin services and support for domestic violence in Indian communities. The act defined family violence as

> any act, or threatened act, of violence, including any forceful detention of an individual which—(a) results, or threatens to result, in physical or mental injury, and (b) is committed by an individual against another individual—
>
> (i) to whom such person is or was, related by blood or marriage or otherwise legally related, or
>
> (ii) with whom such person is or was residing.[5]

Considerable criticism has come from Indian women active in the fight against violence, claiming that tribal governments do not take the problem of domestic violence, rape, and other violent acts against women seriously enough. According to Gunn-Allen (1990), the abuse of women is reaching alarming proportions in their communities, and tribal councils and other official agencies often refuse to recognise the extent of the problem. Indian women face a double-edged sword when discussing violence in their communities. In addition to recognizing and confronting the sexism and violence against women within their communities, they must also deal with the racism and oppression that exist outside the communities. Vio-

Table 3.3 Distribution of Child Sexual Abuse Victims by Age and Sex

Age	Male	Female
< 1 year	40%	60%
1-5 years	21.6%	78.4%
5-10 years	21.4%	78.6%
10-15 years	17.3%	82.7%
15-18 years	20.7%	79.3%

SOURCE: National Indian Justice Center (1990).

lence is rarely an isolated issue, but rather is associated with myriad social ills, including drug or alcohol abuse, unemployment, poverty, isolation, self-hate, and cultural oppression. Although tribal governments continue to be dominated by males, the number of Indian women in elected office is increasing. Also, women in leadership positions—for example, Julia Davis, President of the National Indian Health Board, and Wilma Mankiller, Principal Chief of the Cherokee Nation—are outspoken about the need to turn the Indian national agenda back to the stability and wellness of the Indian family.

A study contracted by the IHS on child abuse and neglect found that up to 34.4% of Indian children are at risk of becoming victims of abuse and/or neglect, with the majority of cases going unreported (National Indian Justice Center, 1990). This same study found that only 25% of communities surveyed tracked child abuse by using computer systems. The majority must depend on reliable manual systems, good memories, and continuity of quality staffing—an unlikely combination.

The study examined 2,035 cases of child abuse from around the United States and provided the first reliable profile of abuse in Indian country. It found that the majority (79.4%) of all abuse occurs in the child's home, with 48.9% of the cases involving neglect, 28% involving sexual abuse, and 20.8% involving physical abuse. Of all the sexual abuse victims, 79.8% were girls. Of the perpetrators of sexual abuse, 90.2% were males, with the majority being biological relatives other than parents (National Indian Justice Center, 1990). The study also found a striking relationship between alcohol and substance abuse and child abuse: Alcohol was a factor in 70.3% of all cases reviewed. Substance abuse was a lesser factor for male offenders; it was involved in 60% of total male offender cases, but was significantly higher for female offenders—70.4%. Male offenders

Table 3.4 Percentage of Indian Adolescents Who Indicated Ever Being Abused by Family Members or Others

Geographical Region	Physical Only	Sexual Only	Both Physical and Sexual
Total Indian sample			
Males (*n* = 1,297)	6.0%	1.1%	1.2%
Females (*n* = 1,360)	9.9%	6.3%	7.8%
Plains subsample			
Males (*n* = 529)	5.7%	0.6%	0.6%
Females (*n* = 585)	11.5%	5.5%	8.2%
Southwest subsample			
Males (*n* = 564)	6.2%	1.6%	1.5%
Females (*n* = 575)	9.4%	6.8%	6.6%
Southeastern subsample			
Males (*n* = 204)	6.0%	0.7%	2.2%
Females (*n* = 200)	6.3%	7.4%	9.7%

SOURCE: U.S. Congress, Office of Technology Assessment (1990).

were more involved in sexual and physical abuse, 90.2% and 59.3%, respectively, whereas Indian women represented 74.7% of all neglect offenders.

For Indian girls who are victims of sexual or physical abuse or neglect, the effects can last a lifetime. The double stigma of growing up in a home with alcoholism or substance abuse and with child sexual abuse can result in myriad problems, including social isolation, depression, low self-esteem, academic failure, sexual promiscuity, and suicidal or self-destructive behavior, which start to emerge in adolescence and can begin a lifelong pattern of sexual victimization (Moz, 1989). Testimony by American Psychological Association representatives before the U.S. Senate Select Committee on Indian Affairs on June 7, 1990, indicated that child neglect and abuse is a generational type of violence and very much a reality in Indian country.

A major survey of Indian adolescents undertaken by the University of Minnesota reveals that Indian girls from every region of the United States suffer disproportionately from both sexual and physical abuse (see Table 3.4). These finding were a part of a major Congressional Office of Technology Assessment inquiry into adolescent mental health (U.S. Congress, 1990).

Little support is available to Indian women and girls who are the victims of violence in their homes and communities. The IHS reports that injuries and poisonings were the fifth most frequent reason for hospitalization of Indian females in 1991. The age-specific mortality rate for motor vehicle accidents for Indian females is higher than for all U.S. races in all age-groups, with the rate twice the national rate for Indian females under age 5 and between the ages of 15 and 34 (U.S. Indian Health Service, 1993). The significant presence of alcohol and substance abuse in the phenomenon of violence in Indian homes should be considered and changes made to bring substance abuse treatment and prevention resources to integrate violence prevention. There have been success stories. For example, in South Dakota an organization of Indian women called the White Buffalo Calf Woman Society has taken on both the state of South Dakota and the Rosebud Sioux Tribe in efforts to get laws and ordinances passed to protect Indian women and children. The Rosebud Sioux Tribal Council adopted a Domestic Abuse Law in 1989 after pressure from the group. Likewise, the IHS has begun a successful accident prevention and education campaign that has had a major impact in reducing unintentional injuries to Indian children.

Diabetes

Diabetes is a problem for both Indian men and Indian women, with a diabetes mortality rate 3 times the rate for U.S. all races. Indian women, however, experience greater complications. Death from diabetes ranks 9th among the top 10 causes of death for Indian men; it ranks 4th among the top 10 causes of death for Indian women (U.S. Indian Health Service, 1993). Diabetes comes in two forms: Type I, or insulin-dependent diabetes mellitus, usually occurs at a young age and requires insulin injections as a part of its treatment; Type II, or non-insulin-dependent diabetes mellitus, usually strikes later in life and is connected with obesity. Type II diabetes could also involve insulin injections in its treatment; this form of diabetes has disproportionately disabled American Indian people, in particular Indian women.

Diabetes is a disease characterized by persistent hyperglycemia associated with an appreciable risk of development of specific microvascular complications. These complications can include retinopathy, peripheral neuropathy, nephropathy, and peripheral vascular disease. The most studied population in the world with regard to diabetes are the Pima Indians of Arizona. The Pima Indians have the highest incidence of non-insulin-dependent diabetes in the world, with up to 50% of the adult Pima population over age 35 affected (Nelson, Goddes, Everhart, Hartner, Zwemer, Petit, L. Knowler, 1980). Amputation is a major complication caused by diabetes and disproportionately affects Indian women. The majority of all amputations performed in Indian hospitals are related to complications of diabetes (Stemple, 1990). Further analysis performed by Sara Dye, an Indian woman physician working for the IHS in the Oklahoma area, found that of all the amputations performed from 1980 to 1989, 365 (51.3%) were to Indian female patients (Dye, Henderson, & Jones, 1990). She also found that 63.1% of all diabetics treated in Oklahoma IHS facilities in 1987 were female. Dye has been an outspoken critic of federal policies that restrict treating foot care and modern prosthesis as a high priority for Indian diabetic patients. She found in her practice that 70% of those Indian diabetics who have a leg amputated will have the second leg amputated within the next 5 years. In a one-woman effort to educate both patients and medical providers that more can be done to save limbs, she travels around the Oklahoma service areas, presenting "Dr. Dye's Dead Toe Show." Her crusade has had an impact (Kauffman, 1991).

Factors that place individuals at risk for developing Type II diabetes include the following:

- *Age and gender:* The incidence rate for men peaks between ages 25 and 44; and for women the incidence peaks between ages 35 and 54.
- *Family history:* Family history and genetics play a part in predicting diabetes. Persons with one diabetic parent are 2.3 times more likely to develop diabetes and 3.9 times more likely to develop diabetes if both parents were diabetic than individuals with no family history.
- *Obesity:* One of the most significant risk factors, particularly for young adults, is obesity.
- *Glucose intolerance:* Bennett et al. (1982), in their years of study, have found that the degree of glucose intolerance is a risk factor separate from the variables of obesity and heredity.

Indian women are also at risk for developing gestational diabetes, which is described as glucose intolerance during pregnancy. Gestational diabetes can cause significant health risks for both the woman and the fetus and thus create increased risk for infant mortality and morbidity. A study in 1987 found that gestational diabetes was present in 6.1% of all

Navaho pregnancies, whereas nationally it appeared in only 1% to 3% of pregnancies of non-Indian populations. An Indian woman who develops gestational diabetes during pregnancy has a 60% chance of developing overt diabetes within 16 years from the time of her pregnancy (Massion, O'Connor, Gorab, Crabtree, Nakamara, & Coulehan, 1987).

Efforts to prevent and treat diabetes are hampered by the poverty that exists in the Indian population. Poverty diets of fast foods, U.S. government commodity food surplus, and fried foods make diet control difficult. It is particularly difficult for Indian women to change their diets when many others within the household are unwilling to make the same diet changes. The cost of cooking two separate dishes at each meal may be prohibitive. Increased patient education that enlists the involvement of the entire family is needed.

Cancer

Malignant neoplasms are the second leading cause of death for American Indian women, second only to diseases of the heart. Cancer is the leading cause of death for Alaska Native women, a finding that suggests variation among certain regions and population groups in the United States. Although the overall cancer mortality rate for Indian women is less than that for U.S. women of all races, new research finds that Indian women are diagnosed later in the disease process than other women and are more likely to die from the disease than other women (Nutting et al., 1990). The poor survival rate of Indian women suffering from cancer is explained by the late diagnosis, combined with inadequate prevention and screening efforts, and an unfortunate confusion among some providers about the allowability of certain diagnostic procedures under severe federal budget constraints. Nutting et al. found that Indian women in the northern plains states and Alaska Native women suffer cancer mortality at rates that exceed U.S. all races rates for all types of cancers. Cervical cancer is a major problem for Indian women; Indian women experience a rate of cervical cancer 2 ½ times the rate of cervical cancer experienced by U.S. all races. Mortality rates from cervical cancer among Indian women in Alaska, the Southwest, and the northern plains states exceed U.S. rates.

It would be a mistake to make generalizations about Indian women and cancer, but the Nutting study has allowed health care professionals to begin to examine the variations from region to region and to target limited resources at those hot-spot areas. The National Cancer Institute (NCI), in coordination with organizations controlled by and for Indian people, has initiated a series of prevention and education campaigns targeting Indian women. This strategy has offered some hope and guidance at the local clinic level.

One of the most disturbing findings of the Nutting study came from a survey of local IHS providers to determine their opinions and practices related to the prevention and treatment of cervical and breast cancer. This survey found that local providers were "confused" about whether the use of mammography is a tool for "screening" high-risk women or a "diagnostic" tool for women who present with a breast lump. This confusion was underscored by the severe budget limitations of the IHS that restricted providers from ordering any procedure not determined to be a priority for the saving of life or limb. The impact of budget-cutting gimmicks on basic life-and-death decisions cannot be understated and was found to have a key role in the confusion of local providers when deciding to order mammographies. The survey uncovered examples of Indian women who had come to the clinic with a detected breast mass and who were placed on a waiting list until such time as the IHS contract funds might be sufficient to pay for the mammography referral (Nutting et al., 1990). Clearly, the intention of budget-cutting directives was not to deny women in need of diagnostic mammography from getting care, but the poor execution of the policy created severe misjudgments that affected the lives of Indian women. The IHS has since moved toward making mammography screening available at all of its service sites.

The same study found that postmenopausal women are at greater risk for receiving inadequate care and failed follow-up. Postmenopausal women are less likely to seek care for an enlarging breast mass and are less likely to be screened routinely by clinic providers (Nutting et al., 1990). The study found that women of childbearing age receive twice as many clinical breast exams as postmenopausal women at the same clinics. For example, 11 postmenopausal women who were discovered with stage II breast cancers had, according to their charts, visited the clinic five or more times in the year before their diagnosis. Even once the diagnosis is made, postmenopausal women are less likely to receive immediate attention and referral: 21% of the postmenopausal women with a diagnosed breast mass waited 3 months or longer before beginning treatment.

The initiatives sponsored by the NCI are having a positive impact. The American Indian Health Care Association, under contract with the NCI, has clinics with trained staffs serving urban Indian populations with computerized patient management systems specifically to improve Pap test followup and referrals. This system is similar to one being implemented by the IHS at IHS and tribal clinics, which is a computerized aggressive patient management system. Originally described by Shorr as "industrial strength triage," the ambulatory patient care system is searching for a less abrasive description (Shorr & Daniels, 1987). The system trains registered nurses to perform rapid, comprehensive patient chart reviews just prior to patient visits for the purpose of identifying unmet health care needs in consultation with the primary provider. The baseline data of Shorr's trial revealed that 84% of women patients had visited the clinic at a time when they would have been due for a Pap screening for cervical cancer; however, fewer than 50% of those patients received a Pap test. After the aggressive ambulatory patient management system was implemented, Pap smear referrals increased from 5% to 58%, immunization rates increased from 8% to 68%, and chronic disease followup improved from 4% to 46%. Indian women have been outspoken in demanding more attention to preventable cancers. A special roundtable of Indian women health experts underscored the need for increased women's health programs, women providers, and increased access to screening.

Reproductive Health

The birthrate for American Indians is almost twice the national rate. Indian birthrate for 1987 through 1989 was 28.8 births per 1,000 population, compared with 15.9 births for U.S. all races (U.S. Indian Health Service, 1993). This rate has been consistent for the last 20 years. Low birth weight babies have not been as significant a problem for Indian women served by the IHS system, compared with other races. Of all Indian births in 1987 through 1989, 5.9% were under 2,500 grams, compared with 6.9% of the babies for all races. This good report does not hold true, however, for the thousands of Indian women who live off a reservation in urban areas. A special study of American Indian and Alaska Native women residing in the Seattle metropolitan area found that the rate of low birth weight babies was considerably higher among urban Indians, compared with that of urban whites and rural Indians (Grossman, Krieger, Sugarman, & Forquera, 1994). The IHS (U.S. Indian Health Service, 1993) reports that, of the Indian women giving birth for the first time, 45% were under age 25, compared with 24% of women under age 25 from other races. The Office of Technology Assessment (U.S. Congress, 1990) found the extent of teenage pregnancy to be an indicator of the need for mental health and social services. In 1980, 25% of Indian births were to girls age 19 and younger, compared with a teenage pregnancy rate of 15% for the U.S. population at large.

Nationally, Indian infant mortality rates approach the U.S. all-races rate. In some geographical regions, however, infant mortality is twice the national rate or higher. These areas include the northern plains states, Alaska, the Southwest, and urban Indian communities. Other states, including California and Oklahoma, do not match birth and death certificates; this practice results in misclassifications by race and unrealistically low Indian infant mortality rates (Kauffman, 1991). The IHS has vastly improved the percentage of Indian women entering prenatal care during their first and second trimesters. Again, Indian women living in urban areas do not benefit from these federal initiatives. The Seattle study (Grossman et al., 1994) found that urban Indian women were less likely to enter prenatal care in the first trimester and more likely to have later prenatal care or none at all.

Sexually transmitted diseases are reported to occur more frequently among American Indian women, compared with other races. Kathleen Toomey, a woman physician who worked for the IHS in Alaska, found that Indian women had a higher rate of asymptomatic chlamydia, which she discovered by initiating routine screening (Toomey, Oberschelp, & Greenspan, 1989). In her research efforts, Toomey found that 114 (23%) of the 493 Alaska Native women studied had chlamydial infections; 39 (49%) of 80 teenagers had chlamydial infections, with rates declining to less than 6% among women over age 35. Left untreated, this infection could lead to other health problems, including sterility. The Centers for Disease Control and Prevention (CDC) also reported that gonorrhea case rates for American Indians and Alaska Natives were higher, compared with non-Indians in selected states, from 1984 to 1988. In clinics where efforts have been made to hold special women's health clinics and to hire women health practitioners, the participation of Indian women has increased. More attention to making Indian women feel comfortable and to providing a confidential, safe environment is important. According to the CDC, the number of American Indians with acquired immune deficiency syndrome (AIDS) as of September 1993 was 731. The data indicate 103 females afflicted with AIDS and 14 pediatric AIDS cases out of the 731 cases reported. The number is relatively low principally because of late reporting by the CDC, which began in the spring of 1987. It has also been noted that improper ethnic identification has contributed to the omission of Native Americans in the AIDS reporting by states and the CDC. The variety of high-risk factors and the limited availability of prevention, screening, and treatment services for AIDS pose a substantial threat for American Indian and Alaska Native women in the future. Numerous

American women may be at greater risk of infection with HIV because of the prevalence of bisexual behavior among Native American men. Family planning and contraceptive care is provided at IHS and urban Indian health clinics. The IHS is still recovering from allegations made in the 1970s that, in the Oklahoma area, sterilizations were routinely performed on Indian women without their consent (Kauffman, 1991). After national publicity, claims of genocide, and Congressional inquiries, the IHS developed an exhaustive patient consent procedure. That shift in vigilance has perhaps tightened the process too much. In addition to requiring a waiting period for sterilizations, many Indian women must wait until the IHS budget controllers assess whether such a procedure fits the definition for emergency care only.

A negative stigma has evolved around the provision of family planning services for Indian women. Staffs at many clinics are worried about advertising family planning services; they fear community claims of genocide. At a national gathering of Indian women sponsored by the Cherokee Nation on the topic of contraceptive services, a panel of Indian women concluded that Indian women, not Indian men or the federal government, should be the ones to decide about the reproductive rights and family planning services available to Indian women. Participants at this meeting also rejected the claims that contraceptive services are equivalent to genocide, and they insisted that Indian women should have the full range of choices available in the overall health system.[6]

Mental Health

One of the most significant pioneers in Indian mental health, Carolyn Attneave, conducted research in 1982 that found that Indian girls experience a higher rate of outpatient psychiatric treatment after age 14 than do Indian boys and a higher rate than boys and girls of other races (Beiser & Attneave, 1982). She found that Indian boys younger than age 14 used the outpatient mental health treatment system at high rates but that Indian girls, on reaching late adolescence, were by far the group at highest risk of entering psychiatric treatment. Data on attempted suicides among Indian adolescents confirm that many Indian girls engage in suicidal behavior. Of the 424 hospitalizations for suicide attempts recorded by the IHS in 1988, 70% were females between ages 15 and 17 (U.S. Congress, 1990). Indian girls represent the significant group at risk for suicide attempts, whereas Indian boys are at a higher risk for suicide completion (May, 1987).

Research on clinical depression among Indians shows that Indian females who are depressed are less likely to also present with alcoholism problems than Indian men. A study by Shore (Shore, Manson, Bloom, Keepers, & Neligh, 1987) found that 75% of the Indian men evaluated with depression also were diagnosed with alcoholism. This finding compared with only 35% of Indian women evaluated with both diagnoses. The Office of Technology Assessment report on Indian adolescent mental health (U.S. Congress, 1990) further found that female mental health patients who were abused as children exhibited more self-destructive behavior than females who were not abused. Boys who were abused exhibited more aggressive behavior than non-abused boys. Candice Flemming, an Indian woman mental health researcher, concurs that Indian women display mental health problems centered around family, spouses, alcohol use by family members, grief, and anxiety, whereas Indian men display mental health problems related to alcohol abuse, violent behavior, or trouble with the law (Flemming & Manson, 1990).

In searching for ways to improve the mental health of Indian women, a panel of Indian women experts concluded that specific factors must be considered, including the following (Kaufman, 1991):

- *Economic issues:* Poverty has had a major impact on the mental health of American Indians. The current federal "welfare" approach to assisting Indian communities has created a stigma of helplessness and paternalism. Indian women are taking on more responsibility as heads of households because of a chronic lack of employment for men in Indian communities.

- *Political issues:* Indian communities have adopted some of the worst traits of the larger political system; this has created divisions and feuding, which slow the growth and harmony of communities and undermine traditional Native values of consensus building. Categorical funding systems and the ever-present federal representatives erode the political empowerment at the grassroots level.

- *Cultural issues:* Indian families cannot insulate themselves from the influences of the dominant culture and the conflicts that are created for Indian youths. The traditional role of Indian women as the primary caretakers is still intact; there are no roles today for Indian men. Women often receive the rage and resentment of Indian men when these gender roles have become unclear in their culture.

- *Lifestyle issues:* To make lasting change will require lifestyle changes and early role models for Indian children. Indian girls need to see empowered Indian women. Indian girls need safe, supportive environments in which to talk about abuses in the home. The tide of self-destructive behaviors must be turned around.

CONCLUSION

The health status of Indian women is improving. Indian women have been the leaders nationally, pushing to focus attention on health care among this population. Principal Chief Wilma Mankiller of the Cherokee Nation of Oklahoma perhaps stated it best: "We all have a responsibility to go out and change things and revitalize health care in our communities. . . . It has been absolutely maddening, to me, the lack of attention paid to women's health care," Chief Mankiller said at the Second Annual Indian Women's Health: Issues and Action Conference in Rapid City, South Dakota, in early May 1994. "There would not be specific funding and bills today, without the women in the United States Congress and Senate working on health care issues."

The roles of American Indian and Alaska Native women in today's society remain quite similar to roles that were traditional for Native cultures, unlike the experience of Indian men who were stripped of their primary roles upon acculturation. Yet, Indian women are more likely to be victimized within their own families and communities. According to studies conducted by Charon Asetoyer, Executive Director of the Native American Women's Health Education Resource Center located on the Yankton Sioux Reservation in Andes, South Dakota, this abuse extended only back to the 1800s, when native children were forcibly placed into boarding schools and subsequently experienced abuse. To reverse this abuse, Asetoyer notes that, "Tribal administrations have the power to ensure that the BIA, IHS, and tribal programs address this very serious problem appropriately. However, until tribal leaders begin to care about the futures of women and children in Native communities around the country and put politics aside, the abuse will continue."

The balance and harmony of emotional, physical, spiritual, and social health of Indian people rests in large part with the balance and health of Indian women. Chief Mankiller has suggested, "It is very important for us to trust our own thinking and regain control of things. I have always thought, if we want to revitalize our communities, we need to do it ourselves." As Indian women are empowered, they will bring along their people and create a world that is safe and nurturing for a new generation of American Indians and Alaska Natives.

NOTES

1. United States Code 25 U.S.C. 13.
2. United States Code: The Johnson O'Malley Act, 25 U.S.C. 452 *et seq.*; the Transfer Act, 42 U.S.C. 2001 *et seq.*; the Indian Health Facilities Act of 1957, 42 U.S.C. 2005; the Indian Sanitation Facilities and Services Act of 1959, 42 U.S.C. 2004; the Indian Self-Determination Act of 1975, as amended, 25 U.S.C. 450 *et seq.*; the Indian Health Care Improvement Act of 1976 as amended, 25 U.S.C. 1601 *et seq.*
3. United States Code, 42 U.S.C. 2001 *et seq.*
4. Testimony of Dr. Everett Rhoades, Director, Indian Health Service, Senate Hearing before the Select Committee on Indian Affairs, 102nd Congress on S.290, to establish an Indian Substance Abuse Program, May 23, 1991, Washington, DC.
5. Public Law 101-630, The Indian Child Protection and Family Violence Prevention Act.
6. Remarks by Wilma Mankiller, Principal Chief, Cherokee Nation, at a national gathering in January 1993.

REFERENCES

Beiser, M., & Attneave, C. (1982). Mental disorders among Native American children: Rates and risk periods for entering treatment. *American Journal of Psychiatry, 139*(2), 000-000.

Brafford, C. J., & Laine, T. (Eds.). (1992). *Dancing colors: Paths of Native American women.* San Francisco: Chronicle Books.

Bureau of Indian Affairs (BIA), Office of Substance Abuse and Alcohol Prevention, Planning Group. (1992). C. Lujan, Director, Proceedings.

Cohen, F. (1982). *Handbook of federal Indian law.* Charlottesville, VA: Mitchie.

Duke, L. (1992, January 8). Study: Infant mortality rates misreported. *Washington Post,* p. 000.

Dye, S. K., Henderson, Z., & Jones, D. (1990). *Standards of diabetic foot care.* Unpublished manual, Indian Health Service, Oklahoma area.

Flemming, C. M., & Manson, S. (1990). Native American women. In R. C. Engs (Ed.), *Women: Alcohol and other drugs.* Dubuque, IA: Kendall Hunt.

Grossman, D., Krieger, J., Sugarman, J., & Forquera, R. (1994). Health status of urban American Indians and Alaska Natives: A population-based study. *Journal of the American Medical Association, 271*(11), 845-850.

Gunn-Allen, P. (1990, July). Violence and the American Indian woman. *Common Ground Common Planes Newsletter,* The Women of Color Partnership Program, July 1990.

Heath, D. B. (1989). American Indians and alcohol: Epidemiological and sociocultural relevance. In U.S. Department of Health and Human Services, Public Health Service, *Alcohol use among U.S. ethnic minorities* (NIAAA Research Monograph No. 18., DHHS Publication No. [ADM]89-1435). Washington, DC: Government Printing Office.

Kauffman, J. A. (1991). *A roundtable conference on Indian infant mortality: Final report.* Rockville, MD: U.S. Indian Health Service.

Kauffman, J. A. (1992). *Indian women's health issues roundtable final report.* Washington, DC: U.S. Department of Health and Human Services, U.S. Indian Health Service.

Massion, C., O'Connor, P., Gorab, R., Crabtree, B., Nakamura, R., & Coulehan, J. (1987). Screening for gestational diabetes in a high-risk population. *Journal of Family Practice, 25*(6), 569-576.

May, P. (1982). Substance abuse and American Indians: Prevalence and susceptibility. *International Journal of Addictions, 17*(7), 1185-1209.

May, P. (1982-83). A pilot project on fetal alcohol syndrome among American Indians. *Alcohol and Health Research World, 7*(2), 3-9.

May, P. (1987, July/August). Suicide among American Indian youth. *Children Today,* pp. 22-25.

Moz, J. M. (1994). *From nightmare to vision: A manual for Native American children of alcoholics.* Washington, DC: National Association for Native American Children of Alcoholics.

National Indian Justice Center. (1990). *Child abuse and neglect in American Indian and Alaska Native communities and the role of the Indian Health Service* (Unpublished final report, U.S. DHHS, Indian Health Service Contract #282-90-036).

Nelson, R., Gohdes, D. M., Everhart, J. E., Hartner, J. A., Zwemer, F. L., Pettitt, D. J., & Knowler, W. C. (1980). *Incidence of lower extremity amputations in non-insulin-dependent diabetes mellitus: A twelve year follow-up study in Pima Indians.* Unpublished manuscript, National Institute of Diabetes and Digestive and Kidney Diseases and Indian Health Service, Phoenix, AZ.

Niethammer, C. (1977). *Daughters of the earth: The lives and legends of American Indian women.* New York: Macmillan.

Nutting, P. A., Beaver, S., Hisnanick, J. Bates, P., Berg, L., Copp, D., & Tyson, H. (1990, May). Preventable cancer mortality in American Indian and Alaska Native women. *Indian Health Service Office of Health Program Research and Development,* . . . .

Population Bulletin, 47,(4), (1992, December).

Shore, J., Manson, S., Bloom, J., Keepers, G., & Neligh, G. (1987). A pilot study of depression among American Indian patients with research diagnostic criteria. *American Indian and Alaska Mental Health Research, 1*(2), 4-15.

Shorr, G., & Daniels, S. (1987, April). *Improving outpatient care with concurrent visit planning: The case for industrial strength triage.* Unpublished manuscript, Indian Health Service Division of Health Systems Development.

Stearns, C., & Wilson, C. (1993). *Indian health care reform, the delivery of Indian health care: The legal and policy foundation.* Unpublished manuscript.

Stemple, T. K. (1990, December). Lower extremity amputations at the Phoenix Indian Medical Center. *IHS Provider,* pp. 165-167.

Streissguth, A. P., Aase, J. M., Clarren, S. K., LaDue, R. A., Randals, S. P., & Smith, D. F. (1991). Fetal alcohol syndrome in adolescents and adults. *Journal of the American Medical Association, 265,* 1961-1967.

Toomey, K. E., Oberschelp, A. G., & Greenspan, J. R. (1989). Sexually transmitted diseases and Native Americans: Trends in reported gonorrhea and syphilis morbidity, 1984-88. *Public Health Reports, 104*(6).

U.S. Congress, Office of Technology Assessment. (1986). *Indian health care* (OTA-H-290). Washington, DC: Government Printing Office.

U.S. Department of Health and Human Services (U.S. DHHS). (1985). *Report of the secretary's task force on black and minority health.* Washington, DC: Government Printing Office.

U.S. Indian Health Service. (1991). *Annual report of the Indian Health Service on sanitation facilities.* Washington, DC: U.S. Department of Health and Human Services.

U.S. Indian Health Service. (1993). *Trends in Indian health.* Washington, DC: U.S. Department of Health and Human Services.

Vogel, V. (1970). *American Indian medicine.* Norman, OK: University of Oklahoma Press.

4

Asian/Pacific Islander American Women

Reiko Homma True
Tessie Guillermo

Although women's health and mental health issues are beginning to attract increased attention and support in the United States, little information is available about the health and mental health issues involving Asian and Pacific Islander American (A/PIA) women. In fact, there is a paucity of any information on A/PIAs, whether men, women, or children, in the United States. Citing methodological problems involved in conducting research among this relatively small portion of the population widely dispersed throughout the country and consisting of widely divergent ethnic and cultural subgroups, most researchers have avoided focusing on A/PIAs in general, including issues related to gender differences. The few national data collected on them until recently were limited to health status reports related to Chinese, Japanese, Filipinos, and sometimes Hawaiians (Yu & Liu, 1994).

Despite these limitations, epidemiological researchers and health care policymakers went so far as to conclude, on the basis of these limited data, that the health status of Asian Americans as a group is remarkably good (U.S. Office of Disease Prevention and Health Promotion, 1987, p. 18) and that "they are, in aggregate, healthier than all (other) racial/ethnic groups in the United States" (U.S. Department of Health and Human Services [U.S. DHHS], 1985, p. 81).

Many A/PIA health care providers active in their communities have learned through firsthand experience that hidden behind the image of healthier Asian Americans are many who are struggling with daily survival issues and suffering from significant health problems that are not being addressed because of barriers in the existing health care system.

The goal of this chapter is to review the information available on the health and mental health issues among A/PIA women, to identify gaps in the knowledge base and service accessibility, and to suggest action strategies to improve the quality of care provided for them.

BACKGROUND OF A/PIA WOMEN

Historical Background

The first group of Asian women to immigrate to the United States were Chinese women, who arrived in the mid 1800s. Because of the prohibitive cost of the long journey from China and the traditional reluctance to send Chinese women overseas, only a small number of them were able to immigrate with their husbands at the early stage of Chinese immigration. Before more Chinese women had the opportunity to immigrate to the United States, strong anti-Chinese sentiment erupted when Chinese male laborers in the United States began to achieve some level of economic success in their various enterprises. They were quickly perceived as potential threats to the socioeconomic security of white Americans, and exclusionary immigration laws were passed, beginning in 1882, to severely limit further entry of Chinese, including women.

In their place, a large number of Japanese males were brought in as cheap laborers to fill the backbreaking jobs no one else wanted. The Japanese government actively encouraged the immigration of women as wives of male laborers as a strategy for preventing problems endemic to bachelor societies, such as prostitution, violence, and gambling. Although the Japanese immigrants subsequently were perceived as a new threat replacing the Chinese, a significant number of Japanese women settled in the United States with their husbands before the restrictive immigration laws were extended to them through the National Origins Act of 1924 (Takaki, 1989, p. 14). The groups that followed the Chinese and Japanese were Korean and Filipino laborers. The number of women who entered the United States in the early years, however, was quite small (Takaki, 1989).

In 1965, the immigration laws were significantly liberalized to permit an increased number of immigrants from Asian countries and to allow the reunion of immigrants' family members, including wives who had been separated from their husbands for many years. This reform made it possible for many Chinese, Filipino, and Korean women to immigrate with or to join their families. After the end of the Vietnam War in 1975, many Southeast Asian refugee women were forced to flee their country, and a large wave of them resettled in the United States with their families.

Demographic Characteristics

In 1990, the U.S. census enumerated a population of over 7.2 million Asians and Pacific Islanders in the United States, doubling in number from 1980. Asian and Pacific Islander women make up a majority of that population, with an average 104 females per 100 males, although this ratio varies widely among the various A/PI ethnic groups.

Although the majority of women, as well as men, live in the western United States, a significant proportion of A/PI women live in other large states. In 1990, the five major states where Asian and Pacific Islander women lived were California (1,452,698), Hawaii (349,724), New York (343,801), Texas (161,371), and Illinois (144,401) (Asian/Pacific Islander Center for Census Information and Services [ACCIS], 1993a).

Asian and Pacific Islander women are, on average, older than men. The median age for females is 31.8 years, which is slightly higher than the median age of 29.0 years for males; this difference reflects the longer life expectancy of females (U.S. Bureau of the Census, 1992).

Asians and Pacific Islanders are not a homogeneous racial minority, and any aggregate analysis of these populations masks the wide diversity within. Up to 48 separate A/PI ethnic populations have been counted in the United States. The major Asian groups are Chinese, Filipino, Japanese, Asian Indian, Korean, Vietnamese, Laotian, Cambodian, Thai, and Hmong. The major Pacific Islander groups are Hawaiian, Samoan, Chamorro (Guamanian), Tongan, and Melanesian (ACCIS, 1993b).

Little information other than census data is available to make distinctions among these ethnic groups and to profile the characteristics relevant for assessing health status. Failure of national and state data systems to break down health data by ethnicity in order to make these distinctions have resulted in inappropriate health policies and programs for A/PI populations.

Sociocultural Characteristics

Among the unique sociocultural characteristics that have been documented as relevant to evaluate the health status of the A/PIA minority are nativity and language. Although at this time, data are not available by gender, it is important to note that 65.6% of all Asians are foreign born, compared with 7.9% of the total U.S. population, and 75.4% speak a language other than English at home, compared with 13.8% of the total U.S. population. Pacific Islanders have a lower percentage of foreign born (12.9%); however, Tongans (60.9%) and Melanesians (77.9%) have a high percentage of persons born outside the United States. Even with the low percentage of foreign-born Pacific Islanders, 31.2% speak a language other than English at home, with only Hawaiians speaking primarily English. The majority (57.5%) of all Asians and Pacific Islanders arrived in the Unites States between 1980 and 1990 (U.S Bureau of the Census, 1993a, 1993b).

In March 1991, 26% of all A/PIA women were never married, 8% were widowed, and 6% were divorced, compared with 28%, 2.5%, and 7% of white American women, respectively (U.S. Bureau of the Census, 1992).

In 1990, 12% of Asian American and 19% of Pacific Islander American family households were headed by women with no spouse, compared with 16.5% of all U.S. households. Among the Asian and Pacific women-headed households, the figures ranged from a low of 5.2% among Asian Indian women householders to a high of 26.2% among Hmong women householders (U.S. Bureau of the Census, 1993a, 1993b). A similar percentage (5.2%) of A/PIA and white family households in the five large A/PIA states were headed by women with children.

On aggregate, educational achievement by A/PIA women is high (74% high school graduate or higher, 31.8% bachelor's degree or higher), compared with the total U.S. population (74.8% and 17.6%; see Table 4.1).

Disaggregated, it is clear that some A/PIA women lag behind. On average, only 9.6% of Pacific Islanders attained a bachelor's degree or higher. Only 19% of Hmong, 25% of Cambodian, 29% of Laotian, and 53% of Vietnamese women have achieved a high school education. In contrast, 48.7% of Asian Indian women have achieved a bachelor's degree or higher.

Table 4.1 Educational Attainment of A/PIA Females 25 and Over

	% High School or Higher	% Bachelor's Degree or Higher
Total U.S.	74.8	17.6
Asian	74.0	31.8
Chinese	70.2	35.0
Filipino	81.4	41.6
Japanese	85.6	28.2
Korean	74.1	25.9
Asian Indian	79.0	48.7
Vietnamese	53.3	12.2
Cambodian	25.3	3.2
Laotian	29.8	3.5
Hmong	19.0	3.0
Thai	66.2	24.9
Other Asian	78.7	34.2
Pacific Islander	75.0	9.6
Hawaiian	79.0	10.7
Samoan	66.5	6.1
Tongan	66.8	5.9
Guamanian	70.6	8.2
Melanesian	56.6	7.9
Other Pacific Islander	76.2	13.5

SOURCE: U.S. Bureau of the Census (1992).

Economic Characteristics

The sociocultural characteristics outlined above for A/PIA women often correlate directly with economic status in 1990. Of women age 16 and over, 60% of Asians and 62.5% of Pacific Islanders are in the labor force, compared with 56.8% of the total U.S. population. Labor force participation by Southeast Asians reflects their lower educational attainment, with only 19.9% of Hmong and 37.3% of Cambodians in the labor force, and with 10.7% of Samoans and 10.5% of Tongans unemployed. Of interest is the lower labor force participation (55%) and unemployment (6.1%, compared with 5.5% for all Asians) of Asian Indian women, which contrasts with their high educational achievement. Filipino women had the highest labor force participation (72.3%); Japanese women had the lowest unemployment rate (2.7%) (U.S. Bureau of the Census, 1993a, 1993b).

The highest rates of employed Asian and Pacific Islander women are in Hawaii (97.1%) and Illinois (94.8%). In both states, the female A/PIA civilian employment rate ranks highest of all population groups (ACCIS, 1993a).

The median earnings of A/PIA women in 1990 was $21,320, compared with A/PIA males at $26,760. The rate for A/PIA women, however, was higher than for white U.S. women ($20,050). When educational attainment is taken into account, A/PIA women made slightly less, compared with white U.S. women with high school level attainment ($16,920, compared with $17,550). Earnings were similar at the college level ($29,150 for A/PIAs, compared with $29,110 for whites) (U.S. Bureau of the Census, 1992).

As with most women, 43% of A/PIA females are employed in the technical, sales, and administrative support positions, in contrast with A/PIA males (26%); 26% of all A/PIA women are employed in the managerial and professional specialty, compared with white females at 29% and A/PIA males at 33% (U.S. Bureau of the Census, 1992). Table 4.2 shows the labor force participation of A/PIA females age 16 and over.

According to census data on the occupational distribution of immigrant women in California, A/PIAs are employed primarily in administrative support occupations. Only Korean immigrant women are employed primarily in sales; this finding probably reflects the extremely high proportion of Korean grocers in the United States overall. Hmong and Thai women are primarily employed in service occupations, excluding protection and household services. Laotian women's occupations differ significantly from those of other A/PI immigrant women, with primary employment in the machine-operating, assembly, and inspection category. The second highest occupational category is craftmaking. Laotian craftsmanship is widely known and valued throughout the A/PIA communities in the United States. Chinese, Filipino, and Asian Indian immigrant women are highly employed in managerial and professional fields.

In 1990, the per capita income of A/PIAs was $1,840 lower than that for whites. Overall, 11.4% of Asian and 15.0% of Pacific Islander families were below poverty, compared with 10% for all U.S. families. Among the poorest Asian families were Hmong (61.8%), Cambodian (42.1%), Laotian (32.2%), Vietnamese (23.8%), and Koreans (14.7%); among Pacific

Table 4.2 Labor Force Participation of A/PIA Females 16 and Over

	Persons in Labor Force	%	Civilians in Labor Force	% Unemployed
Total U.S.	56,672,949	56.8	56,487,249	6.2
Total Asian	1,614,323	60.0	1,610,906	5.5
Chinese	393,077	59.2	392,696	5.0
Filipino	433,262	72.3	431,564	4.7
Japanese	221,857	55.5	221,299	2.7
Korean	185,078	55.5	184,719	6.1
Asian Indian	152,718	58.6	152,621	7.6
Vietnamese	111,282	55.8	111,170	8.9
Cambodian	17,080	37.3	17,080	9.9
Laotian	20,799	49.5	20,786	9.3
Hmong	4,039	19.9	4,039	19.0
Thai	30,268	67.4	30,201	6.2
Other Asian	44,863	53.9	44,731	7.7
Total Pacific Islander	73,822	62.5	73,176	6.9
Hawaiian	45,715	64.5	45,424	5.9
Samoan	9,524	54.8	9,405	10.7
Tongan	2,730	58.3	2,729	10.5
Guamanian	10,404	62.7	10,217	6.5
Melanesian	1,787	68.9	1,787	6.0
Other Pacific Islander	2,264	66.6	2,227	8.1

SOURCE: U.S. Bureau of the Census (1992).

Islander families, Samoans (24.5%) and Tongans (20.6%) were the poorest (U.S. Bureau of the Census, 1993a, 1993b; see Table 4.3).

Of all Asian and Pacific Islander families in the United States headed by women, 22% were below the poverty level. Of those below poverty, 36% were women-headed households with children under age 18.

Health Status Data

Although some of the national health data collection agencies added additional A/PIA groups for data collection in recent years, most of the national data currently available are limited to Chinese, Japanese, Filipinos, and, in some cases, Native Hawaiians and Vietnamese. To fill the

Table 4.3 1990 Income and Poverty Status of Asian and Pacific Islander
Americans

	Median Family	Per Capita Income	% Families in Poverty	% Persons in Poverty
Total U.S.	35,225	14,143	10.0	13.1
Total Asian	41,583	13,806	11.4	14.0
Chinese	41,316	14,876	11.1	14.0
Filipino	46,698	13,616	5.2	6.4
Japanese	51,550	19,373	3.4	7.0
Korean	33,909	11,777	14.7	13.7
Asian Indian	49,309	17,777	7.2	9.7
Vietnamese	30,550	9,032	23.8	25.7
Cambodian	18,126	5,120	42.1	42.6
Laotian	23,101	5,597	32.2	34.7
Hmong	14,327	2,692	61.8	63.8
Thai	37,257	11,970	10.8	12.55
Other Asian	34,242	11,000	15.6	18.2
Total Pacific Islander	33,955	10,342	15.0	17.1
Hawaiian	37,269	11,446	12.7	14.3
Samoan	27,228	7,690	24.5	25.8
Tongan	26,865	6,144	20.6	23.1
Guamanian	33,020	10,834	12.3	15.3
Melanesian	32,003	9,578	8.5	9.5
Other Pacific Islander	29,271	11,651	18.7	19.7

SOURCE: U.S. Bureau of the Census (1992).

major gaps in available information, we have tried to review and incorporate local or regional data whenever feasible. For this reason, we caution the reader that the data identified in this chapter represent only a small portion of the health-related issues concerning A/PIA women and that significant gaps occur in our understanding of the diverse group of women included in the category.

Cancer

Similar to the pattern for white American women, the leading cause of death among the three Asian American women's groups (Chinese, Japanese, Filipino) is cancer (National Center for Health Statistics [NCHS],

Table 4.4 Average Annual Age-Adjusted[a] Cancer Incidence Rates per
100,000 U.S. Population, Malignant Cases Only, for Chinese,
Japanese, and Filipino Females, Compared With White Females[b]

	Females
All sites	
Chinese	225.9
Japanese	207.4
Filipino	178.7
White	329.0
Stomach	
Chinese	8.4
Japanese	17.2
Filipino	5.0
White	5.5
Liver	
Chinese	2.8
Japanese	1.4
Filipino	2.1
White	1.1
Nasopharynx	
Chinese	7.1
Japanese	0.2
Filipino	1.1
White	0.3
Cervix uteri	
Chinese	10.3
Japanese	5.9
Filipino	8.6
White	8.3

SOURCE: Jenkins & Kagawa-Singer (1994).
a. 1970 U.S. standard.
b. San Francisco and Hawaii SEER Areas, 1977 to 1983.

1991). Although malignant incidence rates for all sites combined for the three groups are lower than for white women, subgroup differences indicate significantly higher rates for certain anatomical sites (e.g., oral cavity/pharynx and nasopharynx for Chinese women; stomach for both

Chinese and Japanese women; liver for all three groups; and cervix uteri for Chinese and Filipino women; see Table 4.4) (Jenkins & Kagawa-Singer, 1994).

When these rates are compared with those for women in their native countries, intriguing changes can be identified that indicate lifestyle and acculturative changes may be contributing to an increase in some anatomical sites and a decrease in other sites (e.g., higher breast cancer rates and lower rates for liver, cervix uteri, stomach, and esophagus for Chinese American and Japanese American women, compared with their counterparts in Asian countries) (Jenkins & Kagawa-Singer, 1994).

In contrast with the three rates for Asian American women, the incidence rate for Native Hawaiian women for all anatomical sites combined is higher, with an excess incidence in the areas of breast, cervix uteri, corpus uteri, esophagus, larynx, lung, pancreas, stomach, and multiple myeloma (U.S. DHHS, 1985, pp. 123, 125, 127). Although national data on Asian Indian, Korean, Vietnamese, Laotian, Kampuchean, Hmong, and other Asian groups are not available, Jenkins and Kagawa-Singer (1994) calculated proportional incidence ratios (PIRs) for those living in California from the California Tumor Registry data. Despite the need for caution in interpreting the data, they are useful in identifying potential problem areas for the group. For example, the cervical cancer proportions for all groups are higher than for white women. The proportion of breast cancer for Asian Indians parallels that for white women, but the rates are lower for all other groups reviewed.

Although the mortality rates for combined sites for Chinese, Japanese, and Filipino women are also lower than those for white women, certain sites are higher than for white women (e.g., oral cavity and pharynx, nasopharynx, cervix uteri, liver, and stomach for Chinese; stomach and liver for Japanese; and nasopharynx for Filipino).

Screening Compliance. Although physicians urge women to receive regular cancer screening to achieve early detection and timely treatment, many Asian immigrant/refugee and Pacific Islander women are not being screened. Although available data are fragmented, Jenkins and Kagawa-Singer (1994) reviewed the CDC survey data and several local community surveys and concluded that the compliance rates of these women were significantly lower than that for white women. For example, although only 5% of white women have never received a Pap smear, the rates for Chinese and Vietnamese women were 45% and 51%, respectively. The percentage of Vietnamese women never receiving a breast exam was 47%; the figure for white women was 12%. Although 30% of white women have never received a mammography, the figures for Chinese, Vietnamese, Hawaiian, and other A/PIA women were 68%, 48%, 55%, and 71%, respectively.

Hypertension and Other Cardiovascular Diseases

Heart disease is the second leading cause of death for A/PIA women (NCHS, 1991). Hypertension is one of several conditions cited as contributing factors. Although available data specific to A/PIA groups, including women, are limited, Tamir and Cachola (1994) reviewed existing data and provided some helpful information. For example, despite considerable subgroup differences, the prevalence rates among most A/PIA groups surveyed were lower than for the general white population. However, among those who were diagnosed with the condition, despite the fact that a significant number were under treatment and on medication, the rate for successfully controlling the symptoms was significantly lower than the rate for the general U.S. population; this finding raises further questions about other contributing factors, such as genetic, cultural, and environmental factors, including diet and lifestyle changes.

Smoking, another contributing factor, is generally low among Asian American women, compared with women in the general U.S. population. Findings from one California survey (Burns & Pierce, 1992) indicate that the prevalence rate for Asian Pacific women was 8.9%, whereas the figure for the general female U.S. population was 19.1%. Considerable variability was found among the subgroups and ranged from less than 1% for Vietnamese in California (CDC, 1992) to 18.6% for Japanese (Klatsky & Armstrong, 1991). The figure for Native Hawaiian women was considerably higher, reported to be 20.2% in one survey in Hawaii (Hawaii State Department of Health, 1991). Indications are, however, that younger women are smoking more and that as A/PIA women become more acculturated in the United States, their smoking may increase as they begin to lose the cultural prohibition against smoking (Tamir & Cachola, 1994).

Hepatitis B

Although the rate of hepatitis B chronic carriers among the U.S. population is only 0.2%, it is a common problem among the A/PIA groups, particularly among the foreign-born groups. The rates for Chinese, Korean, Filipino, Southeast Asian, and Pacific Islander American groups are reported to range between 5% and 15% (Hann, 1994). Among those infected are a significant number of pregnant women. According to the findings from a large-scale screening of pregnant Asian American women, Stevens et al. (1985) found 11.4% of pregnant women from China, Taiwan, and Hong Kong and 11.5% of pregnant women from Cambodia, Laos, and Vietnam were infected with HBsAg(+) (the hepatitis B surface antigen).

Because perinatal transmission is the most common mode of hepatitis B virus (HBV) transmission, it is not surprising that many Asian infants born to Asian immigrant/refugee women are carriers. It is staggering, however, that an estimated 54% of all HBV carrier infants born in the United States were born to Asian Pacific women, the majority of whom were foreign-born (Margolis, Alter, & Hadler, 1991). Because many foreign-born Asian American women receive late or no prenatal care, they are less likely to be screened and are more likely to transmit the virus to their babies. To carry out proper screening and immunization and to reduce the risk of HBV transmission to children, childbearing A/PIA women, particularly immigrant and refugee women, will need to be identified for outreach as a high-risk target group and encouraged to seek early screening, prenatal care, and immunization.

AIDS/HIV Infection

Although the reported number of diagnosed AIDS/HIV cases is still low for A/PIA women, the concern among A/PI health care providers is that the disease will spread rapidly among them and parallel the general U.S. trend of increased rates for women, particularly minority women.

Although the major mode of transmission for other racial groups is intravenous drug use, heterosexual contact is the major mode for A/PIA women. Among those most at risk are those who use drugs, work in the sex industry, have multiple partners, or are sexually active. Because the disease is now rapidly spreading among the general population, however, other A/PIA women are also at risk.

These women's knowledge about the disease is extremely limited. Even if they understand the salient features of AIDS/HIV transmission, many have difficulty putting their knowledge of safe sex into practice because of their cultural background, which taught them to put their own needs last and to defer to the wishes of men (Wilkinson, 1992). At present, little support has been given to identifying AIDS/HIV-related issues among A/PIA women. To better understand the risk factors involving various subgroups and to mount successful prevention and intervention strategies, it is critical that support be sought to deal with this growing problem.

Obesity and Diabetes

Although the prevalence rate for obesity among Asian Americans is low, obesity is a major problem for Pacific Islander groups, both men and women, particularly among Samoans and Native Hawaiians (Crewes, 1994). Because the occurrence of non-insulin-dependent diabetes mellitus (NIDDM) is closely related to obesity, the incidence of NIDDM among Pacific Islanders is high (e.g., 12.2% for Western Samoan women in urban areas vs. 7.3% for U.S. white women, ages 20 to 74). As these people grow older, the rates of increase are much steeper than for the general U.S. population. As a strategy for prevention of both obesity and NIDDM, Crews (1994) advocates the need for focusing on early detection of hyperglycemia, weight control, proper diet, and a culturally appropriate exercise regimen.

Substance Use and Abuse

Although data on drug and alcohol abuse for the A/PIA group is extremely limited, preliminary information includes information on gender differences. Several studies on alcohol consumption patterns among Chinese, Japanese, Korean, Filipino, and Vietnamese Americans (Chi, Lubben, & Kitano, 1989) found that Asian American women are generally moderate drinkers or nondrinkers. Their low rate of drinking behavior is thought to be based on the strong cultural sanction in most Asian cultures against women's drinking. Indications are, however, that the pattern may be changing. For example, research conducted in Japan (Kono, Saito, Shimada, & Nakagawa, 1977) indicated a dramatic increase in the rate of women who drink, from 13% in 1954 to 53% in 1964.

Chi et al.'s survey of Asian Americans in the Los Angeles area (1989) revealed that Japanese women had the highest rate of heavy drinkers (11.7%) and the lowest rate of abstainers (33.4%); the rates for Chinese were 0% and 68.8%; for Koreans, 0.8% and 81.6%; and for Filipinos, 3.5% and 80.0%, respectively, for similar categories. Some contributing factors for these changes may be the impact of social changes, including the blurring of sex roles; greater freedom for women; greater prosperity; and increased psychosocial stresses. The impact of acculturation is another factor to be considered for those living in the United States; it was identified as the key factor for the changes in the drinking pattern among Mexican American women (Markides, Ray, Stroup-Bebham, & Trevino, 1990).

Information on the use or abuse of drugs among A/PIA women is even more limited, but use and abuse appear to be increasing among adolescents and young adults. For example, Nakagawa and Watanabe (1973) interviewed junior and senior high school Asian American students in Seattle and found that the use of hard drugs, excluding marijuana and alcohol, was considerable: 17% of female and 12% of male students were identified as "users." Although gender differences were not cited, the differences between ethnic groups were significant, in that 45% of the Filipino, 29% of the Japanese, and 22% of the Chinese students had some experience with hard drugs. The drugs used included amphetamines, barbiturates, psychedelics, cocaine, and heroin (in descending order of frequency of use).

Domestic Violence

Although data available on the extent of domestic violence against A/PIA women are limited, many social service and women's shelter providers are concerned about the increasing incidence of abuse among A/PIA communities in various parts of the United States (C. Ho, 1990; Rimonte, 1989). Although acts of physical violence against women and wives are not openly condoned in various Asian countries, they do occur with some frequency. Male perpetrators often are not punished, and the victims often do not receive sympathy, are treated as if they themselves are responsible, and are expected to endure the pain and humiliation.

A major contributing factor appears to be the significant level of frustration experienced by A/PI immigrant and refugee males as they try to establish themselves in the new country and find ways to support their families. Despite their desire and effort, many of them have difficulty with English and do not have job skills that are transferable to and marketable in the United States.

However, many job opportunities are open for women, although primarily for poorly paid domestic work or various kinds of unskilled work that U.S.-born women are not willing to accept. When their husbands are unable to find work or to fully support their families with a marginal income, many of the women, who did not work before their immigration, must work to help support the family. Often, in such situations, the husbands feel humiliated and that their masculinity or their authority as the patriarchal family head is damaged because they have to rely on their wives to support their families. At the same time, some of the wives begin to become more assertive, believing that they have a greater role in supporting their family, and expect to share decision-making authority on family matters. These changes in marital roles and relationship dynamics could often lead to considerable marital strife. Unaccustomed to such changes, some husbands take out their sense of powerlessness, rage, and frustration by abusing their wives or escape by drinking or drugs, which often leads to aggression against their wives or children.

Many abused A/PIA women, however, are reluctant to seek outside help, partly because of their feeling of shame, fear of greater reprisals from abusers, and sense of powerlessness. When they finally seek outside help, their plights are often ignored by service providers who do not understand the severity of the situation and are not sympathetic to their situation. What is most appalling is that those with authority to intervene fail to do so and justify their non-action by citing the need to respect the cultural tradition. The case in New York of a Chinese immigrant husband, Dong, Lu Chen, who murdered his wife with a hammer and was given a 5-year probation on a reduced manslaughter charge, is the most galling instance of a failing system that ignores the plight of A/PIA women (Hurtado, 1989; Wang, 1990). Although the argument used to justify such a light sentence for a heinous crime was based on the judgments that such an act is culturally acceptable in the man's native country and that he is unlikely to commit other violent acts in the future, murder is not sanctioned in Asian countries regardless of the family relationship involved. This case is a blatant example of an erroneous cultural assumption and perpetuation of sexist treatment toward A/PIA women.

Suicides

Although suicide rates for combined age categories of A/PIAs is low, data broken down by ethnicity and age categories indicate that some of the subgroups are at higher risk than others. For example, Yu and Liu (1985) analyzed the existing suicide data on Chinese Americans and Japanese Americans and found that the rate for Chinese American women increased dramatically, beginning at the age 45-54 category, which was 13.89 per 100,000, and increased to 44.32 at the age 75-84 category and 49.93 at the age 85 and over category. In contrast, the rates for white American women successively declined during the same age categories, beginning with the high of 11.18 at age category 45-54. The rates for Chinese American males were even more dramatic (see Table 4.5).

Some stress factors that may be increasing the risk for elderly A/PIA women include the death of spouses, on whom they were dependent for dealing with the demands of the external, English-speaking world; economic hardships; deteriorating health; decreasing support from their adult

Table 4.5 Average Annual Death Rates for Suicide: Whites and Chinese
Americans, United States, 1980

| | Deaths per 100,000 Population | | | |
| | White | | Chinese | |
Age Group	Male	Female	Male	Female
All ages, crude	20.57	6.43	8.26	8.28
Age-adjusted	19.41	6.20	7.93	8.08
45-43 years	24.55	11.18	10.77	13.89
55-64 years	26.52	9.59	9.37	15.52
65-74 years	32.41	7.45	25.85	22.61
75-84 years	46.18	6.03	21.82	44.32
85 years+	53.28	4.92	64.10	49.93

SOURCE: Yu & Liu (1985).
NOTE: In calculating age-specific death rates, the numerator consisted of 1979-1981 cumulative
number of deaths; the denominator was based on the total enumerated in the 1981 U.S. census.

children; and the breakdown of the extended family support network.
Although traditional A/PI cultures place a strong value on treating their
elders with respect and care, immigrant families are often separated from
their extended family network and have limited resources to care for aging
parents. Some families have to live and work in areas far from their
parents, so it is not possible to provide the day-to-day support.

As the number of A/PIAs over age 65 is projected to increase dramatically, from 450,000 to 2.1 million by the year 2020, representing a 355%
increase (Ong, 1992), and as A/PIA women, like other women in general,
tend to live longer than men, they will likely continue to experience
significant stresses (e.g., poverty, isolation, lack of support, declining
health) and be at risk for suicide and suicidal behavior.

Mental Health Status

Prevalence Data

No comprehensive epidemiological data are available on the mental
health status of A/PIAs in the United States regardless of gender. Several
studies conducted in Japan, China, and Taiwan, however, may be helpful
in speculating about the mental health status of A/PIA women. For
example, Lin, Rin, Yeh, Hsu, and Chu (1969) investigated the prevalence
of various categories of mental illness in three communities in Taiwan in

1963 and found the overall rate for all mental disorders for men and women to be 16.1 and 18.3 per 1,000, respectively. Although the difference in overall rates for the sexes was not statistically significant, significant differences were found within subcategories (e.g., high rates of mental deficiency and psychopathic personality for males; high rates of psychoneuroses for women, particularly in the middle to older age groups). The findings seem to correspond to some findings from epidemiological studies in the United States, in which women were found to have higher rates of affective disorders, panic/obsessive-compulsive disorders, somatization, and phobias, which appear to have been subsumed under the diagnosis of psychoneuroses in Lin et al.'s investigation. The higher rate of antisocial personality disorder for men in U.S. studies also corresponds with the Taiwan study's finding of psychopathic personality (Mowbray & Benedek, 1988).

In the absence of national data on A/PIA women, it is also helpful to review some findings from studies conducted in areas with a significant concentration of A/PIAs. For example, Ying (1988) attempted to explore the level of depressive symptomatology among San Francisco-based Chinese Americans through a telephone survey, using the Center for Epidemiological Studies-Depression Scale (CES-D; Roberts & Vernon, 1983). Among the 360 subjects who agreed to be interviewed, 182 were women. Their mean depression score was 12.83, which was somewhat higher than the mean score of 10.25 for men. Their score was also considerably higher than the mean score for a predominantly white sample in a study by Radloff (1977), which ranged from 7.94 to 9.25. Among the general population, a CES-D mean of 16 and above was used as indicative of clinical depression. In the sample reported by Radloff for the white population, 19% scored 16 or above, whereas 24% of Ying's combined male and female sample scored 16 or above. Ying also found that those who belonged to a lower socioeconomic level (as measured by education and occupation) scored as significantly more depressed than those who belonged to a higher socioeconomic level.

In another study, in Chicago, Hurh and Kim (1990) conducted diagnostic interviews with 622 Korean immigrants (age 20 and older) to explore the extent of mental health problems among the more recent immigrants by using the CES-D scale, the Health Opinion Survey (HOS; Macmillan, 1957), and the Memorial University of Newfoundland Scale of Happiness (MUNSH; Kozma & Stones, 1980). Their findings indicate that those who were married, highly educated, and currently employed in a high-status occupation had better subjective mental health than others. The authors also found significant gender differences among their sample in that the correlates for mental health for males were a set of work-related variables, whereas family life satisfaction and several ethnic-attachment variables were moderately related for females.

Asian immigrant groups generally agree that the Southeastern Asian refugees are facing the greatest stress in adjusting to a new life in the United States. Many of the women suffered traumatic experiences and major losses of close family members before their immigration and frequently experience recurring symptoms of posttraumatic stress disorder (PTSD), which include depression, anxiety, panic attacks, nightmares, and sleeplessness, as well as somatic symptoms (Rumbaut, 1985). The refugees from rural areas, such as Cambodia and Laos, with little exposure to modern urban living, were particularly ill-prepared for the transition into large, complex urban communities. Many experienced bewilderment and confusion, which were often manifested through psychiatric and somatic symptoms (Chung, 1991; Gong-Guy, 1987). The study reported by Rozee and Van Boemel (1989) provides a glimpse into the psychological impact of the harrowing experience of war trauma, multiple losses, and rape and physical abuse suffered by older Cambodian women, who are now experiencing non-organic visual loss, depression, nightmares, sleep disturbances, and other symptoms associated with PTSD.

Although they were not refugees, many Japanese Americans, including U.S.-born citizens, also were subjected to significant trauma when, during World War II, they were rounded up into concentration camps, euphemistically called "internment camps," located in various deserted parts of the country. The experience of being uprooted from their own homes, labeled as enemy aliens even when they were loyal U.S.-born citizens, deprived of their civil rights, and subjected to subhuman conditions was devastating to those affected. In her interviews with third-generation Japanese Americans, many of whom were women, Nagata (1990) identified how the psychological trauma, the humiliation, and the fears about future persecution were passed on to subsequent generations of Japanese Americans even though they were not personally subjected to the trauma.

Utilization Data

In many communities, mental health service utilization data are often accepted as a substitute for epidemiological data and used to estimate the extent and level of mental health problems present in communities. Such data, however, provide little help in identifying the extent of A/PIA's needs or problems in that their record of service use has been traditionally very low (Sue & McKinney, 1975). Factors affecting low service use are thought to include a cultural stigma against the implication of mental illness; a traditional reluctance to seek outside help; a fear of establishment authorities; the absence of bilingual, culturally sensitive service providers; the cost of seeking help; and other institutional barriers, such as geographical locations or hours of operation.

Despite the limitations, some service utilization data provide information on gender differences among A/PIs. For example, Berk and Hirata (1973) reviewed the California state hospital use records for 1936 to 1945 and found that the admission rate for Chinese females was quite low but that the rate for Chinese males, particularly the foreign-born elderly, increased dramatically in later years. Although the number of clients involved was quite small (23 inpatients and 20 outpatients), the experience of Resthaven Community Mental Health (Brown, Stein, Huang, & Harris, 1972) provides the earliest data on Chinese American clients in a community mental health program. In that program, Chinese males outnumbered females in inpatient admissions, but the outpatient admissions were predominantly females. The women were all poor, foreign-born, and had language problems. The problems that brought them into the outpatient clinic were primarily nonpsychotic and often involved symptoms of anxiety and depression.

Recognizing that the mental health problems in A/PIA communities were much more extensive, community leaders and mental health professionals in key communities began to advocate for and develop programs that were more culturally responsive to their communities (President's Commission on Mental Health, 1978). For this reason, in some of the communities that made the effort to be more responsive to the needs of A/PIA residents, service use by A/PIAs has increased significantly (Sue, 1988). The figure for San Francisco Community Mental Health Services (True, 1989) for A/PIA clients was 10.8%: male, 5.4%, and female 5.4%. Although this figure is a significant improvement over the past 15 years, the figure is still considerably lower than the 25% figure that constitutes the A/PIA population among the overall population in the city. Although the overall use rates of services by A/PIA males and females are the same, differences were found in the types of problems they had: Males had more serious psychotic illnesses (45% vs. 29%), whereas females had more problems related to depression and other affective disorders (36% vs. 25%).

Medical Service Use

In their review of U.S. women's mental health service utilization data, Mowbray and Benedek (1988) noted that a significantly greater number of women than men go to primary care physicians for help with emotional problems. When Yu, Liu, and Wong (1987) reviewed the utilization data of a Chinatown health clinic in Boston, they also found that a significant number of Chinese women seen at the clinic were being treated for symptoms related to depression.

Additional support for this trend was identified by Ying (1990) when she conducted a survey in San Francisco on the help-seeking attitude of Chinese women when dealing with potential psychiatric problems. Using a vignette depicting a major depression in a Chinese married woman, she interviewed a group of Chinese immigrant women at a San Francisco health center to explore the relationship between problem conceptualization and help-seeking behavior. When presented with the vignette, on the one hand, the majority of women conceptualized the problem as psychological and did not suggest seeking professional psychological help, but rather suggested turning to family and friends or trying to resolve the problems by themselves. On the other hand, those who conceptualized the problem as physical recommended seeking medical services.

Psychosocial Stresses

Many sources of stress contribute to the development of mental health problems for A/PIA women. Foremost among them are the stresses related to immigration and acculturation. Research conducted on European immigrants in the mid-1900s indicates that the degree of stress will increase if the difference between the host culture and the immigrant group is great (Furnham & Bochner, 1986); such a difference would seem to be greater for Asian immigrants, particularly those from rural communities, unexposed to industrial, urban, Western lifestyles. Among the stresses in the United States are a new and unfamiliar language, lifestyle changes, and day-to-day survival issues. Although many of these people had to deal with survival issues in their old country, they were able to rely on the supportive extended family and community network for help. In the new community, they have not been able to create a substitute network among their neighbors, perhaps because they are working or because of their traditional reluctance to seek help beyond the family kinship network. At the same time, their husbands are often less available to help because they are also struggling to establish themselves.

These Asian immigrants also experience significant conflict with their children, who become more quickly acculturated and begin to demand greater independence and freedom in making personal choices (e.g., friends, dating, sexuality, field of study, occupation), whereas parents are much more restrictive and expect their children to respect parental authority. Because of the old-world attitude toward women, parents are often more restrictive toward their daughters, believing that they need to work hard to protect the daughters against destructive influences in the external environment. The burden most often falls on mothers, who carry on much of the child-rearing responsibilities, particularly for socializing their daughters into the traditional cultural expectation of subservient, compliant women; this is poignantly portrayed in Amy Tan's novel, *The Joy Luck Club* (1989).

Native-born Asian American women and others who are freer of the basic survival needs faced by immigrant women face different types of stresses. Frequently, they are subjected to the double jeopardy of discrimination in various social and work settings because of their status as members of racial and sexual minority groups (True, 1981). Irrespective of their own individual strengths and abilities, A/PIA women are often perceived and treated with negative stereotypes in all types of situations. These include perception of them as easily exploited sex objects; as subservient, passive handmaidens; and as weak, dependent women. If they are somewhat aggressive, they are quickly typecast as power-hungry, ruthless "dragon ladies" (Lott & Pian, 1979).

Another trend emerging as a potential source of strain for A/PIA women is the increasing phenomenon of interracial marriage. Although such marriages were strongly discouraged in the early years of Asian immigrant communities and by the U.S. public in general, it is begrudgingly recognized now as a phenomenon likely to increase (Kikumura & Kitano, 1973). When many young people are first swept away by their romantic love, they do not realize the many potential conflicts, including hostility from those who do not condone interracial unions, that derive from their divergent cultural backgrounds, values, and beliefs (M. K. Ho, 1990). The biracial or multiracial offspring of these interracial unions also face many stresses and challenges (Root, 1992).

Access to Health Care Services

Although equal access to health and mental health care is touted as the ideal principle to strive toward for the U.S. health care system, A/PIA women face many barriers that prevent them from receiving necessary and appropriate care. In their review of access to health care, Mayeno and Hirota (1994) identified a number of barriers that exist for A/PIAs. Included among the barriers are socioeconomic factors, such as poverty, unemployment, and marginal employment, that deprive them of health insurance coverage for needed care. Although all Southeast Asian refugees are eligible for Medicaid assistance for a limited time period and are able to seek medical care without worrying about the financial burden, most immigrants are not eligible for financial support for their medical care. Although a legal provision allows them to seek medical assistance, most of them are not knowledgeable about it. Even when they are informed that they are entitled to some limited care, they are afraid to seek government assistance because they are led to believe they will be deported for accepting any public assistance or that they may be penalized when they apply for U.S. citizenship.

Other factors that pose barriers for service access include the inability to communicate with service providers in English; a lack of knowledge about Western medical practices and systems; fears about impersonal medical institutions, particularly because hospitals are often seen as places where people go when having serious or terminal illnesses; and a fear of public institutions, based on their own or other people's past experience of discrimination. Their experience with medical service providers, when they had occasion to seek care, was often unsatisfactory because they perceived the providers as unsympathetic to their needs and lacking in understanding and sensitivity about unique cultural differences.

In addition to the issues identified above, which are applicable to all A/PIAs, certain psychological factors unique to A/PIA women create additional barriers for them. For example, throughout their childhood, these women are strictly socialized to sacrifice their own personal needs for the good of their husbands and children. Such training often leads to their ignoring or denying their own pains or symptoms so that their families' needs are properly taken care of. An additional factor that often becomes a deterrent to seeking needed care is their modesty and reserve about their bodies, particularly about such anatomical areas as the breasts, vagina, and cervix. To overcome such psychological reluctance, considerable outreach effort is needed to educate the women about the benefits of early and routine examination and care.

Recognizing these problems in service accessibility, several communities have collaborated with A/PIA health and mental health service advocates and have succeeded in significantly improving the service accessibility for A/PIA communities. Some key elements of effective service strategies recommended for A/PIA individuals in general are applicable for A/PIA women and include the following:

- *Availability of bilingual, bicultural service providers for non-English-speaking clients.* It is critical that every effort be made to make bilingual and bicultural service providers available to non-English-speaking clients. Some providers call on family members, including the client's children, to interpret, without making an effort to find trained interpreters. Such substitutions could lead not only to errors and misunderstandings but also to strained family dynamics (e.g., role reversal between parents and children). In its guidelines for working with ethnic, linguistic, and culturally diverse populations, the American Psychological Association (1991) acknowledges the need for competent interpreters or translators in the absence of bilingual, bicultural professionals but also cautions about the limitations and risk of reliance on interpreters.

- *Location of services within geographically accessible areas during hours convenient for working women.*

- *A multiservice approach.* In addition to health and mental health services, many immigrant/refugee families have multiple problem and service needs. To minimize their trouble of traveling to a variety of locations, it will be helpful to co-locate a variety of services in one area. Such a model was quite popular during the early years of European immigration in the form of "settlement houses." More recently, the Southcove Community Center in Boston's Chinatown has successfully implemented this model, which provides a variety of services in one location, including child care; recreation programs; health, mental health, and substance abuse treatment; social services; educational programs; and job referrals.

SUMMARY AND
RECOMMENDATIONS

Despite the paucity of data on A/PIA women about their health and mental health status or service use, researchers are beginning to learn that A/PIA women suffer from a variety of illnesses and experience considerable stress. Researchers have identified some factors that affect these women's health and mental health status and the fact that the availability of services for them is limited and further hampered by many barriers. With the projection of a continued increase in the number of A/PIA women, their health problems are also expected to increase. It is critical that greater attention and support be given to identify and improve their health and mental health status. The following are some actions recommended to address their health care needs:

- Provide funding and technical support for research focused on the health and mental health needs of A/PIA women, with particular attention given to addressing subgroup and regional differences among them.
- Increase the availability of community-based health and mental health services that are linguistically and culturally appropriate.
- Create health and mental health service financing mechanisms for those with limited financial means.
- Aggressively recruit and support training of A/PI mental health professionals to develop expertise on A/PIA women's issues and linguistic, bicultural capacity.
- Train non-A/PI professionals as well as A/PI male professionals to increase their cultural sensitivity toward A/PIA women's needs.
- Provide support for outreach, prevention, and education activities to eliminate fears and distrust in the community and to encourage health-promoting behavior.
- Provide ancillary services, such as social services, child care, vocational training, housing, and homemaker services, to high-risk populations to reduce the level of psychosocial stresses.

REFERENCES

American Psychological Association. (1991). *Guidelines for providers of psychological services to ethnic, linguistic, and culturally diverse populations.* Washington, DC: Author.

Asian and Pacific Islander Center for Census Information and Services (ACCIS). (1993a). *Asian and Pacific Islander Americans: A profile of socioeconomic characteristics, 1990 (United States of America, California, New York, Hawaii, Texas, Illinois)* (Asian and Pacific Islander American Profile Series Three). San Francisco: Asian/Pacific Islander Data Consortium.

Asian and Pacific Islander Center for Census Information and Services (ACCIS). (1993b). *A profile of Asian and Pacific Islander immigrant populations in California.* San Francisco: Asian/Pacific Islander Data Consortium.

Berk, B., & Hirata, L. C. (1973). Mental illness among the Chinese: Myth or reality. *Journal of Social Issues, 29*(2), 149-166.

Brown, T., Stein, K., Huang, K., & Harris, D. (1972). *Mental illness and the role of mental health facilities in Chinatown* (Resthaven Research Report #6). Los Angeles: Resthaven Mental Health Center.

Burns, D., & Pierce, J. P. (1992). *Tobacco use in California: 1990-1991*. Sacramento: California Department of Health Services.

Centers for Disease Control and Prevention (CDC). (1992). Behavior risk-factor survey of Vietnamese in California, 1991. *Morbidity and Mortality Weekly Report, 41*(5), 69-72.

Chi, I., Lubben, J. D., & Kitano, H. H. L. (1989). Differences in drinking behavior among three Asian American groups. *Journal of Studies on Alcohol, 50*(1), 15-23.

Chung, R. C. (1991, August). *Predictors of distress among Southeast Asian refugees: Group and gender differences.* Paper presented at the Asian American Psychological Association Conference, San Francisco.

Crews, D. E. (1994). Obesity and diabetes. In N. W. S. Zane, D. T. Takeuchi, & K. N. J. Young (Eds.), *Confronting critical health issues of Asian and Pacific Islander Americans* (pp. 174-208). Thousand Oaks, CA: Sage.

Furnham, A., & Bochner, S. (1986). *Culture shock: Psychological reactions to unfamiliar environments.* London: Methuen.

Gong-Guy, E. (1987). *The California Southeast Asian Mental Health Needs Assessment.* Oakland, CA: Asian Community Mental Health Services.

Hann, H. W. L. (1994). Hepatitis B. In N. W. S. Zane, D. T. Takeuchi, & K. N. J. Young (Eds.), *Confronting critical health issues of Asian and Pacific Islander Americans* (pp. 148-172). Thousand Oaks, CA: Sage.

Hawaii State Department of Health. (1991). *Annual report: Statistical supplement 1989.* Honolulu: Author.

Ho, C. (1990). An analysis of domestic violence in Asian American communities. *Women and Therapy, 9*(1-2), 129-150.

Ho, M. K. (1990). *Intermarried couples in therapy.* Springfield, IL: Charles C Thomas.

Hurh, W. M., & Kim, K. C. (1990). Correlates of Korean immigrants' mental health. *Journal of Nervous and Mental Disorder, 178*(11), 703-711.

Hurtado, P. (1980, April 5). Killer's sentence defended: "He's not a loose cannon." *Newsday,* pp. 3, 25.

Jenkins, C. N. H., & Kagawa-Singer, M. (1994). Cancer. In N. W. S. Zane, D. T. Takeuchi, & K. N. J. Young (Eds.), *Confronting critical health issues of Asian and Pacific Islander Americans* (pp. 105-147). Thousand Oaks, CA: Sage.

Kikumura, A., & Kitano, H. (1973). Interracial marriage: A picture of the Japanese Americans. *Journal of Social Issues, 29*(2), 67-81.

Klatsky, A. L., & Armstrong, M. A. (1991). Cardiovascular risk factors among Asians living in Northern California. *American Journal of Public Health, 81,* 1423-1428.

Kono, H., Saito, S., Shimada, K., & Nakagawa, J. (1977). *Drinking habits of the Japanese.* Tokyo: Leisure Development Center.

Kozma, A., & Stones, M. J. (1980). The measurement of happiness: Development of Memorial University of Newfoundland Scale of Happiness (MUNSH). *Journal of Gerontology, 35,* 906-912.

Lin, T. Y., Rin, H., Yeh, E., Hsu, C., & Chu, H. (1969). Mental disorder in Taiwan, fifteen years later: A preliminary report. In W. Caudill & T. Y. Liu (Eds.), *Mental health research in Asia and the Pacific* (pp. 66-91). Honolulu: East-West Press.

Lott, J., & Pian, C. (1979). *Beyond stereotypes and statistics: Emergence of Asian and Pacific American women.* Washington, DC: Organization of Pan Asian American Women.

Macmillan, A. M. (1957). The Health Opinion Survey: Techniques for estimating prevalence of psychoneurotic and related types of disorder in communities. *Psychology Report, 3,* 325-329.

Margolis, H. S., Alter, M. J., & Hadler, S. (1991). Hepatitis B: Evolving epidemiology and implications for control. *Seminars in Liver Disease, 2,* 84-86.

Markides, K., Ray, L., Stroup-Bebham, C., & Trevino, F. (1990). Acculturation and alcohol consumption in the Mexican American population of the Southwestern United States: Findings from HHANES, 1982-84. *American Journal of Public Health, 80,* 42-46.

Mayeno, L., & Hirota, S. M. (1994). Access to health care. In N. W. S. Zane, D. T. Takeuchi, & K. N. J. Young (Eds.), *Confronting critical health issues of Asian and Pacific Islander Americans* (pp. 347-375). Thousand Oaks, CA: Sage.

Mowbray, C. T., & Benedek, E. P. (1988). *Women's mental health research agenda: Services and treatment of mental disorders in women* (Women's Mental Health Occasional Paper Series). Rockville, MD: National Institute of Mental Health.

Nagata, D. K. (1990). The Japanese American internment: Exploring the transgenerational consequences of traumatic stress. *Journal of Traumatic Stress, 3*(1), 47-69.

Nakagawa, B., & Watanabe, R. (1973). *A study of the use of drugs among Asian American youths of Seattle.* Seattle: Demonstration Project for Asian Americans.

National Center for Health Statistics (NCHS). (1991). *Health, United States, 1990* (DHHS Publication No. PHS. 91-1232). Hyattsville, MD: U.S. Public Health Service.

Ong, P. (1992). The growth of the Asian Pacific American population: Twenty million in 2020. In *The state of Asian Pacific America: Policy issues to the year 2020* (pp. 11-24). Los Angeles: LEAP Asian Pacific American Public Policy Institute and UCLA Asian American Studies Center.

President's Commission on Mental Health. (1978). *Report to the president* (Vol. 4). Washington, DC: Government Printing Office.

Radloff, L. S. (1977). The CES-D Scale: A self-report depression scale for research in the general population. *Applied Psychological Measurement, 1,* 385-401.

Rimonte, N. (1989). Domestic violence among Pacific Asians. In Asian Women United of California, *Making waves: An anthology of writings by and about Asian American women* (pp. 327-336). Boston: Beacon.

Roberts, R. E., & Vernon, S. W. (1983). The Center for Epidemiological Studies—Depression Scale: Its use in a community sample. *American Journal of Psychiatry, 140,* 41-46.

Root, M. P. P. (Ed.). (1992). *Racially mixed people in America: Within, between, and beyond race.* Newbury Park, CA: Sage.

Rozee, P. D., & Van Boemel, G. (1989). The psychological effects of war trauma and abuse on older Cambodian refugee women. *Women and Therapy, 8*(4), 23-49.

Rumbaut, R. G. (1985). Mental health and the refugee experience: A comparative study of Southeast Asian refugees. In T. C. Owan (Ed.), *Southeast Asian mental health: Treatment, prevention, services, training, and research* (pp. 433-486). Washington, DC: National Institute of Mental Health.

Stevens, C. E., Toy, P. T., Tony, M. J., Taylor, P. E., Vyas, G. N., Nair, P. V., Guduralli, M., & Krugman, S. (1985). Perinatal hepatitis B virus transmission in the United States: Prevention by passive-active immunization. *Journal of the American Medical Association, 253,* 1740-1745.

Sue, S. (1988). Psychotherapeutic services for ethnic minorities: Two decades of research findings. *American Psychologist, 43,* 301-308.

Sue, S., & McKinney, H. (1975). Asian Americans in the community mental health care system. *American Journal of Orthopsychiatry, 45,* 11-18.

Takaki, R. (1989). *Strangers from a different shore: History of Asian Americans.* Boston: Little, Brown.

Tamir, A., & Cachola, S. (1994). Hypertension and other cardiovascular risk factors. In
    N. W. S. Zane, D. T. Takeuchi, & K. N. J. Young (Eds.), *Confronting critical health
    issues of Asian and Pacific Islander Americans* (pp. 209-246). Thousand Oaks, CA:
    Sage.
Tan, A. (1989). *The joy luck club.* New York: Ballantine.
True, R. H. (1981). The profile of Asian American women. In S. Cox (Ed.), *Female
    psychology: The emerging self* (pp. 124-135). New York: St. Martin's.
True, R. H. (1985). Health care service delivery in Asian American community. In M. M.
    Heckler (Ed.), *Report of the Secretary's Task Force on Black and Minority Health*
    (Vol. 2, pp. 193-205) Washington, DC: U.S. Department of Health and Human
    Services.
True, H. (1989, August). *Mental health issues among Asian American women in the United
    States.* Paper presented at the Annual Convention of the Asian American Psycho-
    logical Association, Boston.
U.S. Bureau of the Census. (1992, August). The Asian and Pacific Islander population in
    the United States: March 1991 and 1990. *Current population reports* (Series P20-
    459). Washington, DC: Government Printing Office.
U.S. Bureau of the Census. (1993a). *We, the American . . . Asians.* Washington, DC:
    Government Printing Office.
U.S. Bureau of the Census. (1993b). *We, the American . . . Pacific Islanders.* Washington,
    DC: Government Printing Office.
U.S. Department of Health and Human Services (U.S. DHHS). (1985). *Report of the
    secretary's task force on black and minority health: Vol. 1. Executive summary*
    (Publication No. 491-313/44706). Washington, DC: Government Printing Office.
U.S. Office of Disease Prevention and Health Promotion. (1987). *ODPHP's prevention
    fact book: Life expectancy in the United States.* Washington, DC: Government
    Printing Office.
Wang, C. (1990, Spring). Combating domestic violence in the Asian community. In
    Perspective. New York: Asian/Pacific American Law Students Association, New
    York University, p. 1.
Wilkinson, W. (1992). A/PI women and HIV: The risk is real. *Focus, 3,* 1, 3.
Ying, Y. W. (1988). Depressive symptomatology among Chinese-Americans as measured
    by the CES-D. *Journal of Clinical Psychology, 44*(5), 739-746.
Ying, Y. W. (1990). Explanatory models of major depression and implications for help-
    seeking among immigrant Chinese-American women. *Culture, Medicine, and Psy-
    chiatry, 14,* 393-408.
Yu, E., & Liu, W. T. (1985). Whites, Chinese, and Japanese: Average annual death rates
    for suicide: United States, 1980. In U.S. Department of Health and Human Services,
    *Report of the secretary's task force on black and minority health: Vol. 5. Homicide,
    suicide, and unintentional injuries* (p. 26) (Publication No. 491-313/44710). Wash-
    ington, DC: Government Printing Office.
Yu, E. S., & Liu, W. T. (1994). Methodological issues. In N. W. S. Zane, D. T. Takeuchi,
    & K. N. J. Young (Eds.), *Confronting critical health issues of Asian and Pacific
    Islander Americans* (pp. 22-52). Thousand Oaks, CA: Sage.
Yu, E. S. H., Liu, W. T., & Wong, S. C. (1987). Measurement of depression in a Chinatown
    health clinic. In W. T. Liu (Ed.), *A decade review of mental health research,
    training, and services* (pp. 95-100). Chicago: Pacific/Asian American Mental
    Health Research Center, University of Illinois at Chicago.

5

Latino Women

Aida L. Giachello

In recent years there has been an increased interest in Hispanic/Latino health. Unfortunately, little effort has been made to document the conditions of Latino women, and even less with regard to issues of health. The limited information available on Hispanic/Latino women reveals a large disparity in their socioeconomic and demographic characteristics, compared with either Latino men or non-Hispanic/Latino women in the United States. This disparity manifests itself in the areas of educational achievement, income, occupation, fertility, and health status. Each area is a component of major social and structural factors that hinder Hispanic/Latino women from developing themselves to the maximum extent possible. The need to study Hispanic/Latino women's health is obvious—not only because of the age structure and youthfulness of the Hispanic/Latino women's population but also because limited studies have found that they are at highest risk for certain health conditions, such as diabetes, HIV/AIDS, and depression. Hispanic women also experience a higher proportion of medical indigence and confront a series of financial, cultural, and institutional barriers in obtaining health care. Some people consider sexism, racism, and classism to be the root causes of Latino women's poor health status (Bracho de Carpio, Carpio-Cedraro, & Anderson,

AUTHOR'S NOTE: This chapter is adapted from Giachello (1994a, 1994b), in C. W. Molina and M. Aguirre-Molina (Eds.), *Latino Health in the U. S.: A Growing Challenge.*

1993); others think it is more a problem of lack of information and access to the health care system.

This chapter presents an argument that poverty and sexism, combined with limited culturally appropriate health and mental health services, are the strongest factors associated with Latino women's poor health. Hispanics/Latinos in general and Latino women in particular experience racial and social inequalities. They are one of the poorer minority groups in the United States. Some (e.g., Puerto Ricans) are characterized by sociologists as belonging to the urban underclass—a socially isolated group experiencing high poverty, high dependence on public assistance, and multiple social problems with limited access to health and human resources.

Hispanics/Latinos in general and Latino women in particular have often been physically segregated from the rest of society, living in ghetto areas, and they have suffered a disproportionate share of social and economic instability. Even though acculturation (adoption of the predominant behavior patterns and language) does take place, structural assimilation (gaining access to U.S. institutions, including the medical care system for prevention, screening, and treatment) continues to be difficult (Giachello, 1988). Socioeconomic factors (e.g., health insurance) appear to be the strongest determinants of gaining entry into the formal medical care system. Once Latino women enter the medical care system, they find that health services are oriented to white males; that a series of policies and practices, as well as biases and attitudes, prevails against women in general; and that the health care system in the United States has limited flexibility to meet the needs of populations who are poor or may have different illnesses, cultural practices, or languages. It has been argued that all of these lead to differential health and medical treatment for women.

Specifically, this chapter (a) provides a brief overview of the sociodemographic and economic characteristics of Latino women; (b) discusses Latino women's health within the context of women's general health and social needs; (c) highlights selected aspects of the Latino culture as they relate to health care; (d) summarizes the limited data on morbidity and mortality and other health status indicators as they affect Latino women; (e) discusses aspects of Latino women's health in which issues of race, class, and gender are manifested; and (f) presents findings and recommendations for programs, policy, and future research. Because of the diversity of the Latino population regarding country of origin, cultures and value systems, migration patterns, health status and living conditions, and the impact of these factors on their health once the people are here, caution is needed as the available information is examined; most of the limited research data available refer to those included in the category of Hispanic or Latino. Hispanic identifiers by national origins are often not available in public health records at the state and local levels, and even when items on Hispanic origin are included, their numbers are very small, and little effort has been made by public health officials to analyze and release these data. The terms *Hispanic* and *Latino* are used interchangeably throughout this chapter. Whenever data are available, specific Hispanic/Latino women's groups are identified by national origins.

BACKGROUND

Selected Demographic and Socioeconomic Characteristics of Latino Women

According to the U.S. Bureau of the Census, Latinos (Hispanics/ Spanish origin) are defined as persons who consider themselves to be Mexicans, Mexican Americans, Puerto Ricans, Cubans, or persons who are born or descended from those born in Central or South America, Spain, or selected locations in the Caribbean. This definition encompasses people who come from more than 20 countries.

In 1990, 22.3 million Hispanics/Latinos were in the United States, representing 9.6% of the total U.S. population. Hispanic women comprised 49.5% of the total Hispanic population in the United States. The gender distribution for the different Hispanic subgroups varies greatly: Puerto Rican females represent the majority of the Puerto Rican population in the continental United States (52.5%), and Central or South American males represent the majority (51.1%) of the Central or South American population. Migration patterns, as well as birth and mortality rates, affect gender distribution. The Hispanic/Latino female population as a whole is expected to increase by one fourth, from 8.6% of the total women population in the U.S. in 1990, to 10.7% in 2010 (National Council of La Raza [NCLR], 1993).

Demographic characteristics indicate that Hispanics/Latinos are one of the youngest population groups in the United States, with a median age of 26.7 in 1993, compared with 34.4 for non-Hispanics/Latinos (see Table 5.1). Age differences by gender indicate that Hispanic women are slightly older than Hispanic men but much younger than black and white females (data not shown in Table 5.1). Hispanic women tend to be concentrated in two age-groups—the extremely young group (21 years or younger) and the prime-age worker group (22 to 55 years). Very few of them are of retirement age (NCLR, 1993). Hispanic/Latino women suffer from a

Table 5.1 Select Sociodemographic and Economic Characteristics of
Latinos in the United States by Latino National Origin, by Total
Latino and Non-Latino Population, March, 1993

Characteristic	Total Latino	Mexican	Puerto Rican	Cuban	Central or South American	Total Non-Latinos
Gender						
Male	50.1	50.5	47.5	49.1	51.1	48.7
Female	49.9	49.5	52.5	50.9	48.9	51.3
Median age (years)	26.7	24.6	26.9	43.6	28.6	34.4
% 4 years of H.S. or more*	53.1	46.2	59.8	62.1	62.9	82.5
Mean family size	3.8	4.0	3.3	3.1	3.6	3.1
Median male earnings, 1992	14,706	13,622	18,386	18,416	14,358	23,301
Median female earnings, 1992	10,813	10,098	14,200	14,117	10,249	14,046
Median family income, 1992	23,912	23,714	20,301	31,015	23,649	38,015
% female head of household	23.3	19.4	40.5	18.2	24.7	17.0
% female in civilian labor force	51.9	51.6	46.2	48.4	57.2	57.6
% unemployed**	11.9	11.7	14.4	7.3	13.2	7.1
% females unemployed	11.1	11.1	11.0	7.3	14.4	5.8
Occupation of employed female:						
Managerial and prof. spec.	15.4	13.6	18.5	18.4	15.7	29.8
Tech., sales, and adm. supp.	40.9	40.7	48.5	49.0	31.3	42.9
Services occupations	24.6	24.9	19.9	20.1	31.6	17.5
Farming, forestry, and fishing	1.8	2.8	–	–	0.4	0.8
Precision production	2.5	2.8	2.4	2.0	1.8	1.8
Operators, fabrication, and lab.	14.8	15.2	10.8	10.6	19.2	7.2
% families below poverty level, 1992	26.2	26.4	32.5	15.4	27.0	10.4
% families below poverty level with female-headed household	48.8	46.0	60.3	N/A	51.3	33.3
% without telephone	11.9	12.0	17.2	41.1	13.2	3.9

SOURCE: U.S. Bureau of the Census (1994).
*For those 25 years of age or older; **For persons 16 years old and over.
N/A: Base too small to show derived measures.

series of social and economic disadvantages reflected in low education levels, low income, high unemployment, and a high level of poverty (see Table 5.1).

Factors Associated With Poverty Among Hispanic/Latino Women

Studies indicate that high poverty rates for Hispanics/Latinos in general and Latino women in particular are linked to a number of factors. First, the median earnings of Hispanic/Latino women are lower than those of Latino men and non-Hispanic women. In 1993, the median annual earnings for Latino women were $10,813, compared with $14,046 for non-Latino females and $14,706 and $23,301, respectively, for Latino and non-Latino males. This discrepancy may be related to the fact that Latino women tend to be disproportionately represented in low-paying occupations such as in the service industries and in factory-related jobs, compared with Latino men and non-Latino women (see Table 5.1) (U.S. Bureau of the Census, 1994). A shift in job creation from manufacturing to the service sector has resulted in a decrease in jobs with high pay and benefits for Latinos in general, as well as for Latino women. In addition, a recent report by the Inter-University Program for Latino Research cited by NCLR (1993) indicates that the principal dynamics driving increased wage inequality among Latinos since the mid-1970s include widening gaps in higher and lower educational achievement, renewed or increased ethno-racial wage discrimination, and a widening gap between immigrant and non-immigrant incomes.

Second, a Hispanic family with a worker is more likely than a comparable black or white family to be in poverty. In 1991, 15.5% of Hispanic families with a full-time worker were living in poverty, compared with 9.9% of black families and 3.9% of white families (NCLR, 1993).

Third, Hispanic married-couple families are more likely than black or white married-couple families to be poor. This finding may be related to the fact that Hispanic two-parent families are less likely to have two wage earners than non-Hispanic families. For example, in 1993, 26.2% of Hispanic two-parent families were poor, compared with 10.4% for non-Hispanic two-parent families. Among Hispanic two-parent families, the incidence of poverty was 26.4% in 1993 for those of Mexican origin, 32.5% for Puerto Ricans, 15.4% for Cubans, and 27.0% for those of Central and South American origin. High poverty among two-parent families is partly related to their relatively low participation in the labor force. For example, in 1993, the labor force participation of Latino women was lower overall, compared with that of non-Latino women (51.9% vs. 57.6%). The percentage of Latino women in the civil labor force varies by national origins, the highest being for women of Central or South American origin and the lowest among Puerto Rican women (57.2% and 46.2%, respectively; see Table 5.1).

Fourth, families headed by women are at greater risk of poverty. This is particularly true for Latinos. The proportion of Hispanic families maintained by a female with no husband present has increased since 1970. In 1970, 15% of Hispanic families were maintained by a female with no husband present. By 1990, the percentage had increased to 22% (NCLR, 1993). In 1992, the proportion of Latino families below the poverty level headed by a woman was 48.8%. This percentage is twice as high as that for Latino families below poverty level (26.2%) and for non-Latino families headed by a female (33.3%). The proportion of families living below the poverty line with female-headed households in 1992 varied from 46.0% for Mexican families to 60.3% for Puerto Rican families. The proportion of families of Central and South American origins headed by women was 51.3%. Information was not available on poverty levels for Cuban American families headed by a female (see Table 5.1).

A major reason for the poverty of female-headed families is the failure of noncustodial fathers to fulfill their economic responsibilities. In 1989, only about half of all single mothers obtained child support awards. Hispanic women were much less likely to receive child support, possibly because of the lower income of Hispanic fathers (NCLR, 1993).

The relationship between gender and poverty is clear. According to the NCLR report,

> female-headed households are faced with both a weakened family support structure and social policy which creates disincentives to improving their economic situation. As a result of few employment options, jobs that restrict benefits, and lack of child care, many single mothers are forced to depend on public assistance to support themselves and their families. (NCLR, 1993, p. 4)

On the basis of focus group research, the NCLR found that Mexican and Puerto Rican recipients of Aid to Families with Dependent Children (AFDC) confront a series of barriers to self-sufficiency: family responsibilities, lack of basic skills and relevant job training, the cost and logistics of transportation, and housing costs. In addition, child care and lack of health insurance were critical factors in determining Latino women's need for welfare assistance (NCLR, 1993, pp. 13-14).

Fifth, unemployment is associated with poverty among Hispanic/Latino women. In 1993, the unemployment rate for Hispanic/Latino women was 11.1%. This was more than twice as high as for non-Hispanic women (5.8%). The rate of Latino female unemployment varied by national origins, with women of Central or South American origin experiencing the highest levels of unemployment (14.4%) and Cuban women the lowest (7.3%) (see Table 5.1). The proportion of workers receiving unemployment insurance has fallen markedly in recent years and has disproportionately affected Hispanics. A recent report by the Center on Budget and Policy Priorities cited by NCLR (1993) indicated that fewer than one in five unemployed Hispanic workers received insurance benefits in an average month. This low level of recipients is because of, according to NCLR, state unemployment insurance rules and policy and administrative decisions that restrict eligibility (p. 9).

Sixth, the increase in adolescent pregnancy and parenthood is also associated with poverty among Hispanic/Latino women. In 1990, 16% of Hispanic/Latino mothers were under 20 years of age, compared with 10% for white women and 23% for African Americans. Puerto Rican women had the highest incidence of adolescent pregnancy (22%) among Latinos. The percentages for other Latino women are as follows: 18% for Mexican Americans, 8% for Cubans, 9% for mothers of Central or South American origins. Increasingly, teenage mothers do not marry the fathers, choosing instead to raise their children on their own, sometimes with the assistance of parents and often with some financial support from the government. Therefore, single teenage parents and their children are most likely to live in poverty.

Impact of Poverty on Women's Health

It is impossible to talk about the well-being of women without talking about their economic circumstances. Many poor women are undereducated, face employment and housing discrimination, are geographically concentrated in central cities and in ghetto areas where the economic impact is the greatest, and, if employed, are in low-paying jobs that do not enable them to lift their families above poverty. Poor women and their children have inadequate housing, poor nutrition, poor sanitation, and high rates of physical, emotional, and sexual abuse. People of low socio-economic status experience poorer health that is reflected in a higher incidence of chronic diseases, higher mortality rates, and poorer survival rates (Cooper, Steinhauer, Miller, David, & Schatzkin, 1981; Haan, Kaplan, & Camacho, 1987; Miller, 1987; U.S. Department of Health and Human Services [U.S. DHHS], 1990; Woolhandler et al., 1985). Therefore, poverty is a major influence in the production of disease. Poverty increases not only the likelihood of having poor health but also the ability to afford preventive and routine health care. Women and children represent 80% of poor people in the United States. The majority of them are people of color (NCLR, 1993). Hispanics in general and Hispanic women in particular are more likely than other Americans to be among the working poor, and these working poor are most likely not to have health insurance coverage. Leigh (1994) states that they face double jeopardy with respect to health care. They cannot afford to pay costly medical bills out-of-pocket and do not qualify for federal programs such as Medicaid. Leigh argues that many of the working poor are not U.S. citizens and therefore are not eligible for federal health assistance programs.

Latino women with the worst health status and poorest access to health care live in poor communities where living conditions are unhealthful and where health problems such as tuberculosis, use of alcohol and other drugs, HIV/AIDS, and mental illness and multiple social problems such as family violence, crime, and gang activities are much more prevalent. The fact that women experience a disproportionate share of these problems suggests a strong association between poverty and poor health, both of which result from institutional racism, sexism, and classism.

EFFECTS OF INSTITUTIONALIZED RACISM, SEXISM, AND CLASSISM ON LATINO WOMEN'S HEALTH

Institutionalized racism refers to the established and customary ways in which society operates to keep the minority in a subordinate position (Baca Zinn, 1989). *Racism,* then, is any policy, practice, belief, or attitude that attributes characteristics or status to individuals based on their race. Classist and sexist policies do the same thing according to class and gender (Rothenberg, 1992). Racism, sexism, and classism can be either conscious or unconscious, intentional or unintentional.

Probably the most significant manifestation of the effects of racism, sexism, and classism on Latino women's health is reflected in the limited research and data available on this population and the presence of inefficient health policies that lead to poor health and health practices, particularly among poor women.

Limited Research and
Inefficient Health Policies

Despite the fact that the U.S. Hispanic/Latino population continues to increase at a faster rate than any other population, little effort has been made by the federal government, academic institutions, and the private sector to provide empirical health data on all Hispanics/Latinos. Even less information is available on issues relevant to Hispanic/Latino women.

Real limitations and barriers impede addressing the health needs of Latino women. Few data are available on Hispanics in general, and the data do exist tend to focus on the largest Hispanic subgroup, the Mexican American population. These data, however, do not address the problems of cultural, national, and lifestyle differences that may affect the health of other Latino populations. Nor do the data allow for differences in levels of acculturation, immigration history, or socioeconomic status, all of which have been shown to affect the rates and types of certain diseases, as well as patient access to the health care system. Levels of education, literacy, assimilation, and socioeconomic status similarly reflect the diversity of the Hispanic population in the United States.

There are a number of reasons why limited health information is available on Latinos. Some reasons have to do with government data organization, classification practices, and the inadequacy of the Latino data collection process. Latinos have usually been merged into categories such as "white," "nonwhite," "others," and "racial and ethnic minorities." Latino items have been routinely omitted, at least until recently, from the major national and state data resources. The National Center for Health Statistics (NCHS) did not incorporate an item for the identification of Latinos in its Health Interview Survey until 1976. At present, a number of states continue to omit Latino items and Latino identifiers (place of birth, language preference, Spanish surname lists) from their state forms, records, and data-gathering process. In recent years, some states have become aware of this deficiency and are in the process of making changes to the data collection systems, especially among birth and death records. Nevertheless, interstate comparison of health data remains a nearly impossible task. Moreover, data, when available, continue to depict Latinos as a homogenous whole. Rarely do the available data provide a breakdown among the different Latino ethnic and racial groups (e.g., Cubans, Mexicans, Puerto Ricans, Indian ancestry) or by gender, education levels, socioeconomic status, and other necessary information. Most studies in the 1980s focused exclusively on the Mexican American population and led to a tendency to use this data to address other Latino subgroups. Although this tendency perhaps has been the result of the overall lack of data available to measure the health status of the variety of Latino populations, such generalizations are inappropriate and may lead to hypotheses and conclusions that are wholly inadequate toward addressing each population's specific health needs.

Finally, large surveys that contain Latino data based on national probability samples in which Latinos are included according to their percentage of the total U.S. population result in small Latino numbers among the sample. This practice makes it difficult to conduct detailed analyses and to offer valid generalizations about Latinos and Latino subgroups. Yet, because of the small proportion of Latinos in the total U.S. population, it has been difficult to justify the allocation of resources for large-scale surveys or for the oversampling of the Latino population. This was particularly true in the case of the Hispanic Health and Nutritional Examination Survey (HHANES), which excluded Chicago and the Midwestern region from its scope. HHANES III did include the city of Chicago, but oversampled only Mexicans/Mexican Americans. These practices have made it much harder to obtain any accurate data not only on Latinos but also for all racial and ethnic populations. Hispanic identifiers are lacking from public health records at the state and local levels, and even when items on Hispanic origin are included, little effort has been made by public health officials to analyze and release these data.

Also lacking is epidemiological data on such significant factors as mortality rates, incidence rates, and morbidity and survival rates for certain illnesses such as cancer (Giachello, 1988). In public health, databases (or registries) are lacking in key areas related to chronic disease and mental health. Therefore, researchers are dependent on use and mortality data, when available. In addition, data on hospital use lack Hispanic/Latino identifiers in all states (Arrom, 1993). An added difficulty is the small number of studies conducted among the Hispanic population as a whole and the even smaller number that address Hispanic women by national origin. Because of the diversity of backgrounds, cultures, value systems, migration patterns, health status, and living conditions of Latinas prior to migration and because of the impact of these factors on health status once in the United States, caution must be exercised when examining the existing data.

Little intervention research has been conducted on Hispanic/Latino women, and even fewer clinical trials have included or focused on Hispanic/Latino women; this paucity hampers effective intervention in the lives of Hispanic/Latino women.

In summary, the limitation of data on Latino women is severe. Assumptions have to be made—at times based on observations and anecdotal stories, which may lead to poor formulation of hypotheses—in describing the health needs of Latino women. The inadequacy of data collection measures have contributed to the development of bad policy and poor health status among Latino women.

Institutional racism, sexism, and classism are reflected in the types of policies developed and implemented in the United States, as well as in the lack of action on behalf of disadvantaged groups. According to McKenzie, Bilofsky, and Sharon (1992) and summarized by Bracho de Carpio et al. (1993), between the years 1980 and 1990 poor women suffered reduced federal funding that amounts to a

14% cut in maternal health benefits,

40% cut in community clinics,

35% cut in health benefits to children and the elderly,

67% decrease in employment assistance,

74% decrease in housing assistance, and

66% cut in Title X funds (contraceptive services for poor women).

These cuts have had an even greater negative impact on the few services that were available for poor women and children.

Poor Health and Lifestyle Practices

Minority women in general are affected by institutionalized racism, sexism, and classism in the sense that they live in ghetto areas where there is a sense of despair and a lack of hope, where they engage in daily survival with limited knowledge about opportunities available to them. In developing this argument, Bracho de Carpio et al. (1993) cite Knowles and Prewitt (1970), who stated the following:

The institutions of society have great power to reward and penalize. They reward by providing career opportunities for some people and foreclosing them for others. They reward as well by using the way social goods and services are distributed, by deciding who receives training and skills, medical care, formal education, political influence, moral support and self-respect, productive employment, fair treatment by the law, decent housing, self-confidence and the promise of a secure future for themselves and their children. (Bracho de Carpio et al., 1993, p. 10)

Racism, sexism, and classism are powerful forces in society that negatively affect all aspects of life, including the health of people of color and Latino women, as is discussed in the remainder of this chapter. Latino women experience discrimination, prejudice, and exclusion (based either on language or skin color), perhaps for the first time, affecting their social and psychological well-being.

LATINO WOMEN: CULTURE

Before providing an overview of Latino women's health issues, this section presents a summary of selected aspects of the Latino culture: (a) definition of health, (b) family system, (c) religion, and (d) health attitudes and practices.

Definition of Health

The Hispanic culture has been described as one with a holistic view of health and illness in which good health means that a person is behaving in accordance with his or her conscience, God's mandate, and the norms and customs of his or her group—church, family, and local community (Gregory, 1978). There seems to be no separation between the psychological and total well-being of the individual according to this view (Giachello, 1985).

Illness, then, has been perceived as the result of the following causes: (a) psychological states, such as embarrassment, envy, anger, fear, fright, excessive worry, turmoil in the family, improper behavior, and violations of moral or ethical codes; (b) environmental or natural conditions, such as bad air, germs, dust, excess cold or heat, bad food, or poverty; and (c) supernatural causes, such as malevolent spirits, bad luck, witchcraft, and living enemies (believed to cause harm out of vengeance or envy) (Giachello, 1985, p. 163).

Family System

The importance of the family to Hispanic culture has been well documented. The family rallies in times of crisis to provide support to its members in return for loyalty and support from the individual (Giachello, 1985). Frequently, persons not related by blood are considered part of the family, and this extended family provides a larger support network. Latino families have frequently been described as being highly integrated and having strong family ties (Ramirez, 1978; Sena-Rivera, 1979). The family assists in coping with social problems and emotional stress by bonding together to form a cohesive network that provides mutual help, social interaction, and protection. Relatives live in close proximity, and it is still quite common to find several generations of family members living in either the same household, within the same block, or within a mile of each other.

Empirical studies of Hispanic families document that these groups depend more on relatives and friends for services, emotional support, and advice than on health professionals. Health and illness have been perceived as family problems, and family members are involved in health problem-solving behavior. Self-care within the Latino groups has consisted, according to the literature, of routine daily care, common first aid, use of home remedies, seeking lay health advice, and actual "care" of the ill one. The maintenance of these strong family and friendship ties has been considered important self-care practice per se (Ferguson, 1979). A Hispanic without a family network frequently does not have another support system available.

Within the family system, the roles of males and females have often been studied. Men have been expected to dominate in all realms of family life, to live up to the traditional concept of machismo. The role of Hispanic women is changing. Traditional cultural expectations included being submissive to their husbands or fathers and remaining at home. With the number of female-headed Hispanic households on the rise, Hispanic women must work to support themselves and their children. In a two-parent family, the woman often must work to supplement her husband's income. Although changes have occurred in the roles of some women, traditional attitudes and behaviors are still important in the Hispanic community. Traditional values inhibit the discussion of past sexual and drug history, areas that are critical as they relate to health education for women, early screening and treatment of women with sexually transmitted diseases, and women with dependency on alcohol and other drugs.

Religion

Religion is an important institution in the Hispanic community. It provides a framework of beliefs to explain the world, a model for life, a support and advocacy system, a vehicle for the perpetuation of the traditional culture, and sometimes a necessary factor in achieving economic or social success.

Traditionally, Latinos have been assumed to be Roman Catholic. This has been so unquestioningly accepted that research on religious differences among Latinos is usually considered unnecessary. The few studies that have been conducted suggest that membership in the Catholic Church is much more prevalent among Mexican Americans than among Puerto Ricans, who are members of Protestant churches in greater numbers. Protestant denominations have been proselytizing to Mexican Americans in the Southwest in the last decade; the effect of this effort and the assimilation into mainstream culture of second- and third-generation Hispanics remains to be seen (McCready, 1985). According to Medina (1987), 85% of Hispanics are Catholic, and the remainder are members of different Protestant sects, such as Baptist, Jehovah's Witness, Church of Jesus Christ of Latter Day Saints (Mormons), the Pentecostal Church (Charismatic), and alternative religions such as Espiritismo and Santerismo.

The Catholic Church has taken strong stands on several issues related to reproductive health, such as abortion and HIV/AIDS. Research must be conducted to ascertain the influence of the teachings of the Catholic Church on Hispanics and how these teachings affect receptiveness of women toward certain health education and disease prevention issues.

Health Attitudes and Practices

Many studies on Hispanic health have stressed the existence of a health subculture that has played an important role in determining values, actions, and perceptions about health and illness (Clark, 1959; Giachello, 1995; Saunders, 1954). The Hispanic health subculture described in some of these studies clearly documents the existence of traditional self-care activities and the importance of the family and other social networks in its preservation. Hispanics have been described as highly traditional in their health care practices, with health beliefs characterized by a distrustful attitude toward doctors and modern medical techniques and by the view that professional diagnoses are no better than self-diagnoses. The practice of folk medicine and the use of patent medicines and home cures to treat common aliments is frequent (Clark, 1959; Welch, Comer, & Steinmann, 1973). For example, Stern and Giachello (1977) found that 55% of pregnant women in a sample from a Mexican community on Chicago's West Side were using home remedies (chamomile and cinnamon teas) and over-the-counter drugs for problems related to pregnancy. A study of the use of home remedies in the U.S.-Mexican border area confirms a core group of most frequently used remedies that constitute the bulk of the home treatment of common ailments in that area (Trotter, 1981). Studies further indicate a relatively well-defined group of ailments considered to be more amenable to ethnopharmacological intervention than to treatment by the conventional medical system (Chesney, Thompson, Guevara, Vela, & Schottstasedt, 1980; Martinez & Martin, 1966; Sandler & Chan, 1978; Trotter, 1981). Another group of researchers also found that 21% of the Hispanic population in the Southwestern United States reported the use of herbs and other home remedies to treat episodes of illness, compared with 12% of the total U.S. population. They also found that 33% of the Hispanic population thought illness can be treated more effectively with home remedies than with prescribed medicine, in comparison with only 24% of the total U.S. population. Professional care is sought when self-treatment and folk healing practices have not been successful (Giachello, 1988). Preference for self-treatment may partly be attributed to negative experiences with health providers, manifested particularly in poor relationships between Hispanic patients and their physicians (Hayes-Bautista, 1978).

In addition to folk medicine and home remedies, help from folk practitioners as major alternative resources to the formal medical care system is prevalent (Kiev, 1968; Madsen, 1964). Few studies, however, have presented empirical data about folk practitioners (e.g., *curanderas, espiritistas*), their quantity, location, sociodemographic characteristics, or clients served. Some studies claim that folk practitioners have virtually disappeared (Martinez & Martin, 1966), and their salience as a health resource alternative has been questioned in the work of Edgerton and Karno (1969).

OVERVIEW OF
LATINO WOMEN'S HEALTH

Life Expectancy

In 1991, life expectancy for Latino women was higher than for Latino men (77.1 years vs. 69.6 years), lower than for non-Latino white women (79.2 years), and higher than for non-Latino black women (73.5 years). Life expectancies for white and black men are 72.7 years and 64.8 years, respectively. These statistics seem positive, but researchers must interpret them with caution, considering the increase of certain diseases that women in general experience as they get older. For example, osteoporosis and Alzheimer's disease are increasing among women in general, and little is known about them in reference to Latino women. In addition, women in general and Latino women in particular experience more acute symptoms, chronic conditions, and short- and long-term disabilities arising from health problems. The higher life expectancy rate has provided the white-male-dominant establishment an excuse for not focusing on women's health and on the health of women of color.

Causes of Death

In 1992, the leading cause of death among Latino women was cardio-vascular disease, which claimed 19,829 lives. Cancer is the second major cause of death to Latinas, with 7,235 deaths for that year. In 1992, these two leading causes of death accounted for 49% of all deaths to Latino women. The third and fourth leading causes of death among Latinas in 1992 were cerebrovascular disease (2, 177 deaths) and diabetes (1, 352 deaths). The remaining leading causes of deaths to Latino women were as follows: accidents and adverse effects (1,562 deaths), pneumonia and influenza (1,068), motor vehicles (938), conditions originating in the perinatal period (845), chronic obstructive pulmonary diseases (COPD), including asthma, and congenital anomalies (NCHS, 1995).

Selected Illnesses

HIV/AIDS

Through June 1994, women represented 13% (46,882) of all U.S. AIDS adult/adolescent cases (361,509) and constituted the fastest growing group of AIDS cases in the United States. For example, between December 1992 and October 1993, new AIDS cases among U.S. women increased 54.3%, compared with 31.7% among U.S. males. The CDC estimates that more than one million people in the United States are infected with HIV and that at least 100,000 of them are believed to be women, 80% of childbearing age.

AIDS is the fifth cause of death among women of childbearing years. Presently, in New York and New Jersey, it is the number one killer of women ages 15 to 44 ("HIV/AIDS in New York City," 1991). Some reasons for the increased AIDS cases among women as summarized by Giachello (1991) are as follows:

1. AIDS is perceived as a men's illness that affects only gay white men and men who are intravenous drug users (IVDUs). Therefore, there is a denial that women are at risk, and many health care workers may not screen women for HIV or AIDS.

2. Women are misdiagnosed or diagnosed late because they do not have equal access to medical care and because AIDS manifests differently in women. The opportunistic infections and illnesses (e.g., herpes, candidiasis, cervical cancer, infection of fallopian tubes) that affect women with HIV/AIDS were until recently not conditions officially recognized by the CDC as related to AIDS. Physicians, as a result, may not think about HIV/AIDS when some of these conditions are present in women.

3. Women's traditional role as primary caretakers of their families serve as barriers because women "don't suppose to get sick." When symptoms of illness emerge, a woman may address them only after the needs of her immediate family have been taken care of.

4. Women discover their seropositive status late in HIV progression.

5. Once women are diagnosed with HIV/AIDS, they do not have equal access to ongoing medical care or to clinical trials (only about 6% of all persons enrolled in the AIDS clinical trials group system are women). This is particularly true for IVDUs.

6. Women cannot afford the expensive drugs that may alleviate the symptoms.

For these and other reasons, women tend to be sicker at time of diagnosis and have a shorter survival rate (Giachello, 1991, 1994b). For example, the life expectancy for men from day of diagnosis currently ranges from 24 to 36 months. Life expectancy for women from day of diagnosis averages from 3½ to 6 months. The average life expectancy for black women with AIDS in New York City is as little as 15 days. Women who live longer experience a series of medical, financial, and social consequences. Because the definition of AIDS prior to December 1992 did not reflect the symptomatology of women, women were not entitled to social security benefits because eligibility for disability is based on the CDC's official AIDS definition. All of this clearly reflects sexism in the AIDS epidemic in the United States (Giachello, 1991, 1994b).

Of all women with AIDS in the United States, 21% are Latino and 53% are blacks, although black and Latino women make up only 19% of all U.S. women. Furthermore, recent studies have indicated that the chance of acquiring AIDS for Latino women is over 8 times greater than that for white women (Holmes, Karon, & Kreiss, 1990; Selick, Castro, & Pappaioanou, 1988). Most of the HIV/AIDS cases among Latinos are among Puerto Ricans, who are 7 times more likely than non-Hispanic whites to be diagnosed with HIV/AIDS. The high incidence of AIDS among women has been associated with increased exposure to HIV-infected needles through injecting drugs or by having sexual partners who are current or former needle-injecting drug users (NIDUs). For example, 51% of all AIDS cases among U.S. women are due to intravenous drug use, and 33% are due to heterosexual contact. Heterosexual transmission was the result of having sex with needle-injecting drug users (62%) or with bisexual males (9%). For Hispanic women, heterosexual transmission due to these causes accounted for 80% and 5%, respectively. Actually, Latino women are more vulnerable than white women to heterosexual transmission of HIV/AIDS through sex with bisexual men. This is particularly related to the fact that 20% of Hispanic gay men report having sex with both men and women, compared with 13% for white gay men.

A women's health report of the Women's Research and Education Institute (Leigh, 1994) indicates that acculturation among Hispanics seems to play a role in the transmission of HIV/AIDS, with intravenous drug use most prevalent among more acculturated Latinas. Less acculturated Latinas report a low perceived risk of AIDS and less likelihood of using illegal drugs or engaging in sexual activity with multiple partners.

The number of AIDS cases is expected to increase rapidly among Latino women because high seropositivity rates have also been found among (a) Hispanics (of both sexes) applying for military services during October 1985 and December 1989 (CDC, 1990), (b) Hispanic runaway and homeless adolescents in New York City (Stricof, Kennedy, Nattell, Weisfuse, & Novick, 1991), (c) Latino newborns in New York City (Novick, Glebatis, Stricof, McCubbin, Lessner, & Berns, 1991), and (d) Latino women of childbearing years at a New York City family planning clinic (Stricof, Nattell, & Novick, 1991). Seropositivity has been reported as being the highest among Latino women entering the New York State prisons (29%), compared with black women (14%) and white women (7%) (Smith, Mild, & Truman, 1991), and for Latino women in HIV testing and counseling sites who reported self-injecting illicit drugs. The seropositivity rate for these Latino women was 15.2%, compared with 16.9% for black women IVDUs and 3.8% for white women with similar behavior ("HIV/AIDS in New York City," 1991).

The highest numbers of Latino women with AIDS are found in the northeastern and southeastern United States (New York, New Jersey, Florida, and Puerto Rico). The southwestern states, where most Mexican American women live, have a much smaller number of reported AIDS cases. AIDS among female IVDUs in the Southwest, however, particularly among Mexican Americans, has been described as being in the initial stage of the epidemic (Mata & Jorquez, 1988).

Bracho de Carpio et al. (1993) argue that poverty increases the vulnerability for HIV infection and decreases the capability of prevention among individuals, particularly among Latino women. These researchers analyzed the prevalence of HIV/AIDS in certain geographical areas, such as New York City (Bronx), Chicago (Logan Square, Humboldt Park, and West Town), Texas (Houston, Dallas, and San Antonio; border counties Cameron, Hidalgo, and Webb; and the city of El Paso, which is the fourth poorest city in the United States) and found that the high prevalence of HIV/AIDS among Latino women was among those living in areas of extreme poverty. They recommend that the strategy needed to combat AIDS is confronting "poverty itself."

Leigh (1994) argues that among women with HIV/AIDS, others in their households—lovers, spouses and/or children—are also likely to have the disease. Women with AIDS who must also fulfill their traditional roles as caregivers are likely to live shorter periods of time than women who do not have the added stress of providing care to others. In addition, women with AIDS often leave behind orphans with HIV/AIDS, many of whom subsequently are raised by their grandmothers, an ordeal that increases the stresses in the lives of these older women.

In summary, AIDS is one of the most serious health problems facing Hispanics in the United States. The number of AIDS cases is expected to increase rapidly because of the high seropositivity rates in the Hispanic communities. This is particularly true for Hispanic women, children, and adolescents. Sexism is manifested in the way public officials have dealt with this condition as it relates to women. The definition of HIV/AIDS excluded the symptoms and illnesses that affect women, and women have been excluded from clinical trials. Racism is reflected in the way organizations of color have been receiving a disproportionately low share of resources for prevention and treatment.

Sexually Transmitted Diseases (STDs)

Most of the clinical research on STDs among Hispanics has been conducted in the adolescent population. When compared with other populations, Hispanic teenagers have shown the highest rates of chlamydia, gonorrhea, and trichomoniasis (Eager, 1985). One study revealed that Hispanic teenagers aged 15 to 17 have the highest rate of chlamydia (Smith, 1988). Another study, conducted in South Texas, found that approximately 10% of Hispanic women of all ages who participated in the study were infected with this sexually transmitted disease (Gleeney, Glassman, Cox, & Brown, 1988).

The incidence rate per 100,000 of primary and secondary syphilis in the United Stated slowly increased between 1981 and 1983. It then declined between 1985 and 1986 but has increased rapidly ever since. This pattern is particularly true for women, primarily Hispanic and black women (CDC, 1990). This trend is also true for teenagers 15 to 19 years of age, but the rate of increase of syphilis cases has been more dramatic, particularly for black and Hispanic teen women. For example, the rate of primary and secondary syphilis for Hispanic teen women increased from 17 per 100,000 in 1986 to 22 per 100,000 in 1987, although it slightly declined after that year (Hispanic Health Council [HHC], 1989).

States and cities with the highest concentrations of Hispanics also have the highest numbers and incidence rates per 100,000 population of syphilis in the United States. These same states (e.g., New York, New Jersey, Florida, California) and selected cities (e.g., Miami, New York, Los Angeles) have also experienced a considerable increase in total syphilis cases between 1985 and 1989 (CDC, 1991).

The incidence rate of gonorrhea per 100,000 is higher overall, compared with that of syphilis. Gonorrhea has dropped considerably for both men and women of all ethnic/racial groups between 1981 and 1989. The decline in rates was most pronounced among whites and Latinos of both sexes. Rates for teenagers 15 to 19 years old per 100,000 showed overall decreases in the last decade, particularly for females. At the same time, the black population experienced a considerable increase of gonorrhea, particularly among black male adolescents. States with high concentrations of syphilis also have high concentrations of gonorrhea, although the incidence rates for gonorrhea declined between 1984 and 1988.

STD screening is critical for early diagnosis and treatment. Anecdotal information from health providers suggests that both Latino men and women deny the possibility of having any STD condition and that they are unlikely to seek health care for STDs unless symptoms are noticeable or are accompanied by pain. It is well known that chlamydia-related consequences for women include pelvic inflammatory disease, infertility, and ectopic pregnancy and that infected pregnant women are at risk for spontaneous abortion and stillbirths. Chlamydia has also been associated with conjunctivitis in infants born to infected mothers. In general, infants born to mothers with STDs are at risk of blindness, mental retardation, and death.

Studies show that persons with syphilis or gonorrhea also have a higher incidence of HIV infection. Persons at risk for HIV are also at risk for STDs. Minorities (Latinos and blacks) most at risk for STDs are sexually active persons, particularly under age 25, and those with multiple sexual partners.

In summary, Hispanic adolescents have shown the highest incidence of chlamydia and trichomoniasis. Trends in syphilis and gonorrhea incidence in the United States show that the number of cases for gonorrhea was overall higher, particularly between 1985 and 1988. This was particularly true for the black population. The number of gonorrhea cases has declined for whites and Latinos, although the decline for Latinos was slightly less. For the adolescent population, the incidence of gonorrhea declined for white adolescents but increased considerably for black adolescents, particularly males. The incidence of syphilis has declined for whites and increased for Latinos and blacks. This increase was most pronounced for blacks, particularly for 1988 (CDC, 1990). Screening for STDs is critical to the health of Latino and other minority populations.

Diabetes Mellitus

The prevalence of diabetes mellitus among Latinos is reaching epidemic proportions. An estimated 1.3 million Latinos (11.8% of an estimated total of 11 million Americans) over age 21 have diabetes mellitus (American Diabetes Association, 1991). Diabetes mellitus is a chronic condition characterized by abnormal metabolism. Diabetes affects the circulatory system and is frequently associated with conditions such as arteriosclerosis (hardening of the arteries), kidney failure, vision loss, and amputations. In 1988, diabetes was the ninth leading cause of death among Mexican Americans. Because the risk of diabetes increases with age, it also represents the fifth leading cause of death among Latinos 65 years of age and over. The diabetes mortality rate for Latinos is twice the rate for non-Latino whites.

According to the American Diabetes Association (1991), Mexican Americans and Puerto Ricans experience 110% to 120% higher diabetes rates, compared with whites. The rate for Cuban Americans ranges from 50% to 60%. Mexican Americans and Puerto Ricans also have 2 to 3 times greater risk of non-insulin-dependent diabetes (NIDDM) than non-Latinos (American Diabetes Association, 1991). Data from the National Center for Health Statistics (NCHS) Health and Nutrition Examination Survey (HANES II) and 1982-1984 Hispanic HANES show that 42% of Mexican Americans, 40% of Puerto Ricans, and 58% of Cubans who had diabetes did not know they had the disease. The prevalence of undiagnosed diabetes was higher among Puerto Ricans and Mexican Americans than among whites. The prevalence of diabetes is related to low socioeconomic status, lack of insurance, and hesitation of Latinos to visit a physician (General Accounting Office [GAO], 1992).

Latinos' increased risk may be due to genetic predisposition, age, diet, obesity, family history of diabetes, and sedentary lifestyle, which are all risk factors for the development of NIDDM. Regarding Latino women, one study found that 10% of Mexican American women over age 45 were diabetic, compared with the national rate of 3.7%. Latino women have 3 times the risk of developing diabetes and greater metabolic severity than non-Latino whites.

Gestational diabetes, which occurs only during pregnancy, is another risk factor for NIDDM. Women who have had gestational diabetes have a 30% to 40% chance of developing NIDDM; 25% of women who had gestational diabetes will develop diabetes mellitus afterward. Women who are older, overweight, have a family history of diabetes, a history of multiple, unexplained miscarriages, or unusually large babies are prone to gestational diabetes (U.S. DHHS, 1986). Fetal and perinatal deaths are 3 to 8 times greater in pregnancies of diabetic mothers than nondiabetic mothers, as well as congenital malformations in children. Given these factors, Mexican American women are believed to be at increased risk for gestational diabetes, although no studies have been conducted regarding the incidence of this condition among women in this group.

Because compliance with the regimen to treat diabetes requires monitoring by health care providers and family support, treatment poses particular challenges for Hispanics/Latinos. The middle-class mentality and lack of cultural sensitivity among health care providers are explanations for the treatment practices that focus on the individual, rather than on the family. These factors, combined with lack of bilingual staff, make adherence to treatment for Latino women more difficult.

Cancer

A recent review by Carter-Pokras (1994) offers more comprehensive examinations of the available literature and site-specific analysis of cancer among the U.S. Hispanic population. The limitation of data makes it extremely difficult to draw conclusions or to extrapolate data from the general Hispanic population to specific subgroups or from one subgroup to another. The best source for cancer incidence data has been the National Cancer Institute's Surveillance, Epidemiology, and End Results (SEER) program. The SEER program is composed, however, of only 11 locally based cancer registries that cover only 9% of the U.S. population. Of those 11 sites, only those in New Mexico, Puerto Rico, and New Jersey offer any usable data on Hispanic cancer incidence and mortality rates, and these are primarily for Mexican Americans and Puerto Ricans. In addition, although cancer survival data are available from cancer registries in New Mexico, California (San Francisco, Oakland), Connecticut, and Puerto Rico, none of these data sources is representative of the total Hispanic population or of the many subgroups among Hispanics in the United States (Giachello, 1988). Furthermore, cancer registries operate outside the SEER network and do not always operate under a recognized set of procedures. Therefore, the quality and completeness of the resulting data are subject to great variability (Carter-Pokras, 1994).

According to the available data, cancer is the second leading cause of death for Hispanic women. Cancer is characterized as abnormal microscopic cells that grow uncontrollably. It tends to spread to different parts of the body and eventually results in death, especially if not treated promptly. It can be caused by external or environmental factors, such as chemicals, radiation, and viruses, or internal conditions such as hormones or a failing immune system. The leading external factor contributing to the rise in the number of preventable cancer cases among women is cigarette smoking. The American Cancer Society (ACS, 1991) reports that smoking is responsible for approximately 76% of lung cancer deaths among women and is a major cause of heart disease and other pulmonary conditions, such as colds, chronic bronchitis, and emphysema. Although Hispanic women are less likely to smoke than white women and black

women, dramatic increases have occurred as a result of the heavy marketing of the tobacco industries in the Latino communities, targeting Latino
youth and women (Maxwell & Jacobson, 1989). As a result, a Denver
study covering 1970 and 1980 document a doubling of lung cancer rates
among Latino women and men. During this period, lung cancer among
Latino women grew by 109%, compared with 95% for white women
(ACS, 1991).

In addition to lung cancer, the other three most frequently reported
types of cancer among women are colorectal, breast, and uterine cancers.
Mexican American women from New Mexico are as likely to suffer from
colorectal cancer as from lung cancer. The incidence of breast cancer
among Latino women is lower, compared with that of non-Hispanic
whites, but they are more likely than white women to die of breast cancer.
The differences in survival rates are reflective of the stages in which breast
cancer is diagnosed and treated; early diagnosis and treatment are considered critical for survival. According to the NCLR (1993) Latino women,
particularly Mexican Americans, are most likely to develop cervical
cancer than uterine cancer. Uterine cancer survival rates, however, are
slightly better for Mexican American women than cervical cancer survival
rates.

Finally, the relatively high prevalence of cancer among Latino women
is related to the fact that Hispanic women are less likely than white women
to have received common types of cancer screening. They are either
unaware that such screening exists, or financial, cultural, and system
problems related to the delivery of health services have served as barriers
in prevention. The American Cancer Society, for example, found that in
1987, a larger percentage of Hispanic women had never heard of or
received a Pap smear, breast exam, or mammogram, as compared with
other women (ACS, 1991; NCLR, 1993).

Mental Health

Relatively little is reported on the specific mental health status and
issues of Latino women, considering the rapidly growing literature on
Latinos and the large number of women mental health practitioners. The
literature on Latino women and mental health tends to be scattered across
many topics. Few large studies compare women and men. The few studies
available document that depression, particularly among older women, is
three times higher than men. The epidemiological studies on Latinos have

focused on the relationship of acculturation and the prevalence of mental disorders (Rogler, Cortes, & Malgady, 1991). Other studies have focused on the limited utilization of the mental health servies by Latinos (Treviño and Rendón, 1994) as a result of cultural, financial, and institutional barriers. Most recently, studies have documented differential utilization of mental health services among Latino men and women. Wells and associates (1989) reported Mexican-American females were most likely to use medical inpatient services, have a general visit, use the general medical sector for dealing with emotional problems, use a specialty mental health service, and use more human services. In addition, they found those persons enrolled in the Medicaid program or with higher levels of acculturation, or both, were more likely to use more services.

Violence

Violence, particularly continous violence from domestic assault, war, and torture, impacts mental health through posttraumatic stress disorder. This disorder has been shown to be a mediator between trauma and physical health, manifested by increased health services utilization, cardio-vascular morbidity, poor self-reported health, and shorter life expectancy (Friedman, & Schnurr, 1995). Certain nationalities of Central and South American women are more likely to be affected by state-sponsored violence. Latino women living in inner cities will be more affected by witnessing or having a close relative injured or killed by gang-related violence.

Regardless of the population group, Lation women will be impacted by domestic violence. In Chicago and nationally, Latino women have mortality rates from violence equally or lower than non-Hispanic white women. It is believed that some cultural factors may be "protective" of men killing women; however, their rates of injury and mental trauma are not shown to be lower than for non-Hispanic whites. Even though mortality indicators do not differentiate for national origin or socioeconomic status, there may be differences between groups.

Selected Lifestyle Practices

Alcohol Consumption

The available literature on levels of alcohol use and abuse among Latinos indicates great variance across gender, levels of acculturation, and national origin. Most of the available research is based on one of two methodologies: (a) retrospective self-reporting of consumption and (b) indirect indicators of alcohol consumption. Both of these research techniques are problematic for a variety of reasons. Self-reporting is subject to the truthfulness and awareness of the respondents. Latino women have been found to underreport their consumption, possibly because of strong cultural inhibitions against women drinking. The use of indirect indicators of alcohol consumption is also problematic for research on Latinos because, in the past, no mortality data were collected on Latinos and because only recently death certificates have been modified in some states to include a Hispanic identifier. In addition, police statistics of public drunkenness or drunk-driving arrests for Latinos may be influenced by the possibility of greater police surveillance of Latinos (Caetano, 1983).

Studies on alcohol consumption among Latinos indicate that Latinos drink less than whites overall and that younger Latinos, particularly those under age 25, drink more than older age-groups. Data indicate that males drink considerably more than females. The differences found in the Hispanic Health and Nutrition Examination Survey (HHANES) (Christian, Zobeck, & Martin, 1985), showing that Latino men are twice as likely to be drinkers as Latino women, are in agreement with most of the literature. In addition, women seem to drink much less than men, and then primarily at culturally appropriate events (Arredondo, Weddige, Justice, & Fitz, 1987; Holck, Warren, Smith, & Rochat, 1984). This pattern is changing, with increased participation of women in the labor force and in traditionally male-dominated jobs that are more stress producing. Also, the percentage of alcoholic women is expected to increase approximately 10% because women live longer (Giachello, 1991).

Latino subgroups are comprised of both abstainers and heavy drinkers. Data by place of birth indicate that heavy-drinking Latino men tend to be first-generation U.S. born, followed by Mexican-born men. Heavy-drinking females were most likely to have been born in Latin American countries other than Mexico, Puerto Rico, and Cuba. Drinking behaviors among Latinos have been strongly associated with high levels of acculturation, measured by high income and high education and English language dominance.

Acculturation into the mainstream culture, along with employment outside the home, seems to affect the rate and quantity of drinking among Latino women. Holck et al. (1984) found that Mexican American women were more likely to abstain than Anglo women and that Anglo women were 3 times more likely to be heavy drinkers. Drinking increased for both groups of women as their level of education increased. Once the level of education was controlled, no significant ethnic differences were found. With education as a measure of socioeconomic status and acculturation, these data suggest that as Mexican American women become more acculturated and achieve higher levels of education, their rate of drinking increases. Evidence seems to suggest that never-married women and those divorced or separated have higher rates of heavier drinking.

A recent study using data from the Southwestern sample of the HHANES compared the patterns of alcohol use among Mexican American mothers and children in female-headed households with use patterns among mothers and children in dual-headed households (Stroup et al., 1988). The study found that, regardless of age, education, income, and acculturation, Mexican American single female heads of households drank more alcoholic drinks, drank more days, and had more drinks per occasion than did the female heads of dual-headed households. Cultural factors (e.g., Latino women's self-sacrificing role) and multiple, and at times conflicting, roles led to higher stress. As a whole, children of single heads of households did not drink significantly more than children from dual-headed households, although there was some tendency for male children of single heads of households to drink the most.

Illicit Substance Abuse

Substance abuse has been associated with the general health status of the mother and with birth outcomes. Data available on illicit substance abuse in the Latino community is very limited. The available data obtained through the 1988 Household Survey, summarized in a National Council of La Raza report (1993), show that Latinos are less likely than whites or blacks to report ever having tried illicit drugs, although they were most likely to report being current users. For example, close to one third of Latinos (32.3%) reported that they "ever used" any kind of illicit drug, compared with 35.9% of blacks and 37% of whites. However, 14.7% of Latinos reported using illicit drugs in the past year, and 8.2% reported using drugs in the past month. These data compare with 13.9% and 7.0%, respectively, for whites and 13.3% and 7.8%, respectively, for blacks.

The 1988 Household Survey also found that Latinos were more likely than whites to report current use of certain illicit drugs, such as heroin, cocaine, crack, and PCP. These types of drugs are usually associated with physical addiction, excess mortality, and other negative social consequences for the individual, for his or her family, and for the community. These problems are expected to increase because the percentage of

Latinos reporting ever having used cocaine increased from 7.3% to 11.0% between 1985 and 1988 and because users of crack appear to be more prevalent among the Latino population between ages 18 and 25. The literature suggests that whites may be more likely to experiment with illicit drugs, whereas blacks and Latinos are more likely to use them regularly. Latinos were also most likely to report current use of any psychotherapeutic drugs, such as sedatives, tranquilizers, stimulants, or analgesics, than whites or blacks.

Data on Latinos by national origin are available for marijuana, cocaine, inhalant, and sedative use through the HHANES. The survey (which cannot be generalized to the national Latino population because of possible regional differences) found that 42% of Mexican Americans in the Southwest, 43% of Puerto Ricans in New York, and 20% of Cuban Americans in Florida had used marijuana at some time. Twelve percent of Mexican Americans were current users, as were 15% of Puerto Ricans and 5% of Cuban Americans. Many more Puerto Ricans than Mexican Americans or Cuban Americans had tried cocaine (22%, 11%, and 9%, respectively). The use of inhalants and sedatives was not found to be widespread in any of these populations.

The HHANES also found that the use of any of these substances was much higher among males than females for the three ethnic groups. Although it is believed that traditional Latino women's roles discourage women from substance abuse, this may not hold true in the 1990s; data for seven cities with significant Latino populations indicate that 40% of Latino female arrestees tested positive for some drug. For example, in Los Angeles, Latino female arrestees were more likely than Latino males to test drug positive.

Studies on Latino women and substance abuse are limited. Available data indicate that Latino women are less likely to use illicit drugs than Latino men and black or white women. For example, 37.8% of Latino men and 26.9% of Latino women reported ever using illicit drugs, whereas the numbers for white and black women were 34.8% and 29.6%, respectively.

Some demographic characteristics of Latino users, according to HHANES findings, indicate that they were more likely to speak English and to have higher levels of income and education; they were most likely to be single (either [a] never married or [b] divorced or separated); and most likely to be born in the United States.

A series of legal and ethical controversies has emerged regarding women's use of alcohol and drugs during pregnancy. There is much debate about whether women who use drugs during pregnancy should be criminally prosecuted for their conduct. The National Association for Perinatal Addiction Research and Education (NAPARE) (1992) indicates that more than 40 women have been charged nationwide with felony crimes—as diverse as delivery of a drug to a minor and use or possession of a controlled substance—on the basis of their prenatal drug use. It has been argued that criminalization of prenatal drug use may lead pregnant drug users to either delay their entry into the medical care system or not use the system at all for prenatal care because of fears of prosecution. This behavior would not serve either the baby's or the mother's health. This behavior also may have particularly negative consequences to Latino women who already delay seeing a health care provider for prenatal care or just do not see one at all. This is particularly true of Puerto Rican and Mexican women (Giachello, 1991).

Once again, the patterns of illicit drug use among Latino women require attention and monitoring because of the current emergence of pregnant addicted women, who require special intervention and attention. Currently few drug treatment rehabilitation programs are available for women, and even fewer would accept pregnant women.

In summary, studies on illicit drug use are limited among Latinos and Latino subpopulations. Available data indicate that Latinos overall are less likely to use illicit drugs than whites or blacks, although some new evidence shows that, for certain types of drugs (e.g., crack), the proportion of Latino users is increasing relative to white and black users. Data by Latinos of national origin indicate that Puerto Ricans and Mexicans are equally likely to report the use of marijuana but that Puerto Ricans are most likely to use cocaine. Hispanic men are more likely than Latino women to use illicit drugs, although recent studies from New York City and data from CDC HIV/AIDS Testing and Counseling Centers document high numbers of Latino women who are IVDUs. Latino drug users tend to be U.S. born and to have higher levels of acculturation.

Smoking

Studies have shown that Latino women have lower smoking rates, smoke less frequently, and smoke fewer cigarettes than women in the general population. Data from the 1989 Current Population Survey indicate that 13% of Latino women were current smokers, compared with 23% of women in the total U.S. population. Data from the 1991 birth certificates in 45 states and the District of Columbia support these findings: On average, 6% of Latino mothers smoked during pregnancy, compared with

21% of white mothers and 15% of African American mothers. Tobacco use was especially high for Puerto Rican mothers (13%), particularly those between ages 20 and 24; next highest was for mothers of other/unknown Latino origin (11%). It was especially low for mothers of Central and South American origin (3%), followed by Mexican (6.3%) and Cuban (6.2%) mothers.

Aside from being one of the primary risk factors for heart disease, lung disease, hypertension, and cancer, smoking has a strong negative impact on pregnancy outcome. Scientific evidence indicates that smokers have a higher risk of miscarriage, stillbirth, and premature and low-birth-weight babies. Low birth weight for Latino mothers who smoked during pregnancy varies by place of birth of the mother. U.S.-born Mexican mothers who smoked during pregnancy were more likely to deliver low-birth-weight babies than their foreign-born peers (11% vs. 7%). The opposite was true for Puerto Rican and Cuban mothers (13% vs. 15%, 7% vs. 17%). No differences were found in birth weight by Central and South American women who smoked during pregnancy and prior to birth (Ventura, 1993).

Cholesterol

Hispanic females appear less likely to have high serum cholesterol levels than non-Hispanic black or non-Hispanic white females. The 1982-1984 HHANES indicated that cholesterol levels were higher for non-Hispanic white women (28.3%) than for non-Hispanic black women (25.0%) or for the three Hispanic subgroups surveyed. The HHANES data indicate that Cuban women (16.9%) were less likely than Mexican American (29.0%) or Puerto Rican women (22.7%) to have high cholesterol. Overall, Hispanic figures are unavailable because HHANES data cover only particular Hispanic subgroups in certain areas.

Hypertension

Data suggest that Hispanic women are less likely than non-Hispanic women to have hypertension. According to the HHANES, 43.8% of non-Hispanic blacks and 25.1% of non-Hispanic whites between ages 20 and 74 were hypertensive. Among the three Hispanic subgroups studied, the prevalence was lowest for Cuban females (14.4%), followed by Puerto Ricans (19.2%) and Mexican Americans (20.3%). Yet, these numbers may be deceptive because hypertension increases with age and because the relative youth of the Hispanic population may cause underestimation of the extent of the problem.

Reproductive Health

Family Planning

Latino women are less likely to use family planning services than non-Latino white women and African American women (e.g., Garcia, Salcedo-Gonzalez, & Giachello, 1985; NCHS, 1981a). Use of services varies by age, education, and access barriers. Those who visit a family planning clinic are more likely to have been referred by parents, doctors, or clinics and by other relatives.

The use of family planning services is an important determinant of use of birth control methods. Two researchers found that Latino women who made a family planning visit were slightly more likely than non-Latino white women to begin a birth control method (51% and 49%, respectively) but much more likely than African American women (43%). Latino women were as likely as African American women to make a family planning visit before first intercourse (16% and 17%, respectively) but were significantly more likely to make no visit for family planning services, compared with African American women (33% and 18%, respectively).

Data on patterns of use of various contraceptive methods based on the 1988 National Family Growth Survey show that the pill is the contraceptive method most often reported by Latino women between ages 15 and 44 (33%). This percentage is slightly higher than those reported for non-Latino whites (30%) but lower than those reported by African American women of the same age-group (38%). The percentage of Latino women who reported the use of the pill is also higher, compared with the aged-adjusted percentages found by two researchers in 1991, using 1982-84 HHANES data in their study on reproductive characteristics of selected Latino women aged 15 to 45. They found that 15.7% of Mexican American, 8.7% of Puerto Rican, and 8.2% of Cuban American women reported current use of oral contraceptives (p. 225).

The 1988 National Family Growth Survey also found that condom use was reported by 14% of the Latino population. The percentage use is similar to that for whites (15%) but higher than that for African Americans (10%). The use of condoms for Latinos doubled between 1982 and 1988 (p. 201). Those most likely to use condoms for the total 1988 sample were teenagers, never-married women, and those who intended to have children in the future. The intrauterine device (IUD) and the diaphragm were the contraceptives least used by Latinos (5% and 2%, respectively). The percentage of IUD use represents a decline from 19% use by Latino women in 1982. Sterilization as a contraceptive is discussed below.

Sterilization

Hysterectomy is one of the most common major surgical procedures in the United States. Studies show little or no difference in race or ethnicity in average age at the time of the sterilization operation. For all types of sterilization operations, the average age for whites was 30; for African Americans, 29; and for Latinos, 30 (NCHS, 1987).

A study conducted by the Alan Guttmacher Institute (based on the Family Growth Surveys) found an increase in sterilizations among 15- to 44-year-old Latino women between 1982 and 1988. The increase was considerably higher for Latino women, compared with non-Latino white women and African American women. For example, in 1982, 23% of Latino women were sterilized. This increased to 32% by 1988. The increase for non-Latino white women was 22% in 1982, and it escalated significantly to 26%. African American women reported the highest percentage of sterilization in both periods and also experienced a significant increase from 30% to 36%.

Two researchers in 1991 used the 1982-1984 HHANES data in their study of reproductive characteristics of Mexican American, mainland Puerto Rican, and Cuban American women. They found that the incidence of hysterectomy and removal of an ovary or ovaries was relatively low in the sample population, with Mexican American women reporting the highest rates of hysterectomy (5.3%) and Puerto Rican and Cuban American women reporting 3.5% and 3.6%, respectively (p. 225). For ovary or ovaries removed, the age-adjusted percentage was relatively higher for Mexican women (3.9%), followed by Puerto Rican (3.2%) and Cuban women (2.3%). For tubal ligations, all Latino women reported higher percentages, with Puerto Ricans reporting during 1982-1984 the highest age-adjusted percentage (23.0%), followed by Cuban America women (15.4%) and Mexican American women (14.8%).

Since the mid-1930s, sterilization has been used extensively as a means of population control in Puerto Rico. By 1982, over 40% of women aged 15 to 49 who were ever married had been sterilized. A group of researchers in 1988 found that female sterilization has increased to 58%, which is very high when compared with 26% for the U.S. population. This practice has resulted in an estimated decline in the crude birth rate by one half since World War II.

Data from household surveys conducted in Hartford, Connecticut; New York City; and Springfield, Massachusetts suggest that the percentage of Puerto Rican women living in the United States who have been sterilized may be higher than that of Puerto Rican women living in Puerto Rico (Schensul, Borrero, Barrera, Backsttrack, & Guarnaccia, 1982; Torres, 1985). Estimates based on these local studies range from 52% in Hartford and 55% in Springfield to 67% in New York, the site with the largest concentration of Puerto Ricans.

It has been argued that Latino women have experienced forced sterilizations in the United States because of language barriers and poor hospital procedures; these surgeries violate the patient's rights (not requesting patient's written permission or not allowing a period of time for patient to change her mind).

Abortion Issues

The 1988 study by the Alan Guttmacher Institute revealed that Latinas represent 8.4% of women aged 15 to 44 but comprise 12.8% of abortion patients. In 1988, the abortion rate for Latinas aged 15 to 44 was considerably higher (43 per 1,000) than that for non-Latino white women (27 per 1,000) but lower than that for African American women (53 per 1,000). For Mexican American women aged 13 to 19, the age-adjusted abortion rates were considerably lower than those of non-Latino white women (1.7 to 4.8, respectively). The percentage was much higher among adolescents who reported being pregnant at some point in their lives.

Some organizations, such as the Chicago Abortion Fund, provide loans to low-income women seeking abortions. Only 11% of the clients of the Chicago Abortion Fund are Latinas, compared with 69% black and 19% white clients. This low percentage of Latino clients may be a reflection of lack of knowledge about the organization in the Latino community, rather than a lower need for services. The goals of the Chicago Abortion Fund include more outreach to Latinos, but presently no resources are available for hiring Spanish-speaking staff (Toni Bond, Executive Director, Chicago Abortion Fund, personal communication, 1995, September).

The incidence of abortion in the Latino community may be higher than reported because of the relative youth of the Latino population, the number of Latinos below the poverty level, the high fertility rates for Latinas and the lack of Latino identifiers included in the data.

Considerable debates have developed regarding Latino women's reproductive attitudes and decisions. Latino women are often expected to be influenced by their partners and religion, particularly the Catholic Church. Although church membership has not been extensively studied for Latinos, the few available studies indicate that Mexican Americans are more likely than Puerto Ricans to be Catholic. One study found that 85% of Latinos in the United States are Catholic and that the remainder belong to various Protestant sects and a few alternative religions (Medina, 1987).

A study of Mexican Americans in Los Angeles investigated attitudes toward motherhood, pregnancy, contraception, abortion, sexuality, and unwanted pregnancy. It was found that Mexican American women make their own reproductive decisions, particularly regarding motherhood, abortion, and contraception. Mexican American women support the use of contraceptives and abortions, especially for health and legal reasons. The findings of this study seem to indicate that lack of use of different contraception methods is more attributable to barriers to services than to religion. Most of the respondents agreed that motherhood was very important, but most did not want to have more children, and almost half said they would be unhappy if they became pregnant again (Amaro, 1988).

Studies have also found that over two thirds of Latino women favor voluntary abortion, particularly if the fetus is abnormal, if the pregnancy endangers the life or the health of the mother, or if it is the result of a rape (Amaro, 1988). Amaro also found that approximately one third of the Latino women studied favored abortion for economic reasons or if the child was unwanted or if the mother was single.

Thus, although Mexican American women are perceived to be conservative in their beliefs against abortion, their attitudes vary, and are determined in part by socioeconomic status, as well as religious beliefs and practices.

In the case of abortion among adolescents, other factors, such as age, marital status, and education, must also be considered. A study of pregnancy resolution among adolescents in New York found that when socioeconomic status was held constant, younger teens (15 years of age or younger) were more likely to abort than the older teens. Adolescents who carried their pregnancies to term were more likely to be married than those who terminated their pregnancies. Among unmarried teens, those least likely to abort were those who were receiving Medicaid and who were in school.

Family relationships also have a strong influence over pregnancy decisions. A prospective study of 43 pregnant Puerto Rican adolescents found that mothers were most influential in the teens' decisions to carry their pregnancies to full term, whereas sisters and boyfriends were more influential in the girls' decisions to abort. Girls who decided to take their pregnancies to term were highly supported by their families and friends even prior to making that decision, compared with girls who decided to terminate their pregnancies. No correlation was found between church affiliation and the decision to have an abortion in this study.

In some cases, cultural factors may come into play in the decision to take a pregnancy to term. The prevailing belief among many Latino families is that where you can feed one child, you can feed two: *"Donde come uno, comen dos."* Children in the Latino culture are highly valued. They are considered a blessing from God. In the case of teen pregnancy, after the crisis of finding out that a teen is pregnant, members of the family usually become available to provide emotional support and/or financial assistance. Sometimes the pregnant teen stays (on a temporary basis) in the home of relatives (e.g., grandparents) until parents resolve their feelings of anger, disappointment, and guilt.

Breast-Feeding

Breast-feeding provides a child with several advantages: (a) immunological protection against infections, (b) protection from iron deficiency, (c) fewer respiratory infections, (d) lower infant mortality rate, and (e) lower childhood medical costs. It also helps develop a baby's immune system, according to the American Academy of Pediatrics, which recommends exclusive breast-feeding for the first 4 months and supplemental nursing for 1 year. Breast-feeding helps fight allergies, asthma, and ear infections and combats bacterial and intestinal disorders; it also rarely causes allergic reactions. Despite these advantages, Latino women are less likely to breast-feed than white women, and when they do, they do so for a shorter period of time (HHC, 1989; Wright, Holberg, Taussing, & the Group Health Medical Associates Pediatricians, 1988). A survey of mothers conducted by Ross Laboratory found that, in 1990, 59% of all white women breast-fed, compared with 25.8% of black women and 51.8% of Latino women.

Latino breast-feeding rates vary by national origin and by region. Combined results from the 1982 National Survey of Family Growth and from the 1982-1984 HHANES indicate that breast-feeding rates vary from 34% to 51% for Mexican American women, 16% to 26% for Puerto Rican women, and 27% to 40% for Cuban women. According to these data, the percentage of children born between 1971 and 1982 who were breast-fed increased for non-Latino children overall and specifically Mexican American and Puerto Rican children. For example, over 50% of non-Latino children born between 1980 and 1982 were breast-fed at some point (53.2% vs. 50.6% for Mexican American children, near one third of Cuban American children, and over one fourth of Puerto Rican children). The percentage of children born between 1980 and 1982 who were breast-fed for 6 months or more was highest among non-Latino and Mexican American children (18% each), compared with 5% and 7% for Cuban American and Puerto Rican children, respectively.

Latinas are viewed as coming from a breast-feeding culture; however, nursing rates begin to decline as immigrants become acculturated. By the third generation, Latinas breast-feed at the same rate as other women in the same socioeconomic group (Stern & Giachello, 1977). For example, two researchers, in their 1991 examination of reproductive characteristics of Latino women in childbearing years, found, by using 1982-1984 HHANES data and after adjusting the data for age, that only 17.2% of Mexican American women who delivered a child in the past 12 months were currently breast-feeding. The percentages were extremely low for Puerto Rican and Cuban women (1.5% and 1.9%, respectively). The literature cites several factors that may influence the likelihood of breast-feeding. These include mother's age, education, marital status, level of acculturation, employment, perceived benefits of bottle-feeding as opposed to breast-feeding for both the mother's and the child's health, nature of the interaction with the physician, and structural characteristics of the health delivery system (HHC, 1989; Stern & Giachello, 1977; Wright et al., 1988).

Findings of the Mother-Infant Research Study in the Mexican community on Chicago's West Side indicate that the majority of recently arrived Mexican women (primarily from rural or small towns in Mexico) who were bottle-feeding their children at the same of the study had breast-fed their babies in Mexico (Stern & Giachello, 1977). Organizational characteristics of the medical care system were, according to the authors, responsible for the decision to bottle-feed an infant. This decision was made because of the standard hospital procedures that require relatively long periods of time before mother and infant are reunited after delivery. During this time, the staff often bottle-feed the infant, at times without the mother's consent. Language barriers worsen the situation and/or limit the communication that takes place between patient and health care provider regarding mother's intentions about breast feeding. Furthermore, hospital settings have not been instrumental in teaching and/or encouraging Latino mothers to breast-feed their infants.

ACCESS TO HEALTH CARE

Lack of access to medical care is frequently cited as the single greatest problem that Latinos face in the health care system. Access is an indicator of the ability to obtain medical care for an immediate health need. It is also an indicator of the likelihood of receiving preventive and maintenance health care. Lack of access to the health care system results from financial, cultural, and institutional barriers. Latinos lack access to a broad array of health services, especially primary care. Poor and uninsured Latinos who turn to public facilities for routine care confront a lack of bilingual/bicultural services, long waiting times between calling for an appointment and the actual visit, and long waits once they get there. These barriers contribute to their disproportionate use of more costly services, such as hospital emergency rooms, when symptoms of illness persist or when the illness has reached an advanced stage. Access to inpatient care is also a problem in many cities, such as Chicago, where during the past several years as many as 14 community hospitals serving low-income areas and providing charitable care to the poor have closed. There are several indicators of access: (a) whether or not a person has a regular source of care, (b) health insurance coverage/financial barriers, (c) inconveniences in obtaining care, and (d) the actual use of medical services. Research findings on these areas are briefly elaborated below.

The phrase *regular source of care* refers to an established and identifiable facility or medical source that an individual or a family uses on a routine basis. Having a regular source of care is a good indicator of health services use because it facilitates entry into the system and the continuity and quality of care. Studies consistently document that Latinos are less likely than any other group to be linked to a regular source of care. This is particularly true among those with low family income.

The situation appears to be worsening among Latinos. A 1986 national survey conducted by Lou Harris and Associates found that the percentage of Latinos without a regular source of care was almost double that for whites (30% vs. 16%). Furthermore, the percentage of Latinos without a regular source of care almost tripled in 4 years, from 11.8% in 1982 to 30% in 1986.

The 1982-1984 HHANES data show that, within Latino subgroups, the proportion of those having a regular source of care varies by gender and age-group. For instance, only 56% of Mexican American men aged 20 to 30 reported a regular source of care, compared with 69% for those aged 31 to 45 and 78% for those aged 46 to 74. Mexican American women consistently reported higher linkages with a regular source of care (78% for those aged 20 to 30).

Limited Flexibility of the Health Care System

Other inconveniences in obtaining health care for Latinos are related to the fact that the health care system in the United States possesses limited flexibility to meet the needs of populations that are poor or that may have differing illnesses, cultural practices, diets, or languages (U.S. DHHS-HSRA, 1990). Providers' inability to communicate is problematic because they not only do not know the language but also use technical jargon that further confuses the client.

Providers' lack of knowledge and sensitivity about Latino culture and health behavior may also result in a series of stereotypes negatively affecting the provider-consumer relationship. This effect may have implications not only in service delivery but also in patient compliance. For instance, some non-Latino providers may regard Latinos as superstitious, present oriented, uninterested in preventive exams, and noncompliant (Gregory, 1978).

In addition, prejudice and social discrimination against Latinos may maintain and reinforce the social distance between provider and consumer (Aponte & Giachello, 1989; Quesada & Heller, 1977). A mail survey done in Chicago documented providers' knowledge, attitudes, and practices toward Latino patients/clients (Aponte & Giachello, 1989). The study found that more than half of the health care providers who responded to a questionnaire reported not knowing about Latino health status and about the heterogeneity of the Latino population. They also reported not knowing the meaning of the terms *Latinos* and *Hispanics* and how they are used by many Latinos interchangeably. Also, 50% said that Latinos should learn English instead of expecting bilingual services to be provided. Clear differences emerged in this study in levels of knowledge and cultural sensitivity between health care providers serving high numbers of Latino clients as opposed to those serving relatively low numbers of Latinos. Those providers serving few Latino clients showed the least interest in learning about Latino health problems or about how to reach out and serve Latinos.

Language as a Barrier

Much of the literature indicates that language is a major barrier to access and appropriate use of prenatal and obstetrical services. Language becomes a problem when the population to be served is primarily Spanish speaking. Edgerton and Karno (1971) found that language barriers may be linked to other barriers, depending on whether the individual is bilingual or mainly monolingual either in Spanish or English. For example, Latinos who were only Spanish speaking tended to have less education and lower income and tended to be older and more attached to their culture. The inability to speak English fluently has interfered with Latinos' ability to obtain important health information, to communicate with health professionals, and to locate health services available in their community.

Communication and the provider-consumer relationship may be negatively affected by the use of interpreters. Interpreters require a great deal of skill to describe and explain terms, ideas, and processes regarding patient care (Putsch, 1985). Usually, the responsibility for interpretation in a health or mental health facility falls, according to Putsch, to anyone who is bilingual, such as an employee, family members (e.g., child), or friend, usually with no formal interpretation training. This lack of training may lead to inaccuracies, failure to disclose information, violation of confidentiality, and failure of the provider to develop rapport with the patient (but with the interpreter).

The presence of bilingual staff does more than provide translation services. It also promotes a perception of caring about Latinos, opens the way for changes in service delivery that can contribute to better access for Latinos, and improves the quality of service delivery (Giachello, 1985). Understanding a patient's language is the beginning of understanding her or his health and illness beliefs and behavior and facilitates treating the patient as a whole person, and not just as a configuration of disease symptoms.

Even so, a citywide survey of health care providers' perceptions of Latino clients in Chicago found that only 28% of providers made any special efforts to recruit bilingual personnel (Aponte & Giachello, 1989). Nonprofit providers and those located in Latino areas were most likely to make such efforts (47% and 45%, respectively). Of those that did, providers located in Latino areas reported encountering the most difficulty in recruiting such personnel.

Limited provisions are being made in many health facilities that serve a large number of Latinos to establish procedures to handle the case of interpreters. For example, Aponte and Giachello (1989) found that only 40% of health care providers reported having a protocol for dealing with monolingual Spanish-speaking clients. Of those who reported a protocol, close to one third said that the protocol consisted of telling the client to bring her or his own interpreter, and two thirds indicated that an interpreter was available on site. Providers serving primarily Latino clients were least likely to report having any sorts of arrangements for serving their clients who spoke only Spanish.

Health Care Costs

A 1990 study based on the 1982-1984 HHANES data examined specific barriers that Mexican Americans experience in using medical services. Cost of health care emerged as the number one factor, mentioned by 18% of the sample. Similarly, Andersen, Giachello, and Aday (1986) found in their national survey on access to health care that Latinos and African Americans in 1982 had more difficulty than whites in getting medical care because of financial reasons; similar findings were obtained by Garcia et al. (1985).

Analyses of the problem have indicated that lack of insurance among Latinos is related to employment status, type of industry, and income (GAO, 1992). A report issued by the General Accounting Office on Hispanic access to health care indicated that one third of Latinos (more than 6 million persons) were uninsured during all or part of 1989, compared with 19% of African Americans and 12% of whites (GAO, 1992). This report indicated that 78% of Latino family members under age 65 who were uninsured lived in families with an adult worker (p. 12). It also indicated that uninsured Latinos were more likely than whites and African Americans to work in industries that are less likely to provide health insurance coverage, such as construction and agriculture. Because health insurance coverage decreases with income, working Latinos with low incomes, particularly those below the poverty level, were much more likely to be uninsured than those with higher incomes. This finding is particularly true among Latino males with lower incomes. They were twice as likely to be uninsured (64% vs. 30%), compared with Latino males with higher incomes.

Research on uninsured Latinos by gender also indicates differences in coverage among subpopulations. For instance, the 1982-1984 HHANES found that 34% of Mexican American males in the study reported no health insurance, compared with 28% for Cuban American males and 30% for Puerto Rican males. The percentages for Latino women were 34% for Mexican American, 25% for Cuban American, and 17% for Puerto Rican.

The problem of insurance coverage is even more severe among Latino children and adolescents. Two researchers in 1989 found that, in Chicago, 38% of Mexican American children and adolescents were uninsured. Mexican adolescents experienced the greatest disadvantage, with over half of 18- to 19-year-olds (56%) uninsured. Even in a more affluent Latino community, such as that of the Minneapolis-St. Paul metropolitan area, a 1990 telephone survey among Latinos found that only 27% of adolescents aged 16 to 21 had insurance (Giachello & Arrom, 1990).

Studies on type of health insurance coverage have found differences among racial and ethnic groups and among Latinos of various national origins. A group of researchers in 1991, using data from the 1989 Current Population Survey, found that Mexican Americans (43.7%) and Puerto Ricans (43.6%), followed closely by African Americans (45.4%), were least likely to have private health insurance. Furthermore, Puerto Ricans were most likely of all racial and ethnic groups to report Medicaid coverage (32.5%), followed by African Americans (23.3%), compared with Mexican Americans (13.7%), Cuban Americans (11.9%), and compared with the total U.S. population (8.3%).

One explanation for the high percentage of Puerto Ricans on Medicaid programs is that a high proportion of Puerto Rican poor families are female-headed households and thus are more likely to be eligible for Medicaid coverage. This eligibility is because many states exclude two-parent families from the Medicaid program regardless of whether they meet the income requirements. Another explanation is the difference in Medicaid eligibility criteria across states. Texas and Florida, where 3 of every 10 Latinos live in the United States, are the most restrictive states; New York and New Jersey, where Puerto Ricans are mostly concentrated, are not (GAO, 1992). Furthermore, Arizona and New Mexico do not have a medically needy program (GAO, 1992).

The National Coalition of Hispanic Health and Human Service Organizations explored in detail the Medicaid programs of seven states: Arizona, California, Florida, Illinois, New Jersey, New York, and Texas. The Latino population in these states comprise 84.4% of the total Latino population in the United States. The survey found that the percentage of Latino Medicaid recipients varies by state, ranging from 0.4% in Florida to 33.7% in Texas. It also revealed that almost two of every three Latinos (65%) below age 65 and under the poverty level and not covered by private insurance coverage were not covered by Medicaid, compared with 36% of whites. For those covered, the per capita spending under the Medicaid program for a group of preventive care and acute illness services in all the states except New York and New Jersey was lower for Latinos than for whites.

Medicaid has not been a solution to the lack of insurance for all poor people, particularly Latinos and African Americans below the poverty level. Furthermore, studies show that health care providers are least likely to accept Latino patients with Medicaid than with Medicare. Providers located in Latino barrios and with at least 50% of Latino clients were the ones most likely to accept Latinos with Medicaid coverage (Aponte & Giachello, 1989).

Having insurance coverage, however, does not ensure equal access because of (a) inequities in benefits packages, (b) providers' discretion in deciding which health insurance company to accept, and (c) increased search costs due to private cost-containment efforts (e.g., deductibles, copayments). Latinos appear particularly vulnerable to these weaknesses in the current system of financing medical care.

The relationship between health insurance and use of services has been documented. Using data from the HHANES, a group of researchers in 1991 found that lack of health insurance reduces an individual's access to health care; a high proportion of the uninsured did not have a regular source of medical care, had not consulted a physician in the past year, and never had a routine medical examination, compared with the insured. Latinos with only Medicaid coverage were most likely to report a physician visit within the year, followed by those with Medicare and other public insurance programs. In 1989, Medicaid coverage was associated with an increase in the probability of hospital admission for Mexican Americans.

Finally, even the presence of insurance (public or private) may not provide adequate coverage for the needs of Latinos. More than half of private health insurance plans do not cover pre- or postnatal care, both critical time periods for ensuring a child's future health. Of employment-based insurance plans, only 9% cover preventive care, 15% cover eyeglasses, and 32% cover dental care. Similar inadequacies are also found in public programs.

SUMMARY

It is clear that Latino women are experiencing serious health problems and that access to health care continues to be difficult for this population. They are experiencing a chronic lack of access to health care because of financial, cultural, and institutional barriers. Linkages with regular sources of medical care are limited, and differences exist in the sources, patterns, and quality of health care received by Latinos. There is also shortage of bilingual and bicultural health professionals, combined with drastic cuts in health and human services programs.

These problems are occurring at a time when Latino women's medical needs are becoming greater. Latinos with the worst health status and with poor access live in communities that are experiencing a series of health and social problems, such as family violence, crime and gang activities, and high school dropouts. A strong association appears to exist between poor health and poverty, both of which are the result of institutional racism, classism, and discrimination.

RECOMMENDATIONS

This chapter provided a review of the literature on Latino women's health. What follows are a series of recommendations for public policy formulation, for program planning and implementation, and for future research.

1. *It is critical that health care providers and policymakers give the proper attention to the special health needs of Latino women.* In doing so, it is necessary to take into consideration the tremendous diversity of the Latino women population in terms of national origin, age, socioeconomic status, levels of education, assimilation and acculturation into the mainstream society, and regional areas. Health care providers and policymakers must expand the network of Latino health professionals who are consulted on health and human services matters to include representatives

from the different Latino women's health and social organizations and representatives of women of different Latino groups (e.g., Mexican Americans, Puerto Ricans, Cubans) and from different regions of the country.

2. *There is a need is for long-term institutional/structural changes to deal effectively with the health problems of Latino women.* Social changes must occur in society to minimize poverty and to improve levels of education and income among Latinos. For example, the health needs of Latino women cannot be adequately addressed unless the social and economic problems that women confront in society are addressed.

3. *More research and data are needed on Latino women.* Despite an increase of data on Latino women, tremendous gaps exist. For example, no recent data are available on health services use. Insufficient data are available on their health status regarding certain health problems and on health services use patterns. Practically no information is available on the health status of women from Central or South America; yet, this group is the fastest growing Hispanic population. Limited data are available on Latino life expectancy and on socioeconomics, life, and environmental factors that affect their health. More research is needed on the following:

- *Health and mental status of Latino women.* More data are needed on acute and chronic conditions (e.g., gestational diabetes, sexually transmitted diseases), pre- and postpartum depressions, attitudes toward pregnancy and birth, factors responsible for medical high-risk designations, and the long-term physical and mental health effects of bearing many children.

- *The lifestyle practices or personal health habits of Latino women, adolescents, and adults.* The limited data that exist are primarily in the areas of smoking, alcohol consumption, and selected nutritional habits.

- *Factors related to access to medical care.* Aspects that must be examined are financial barriers (e.g., cost of services, health insurance coverage, type of insurance—private as opposed to government sponsored), characteristics of the regular source of health care (e.g., private vs. public), and inconveniences of health care (e.g., clinic hours, appointment system, staff composition).

- *Sociocultural factors, including health beliefs and behaviors and their effects on health outcomes.* Elements of the culture have positive impacts on pregnancy outcome. These elements should be studied, and programs should be developed that can transfer these elements to other at-risk populations.

- *Programs that can educate Latino adolescents of both sexes about issues of sexuality; family planning methods, including abstinence; and the social and medical implications of teen pregnancy.* More important, Latino youths, particularly females, need assistance to increase their communication skills, decision-making skills, and negotiation skills regarding when, how, and under what circumstances they will become sexually active.

- *Programs at the community level that could provide the necessary support (e.g., mental health, training programs, day care service) and financial assistance to Latino women who are female heads of households to break the cycle of poverty for themselves and their children.*

4. *HIV/AIDS policies and funding must be more responsive to Latino women's needs.* A recent shift in policies occurred at the federal level from primary prevention and education to early intervention and treatment. Although proper attention should be given to these areas, drastic reductions are occurring, and more are expected, aimed at the area of primary prevention (e.g., general awareness campaign, HIV/AIDS education activities). Funds for prevention and education should not be taken away from communities of color. This shift may have negative consequences to the Latino communities that have just begun to be exposed to HIV/ AIDS education and prevention activities. Many Latino women, particularly the poor and migrants or those living in small communities in the Midwest, have not been reached at all. For these populations already lacking access to medical care in general, HIV and AIDS are not a "chronic manageable disease," but a sentence to death.

Prevention and education remain the only effective tools in the fight against AIDS and are an inexpensive and extremely cost-effective way to fight the epidemic. A continuum of care policy is needed. In addition, prevention strategies that go beyond awareness levels have not been implemented. Prevention strategies require more intensive efforts at the community level to develop the infrastructure that will provide clear, unequivocal prevention messages and ensure that resources such as the distribution of condoms, which has proven effective, be expanded.

Congress needs to legislate and to recommend that federal agencies develop programmatic means that will minimize the competition for funding among groups at high risk for AIDS. The way the distribution of funds currently works, groups are forced to compete with one another for limited resources—for example, gay/bisexual groups competing for funds against racial/ethnic minorities.

5. *We need to increase Latino women's representation at the federal level.* This is particularly necessary in key administrative and policy-making positions addressing the needs of children and adolescents. A report from the Hispanic Health Policy Summit in 1992 indicates that

Hispanics account for less than 3% of all employees in the federal government workforce. Among federal health professionals with doctoral degrees, Hispanics comprise less than 2% of employees. Of those federal health professionals in the U.S. DHHS who manage significant departmental budgets, Latinos constitute less than 1%. Evidence suggests that the Latino workforce in the federal government is declining.

6. *In the area of alcohol and substance abuse, there is a need for more drug treatment programs for Latino women addicted to drugs.* Practically no culturally appropriate and affordable programs are available for female adolescents and adult women dependent on alcohol and other drugs. The need is to strongly advocate for more treatment slots for women with alcohol and drug addiction who are pregnant. These women tend to be excluded from drug treatment programs. Arguments used are that these programs do not have birth centers and cannot handle complications that require neonatal care. The need is to make provision for the comprehensive care and services delivery for the growing number of drug-addicted Latino women and their babies.

Public health and social policies that promote the prosecution of women who use alcohol and drugs during pregnancy should be reexamined. A series of legal and ethical controversies has emerged regarding alcohol and drug use during pregnancy. Debate has been increasing on whether women who use drugs during pregnancy should be criminally prosecuted for their conduct. Criminalization of drug use during pregnancy may lead pregnant Latino women who are drug users to either delay their entry into the medical care system or not use the system at all for prenatal care because of fears of prosecution or of removal of the child after she or he is born. These actions would serve neither the baby's nor the mother's health.

It is imperative that the war against drugs, as well as any antidrug strategic plans, incorporate and bring for public discussion ways of minimizing and/or ultimately eliminating the abuse of legal (alcohol) and illegal drugs in the United States. The federal government should establish tough measures to keep the alcohol and tobacco industries away from Latino women, children, and youths.

It is important that state and local governments and the public recognize the direct relationship between HIV/AIDS and substance abuse. Funding should be made available for community-based organizations to develop the proper strategies for dealing effectively with this problem.

REFERENCES

Amaro, H. (1988). Women in the Mexican-American community: Religion, culture, and reproductive attitudes and experiences. *Journal of Community Psychology, 16,* 6-20.

American Cancer Society (ACS). (1991). *Cancer facts and figures for minority Americans.* New York: Author.

American Diabetes Association. (1991). *Diabetes, 1991 vital statistics.* McLean, VA: Author.

Andersen, R. M., Giachello, A. L., & Aday, L. A. (1986). Access of Hispanics to health care and cuts in services: A state-of-the-art overview. *Public Health Reports, 101,* 238-252.

Aponte, R., & Giachello, A. L. (1989). *Health care provider's knowledge, attitude, and practices in reference to Hispanics in Chicago: Analyses of a 1988 citywide survey.* Chicago: Hispanic Health Alliance.

Arrendondo, R., Weddige, R. L., Justice, C. L., & Fitz, J. (1987). Alcoholism in Mexican-Americans: Intervention and treatment. *Hospital Community Psychiatry, 138,* 180-183.

Arrom, J. (1993, March). *Issues of research and data regarding Hispanics/Latinos in the Midwest.* Paper presented at the Surgeon General's Regional Meeting on Hispanic/Latino Health, Chicago.

Baca Zinn, M. (1989). Problems of inequality: Race and ethnicity. In D. Stanley & M. Baca (Eds.), *Social problems* (4th ed.). Needham Heights, MA: Allyn & Bacon.

Bracho de Carpio, A., Carpio-Cedraro, F., & Anderson, L. (1993, September). *Latino female poverty and HIV prevention: An overspoken and undeveloped link.* Paper presented at the UCLA Research Conference, Los Angeles.

Caetano, R. (1983). Drinking patterns and alcohol problems among Hispanics in the United States: A review. *Drug and Alcohol Dependence, 12,* 37-59.

Centers for Disease Control and Prevention (CDC). (1990). *HIV/AIDS surveillance report: U.S. AIDS cases reported through June 1990.* Washington, DC: U.S. DHHS, Public Health Service, Center for Infectious Diseases, Division of HIV/AIDS.

Centers for Disease Control and Prevention (CDC). (1991, May). *HIV AIDS surveillance report: U.S. AIDS cases reported through April 1991.* Washington, DC: U.S. DHHS, Public Health Service, Center for Infectious Diseases, Division of HIV/AIDS.

Chesney, A., Thompson, B., Guevara, A., Vela, A., & Schottstasedt, M. (1980). Mexican-American folk medicine: Implications for the family physician. *Journal of Family Practice, 11,* 567-574.

Christian, C. M., Zobeck, T. S., & Martin, H. J. (1985). *Self-reported drinking behavior among Mexican-Americans: Some preliminary findings.* U.S. Public Health Conference on Records and Statistics.

Clark, M. (1959). *Health in the Mexican-American culture.* Berkeley: University of California Press.

Cooper, R., Steinhauer, M., Miller, W., David, R., & Schatzkin, A. (1981). Racism, society, and disease: An exploration of the social and biological mechanisms of differential mortality. *International Journal of Health Services, 11*(3), 389-414.

Eager, R. (1985). Epidemiology and clinical factors of *Chlamydia trachomatis* in black, Hispanic, and white adolescents. *Western Journal of Medicine, 143,* 457-462.

Edgerton, R. B., & Karno, M. (1969). Mexican-American bilingualism and the perception of mental illness. *Archives of General Psychiatry, 40,* 286-290.

Edgerton, R. B., & Karno, M. (1971). Mexican-American bilingualism and the perception of mental illness. *Archives of General Psychiatry, 24*(3), 286-290.

Ferguson, T. (1979). Social support systems as self-care. *Medical Self-Care, 7,* 80.

Friedman, M.J., & Schurr, P. P. (1995). The relationship between trauma, post-traumatic stress disorder, and physical health. In Friedman, M. J., Chaney, D. S., & A. Y. Deutch (Eds.), *Neurobiological and clinical consequences of stress: From natural adaption to PTSD.* (pp. 507-524). Philadelphia: Lippincott-Raven Publishers.

Garcia, R., Salcedo-Gonzalez, I., & Giachello, A. L. (1985). *Access to health care and other social indicators among Hispanics in Chicago.* Chicago: Latino Institute.

General Accounting Office (GAO). (1992, January). *Hispanic access to health care: Significant gaps exist* (GAO/PEMD 92-6). Washington, DC: Government Printing Office.

Giachello, A. L. (1985). Hispanics and health care. In P. Cafferty & W. McCready (Eds.), *Hispanics in the U.S.: The new social agenda.* Brunswick, NJ: Transaction Books.

Giachello, A. L. (1988). *Self-care behavior among Hispanics, blacks, and whites in the United States: Analysis of national data.* Unpublished doctoral dissertation, University of Chicago.

Giachello, A. L. (1991, Summer). Women and substance abuse and HIV/AIDS. In *Common Ground.* Chicago: Illinois Prevention Resource Center.

Giachello, A. L. (1994a). Issues of access and use. In C. W. Molina & M. Aguirre-Molina (Eds.), *Latino health in the U.S.: A growing challenge* (pp. 83-111). Washington, DC: American Public Health Association.

Giachello, A. L. (1994b). Maternal/perinatal health issues. In C. W. Molina & M. Aguirre-Molina (Eds.), *Latino health in the U.S.: A growing challenge* (pp. 135-187). Washington, DC: American Public Health Association.

Giachello, A. L., & Arrom, J. O. (1990). *HIV/AIDS knowledge, attitudes, and behaviors among Hispanics in the Minneapolis-St. Paul area: A 1990 needs assessment study.* Chicago: Midwest Hispanic AIDS Coalition.

Gleeney, K., Glassman, S., Cox, S., & Brown, H. (1988). The prevalence of positive test results for *Chlamydia trachomatis* by direct smear from fluorescent antibodies in a South Texas family planning population. *Journal of Reproductive Medicine, 33*(6), 457-462.

Gregory, D. (1978). Transcultural medicine: Treating Hispanic patients. *Behavioral Medicine, 22,* 22-29.

Guiterrez-Ramierz, A., Burciaga Valdez, R., & Carter-Pokras, O. (1994). Cancer among Hispanics. In C. W. Molina & M. Aguirre-Molina (Eds.), *Latino health in the U.S.: A growing challenge.* Washington, DC: American Public Health Association.

Haan, M., Kaplan, G., & Camacho, T. (1987). Poverty and health; Prospective evidence from the Alameda County study. *American Journal of Epidemiology, 125*(6), 989-998.

Hayes-Bautista, D. (1978). Chicano patients and medical practitioners: A sociology of knowledges, paradigms of lay professional interaction. *Social Science and Medicine, 12,* 83-90.

Hispanic Health Council, Inc. (HHC). (1989). *Puertorriquenas: Sociodemographics, health, and reproductive issues among Puerto Rican women in the United States. A fact handbook.* Hartford, CT: Hispanic Health Council, Inc.

HIV/AIDS in New York City [Special issue]. (1991, May). *American Journal of Public Health.*

Holck, S. E., Warren, C. W., Smith, J. C., & Rochat, R. W. (1984). Alcohol consumption among Mexican-American and Anglo women: Results of a survey along the U.S.-Mexican border. *Journal of Studies in Alcohol, 45,* 149-154.

Holmes, K. K., Karon, J. N., & Kreiss, J. (1990). The increasing frequency of hetero-sexually acquired AIDS in the United States. *American Journal of Public Health, 80*(7), 858-863.

Kiev, A. (1968). *Curanderismo: Mexican-American folk psychiatry.* New York: Free Press.

Knowles, L. L., & Prewitt, K. (1970). *Institutional racism in America.* New York: Prentice Hall.

Leigh, W. A. (1994). *The health status of women of color.* A women's health report of the Women's Research and Education Institute.

Madsen, W. (1964). *The Mexican-Americans of South Texas.* New York: Holt, Rinehart & Winston.

Martinez, C., & Martin, H. W. (1966). Folk diseases among urban Mexican-Americans: Etiology, symptoms, and treatment. *Journal of the American Medical Association, 196,* 147-160.

Mata, A., & Jorquez, J. (1988). Mexican-American intravenous drug users' needle-sharing practices and implications for AIDS prevention. *National Institute for Drug Abuse Research Monograph, 88,* 40-58.

Maxwell, B., & Jacobson, M. (1989). *Marketing disease to Hispanics: The selling of alcohol, tobacco, and junk foods.* Washington, DC: Center for Science in the Public Interest.

McCready, W. (1985). *Culture and religion, Hispanics in the US: The new social agenda.* Brunswick, NJ: Transaction Books.

McKenzie, N., Bilofsky, E., & Sharon, L. (1992, Summer). Women and the health care system. *Health/PAC Bulletin,* pp. 30-32.

Medina, C. (1987). Latino culture and sex education. *Sex Information and Education Council of the U.S. Report, 15,* 3.

Miller, S. (1987). Race in the health of America. *Milbank Quarterly, 65* (Supp. 2).

National Association for Perinatal Addiction Research and Education (NAPARE). (1993). *NAPARE Update 1992.* Chicago: Author.

National Center for Health Statistics (NCHS). (1987). Births of Hispanic parentage, 1983 and 1984. *Monthly Vital Statistics Report, 36*(4), 1-19.

National Center for Health Statistics (NCHS). (1995). Advance report of final mortality statistics, 1992. *Monthly Vital Statistics Report 43(6).* Supplement March 22. Hyattsville, MD: Center for Disease Control, National Center for Health Statistics.

National Council of La Raza (NCLR). (1990). Health Promotion Fact Sheet: Hispanic Women's Health Status. Washington, DC: Author.

National Council of La Raza (NCLR). (1993, July). *State of Hispanic America 1993: Toward a Latino anti-poverty agenda.* Washington, DC: Policy Analysis Center, Office of Research, Advocacy, and Legislation.

Novick, L., Glebatis, D., Stricof, R., McCubbin, P. A., Lessner, L, & Berns, D. S. (1991). Newborn seroprevalence study: Methods and results. *American Journal of Public Health, 81*(Suppl.), 15-21.

Perez, R. (1983). Effects of stress, social support, and coping style on adjustment to pregnancy among Hispanic women. *Hispanic Journal of Behavioral Sciences, 5,* 141-161.

Putsch, R. W. III. (1985). Cross-cultural communication: The special case of interpreters in health care. *Journal of the American Medical Association, 254*(20), 3344-3348.

Quesada, G., & Heller, P. (1977). Sociocultural barriers to medical care among Mexican-Americans in Texas: A summary report by the Southwest Medical Sociology Ad Hoc Committee. *Medical Care, 15,* 93-101.

Ramirez, O. (1978, October). *The role of la familia in Chicano mental help seeking: Preliminary research results.* Unpublished paper presented at the Coalition of Spanish Speaking Mental Health Organizations (COSSMHO) National Hispanic Conference on Families, Houston, TX.

Rogler, L. H., Cortes, D. H., & Malgady, R. G. (1991). Acculturation and mental health status among Hispanics: Convergence and new directions for research. *American Psychologist, 46*(6), 585-597.

Rosenbach, M. L., & Butrica, B. (1991, May). *Issues in providing drug treatment services to racial and ethnic minorities.* Paper prepared for the Second Annual Advisory Committee Meeting for the National Institutes of Health, National Institute on Drug Abuse, Center for Drug Abuse Services Research, Tyngsboro, MA.

Rothenberg, P. S. (1992). *Race, class, and gender in the United States.* New York: St. Martin's.

Sandler, A., & Chan, L. (1978). Mexican-American folk belief in a pediatric emergency room. *Medical Care, 16,* 778-784.

Saunders, L. (1954). *Cultural differences and medical care: The case of the Spanish speaking people in the Southwest.* New York: Russell Sage.

Schensul, S., Borrero, M., Barrera, V., Backsttrack, J., & Guarnaccia, P. (1982). A model of fertility control in a Puerto Rican community. *Urban Anthropology, 11,* 81-100.

Selick, R. M., Castro, K. G., & Pappaioanou, M. (1988). Racial/ethnic differences in the risk of AIDS in the United States. *American Journal of Public Health, 78,* 1539-1544.

Sena-Rivera, J. (1979). Extended kinship in the United States: Competing models and the case of la familia Chicana. *Journal of Marriage and the Family, 41,* 121-129.

Smith, P. (1988). Predominantly sexually transmitted diseases among different ages and ethnic groups of indigent sexually active adolescents attending a family practice clinic. *Journal of Adolescent Health Care, 9*(3), 291-295.

Smith, P., Mild, J., & Truman, B. (1991). HIV infection among women entering the New York State correctional system. *American Journal of Public Health, 8,* 35-39.

Stern, G., & Giachello, A. L. (1977, November). *Applied research: The Latino mother-infant project.* Unpublished paper presented at the Annual Meeting of the American Anthropology Association, New York City.

Stricof, R. L., Kennedy, J. T., Nattell, T. C., Weisfuse, I. B., & Novick, L. F. (1991). HIV-seroprevalence for runaway and homeless adolescents. *American Journal of Public Health, 81*(Suppl.), 50-53.

Stricof, R. L., Nattell, T., & Novick, L. F. (1991). HIV seroprevalence in clients of sentinel family planning clinics. *American Journal of Public Health, 81*(Suppl.), 50-53.

Stroup, M., Trevino, F. M., & Trevino, D. (1988). Alcohol consumption patterns among Mexican-American mothers and children from single- and dual-headed households. *American Journal of Public Health, 80*(Suppl.), 36-41.

Treviño, F. M., & Rendón, M. I. (1994). Mental Illness/Mental Health Issues. In Molina, C. W., & M. Aguirre-Molina (Eds.) *Latino health in the U.S.: A growing challenge.* (pp. 447-475). Washington, DC: American Public Health Association.

Trotter, R. T. (1981). Folk remedies as indicators of common illnesses; Examples from the United States-Mexico border. *Journal of Ethnopharmacology, 4,* 207-221.

U.S. Bureau of the Census. (1994). *The Hispanic population in the United States: March, 1993* (Series CPR, No. 455). Washington, DC: Government Printing Office.

U.S. Department of Health and Human Services (U.S. DHHS). (1986). *Report of the Secretary's Task Force on Black and Minority Health: Vol. 3. Chemical dependence and diabetes.* Washington, DC: Government Printing Office.

U.S. Department of Health and Human Services, Health Resources and Services Administration (HRSA). (1990). *Health status of the disadvantaged chartbook 1990* (Publication No. HRSA-HRS-P-DV 902D1). Washington, DC: Government Printing Office.

Ventura, S. (1993, October). *Maternal and infant health characteristics of births to U.S. and foreign-born Hispanic mothers.* Paper presented at the meeting of the American Public Health Association, San Francisco.

Welch, S., Comer, J., & Steinmann, M. (1973). Some social and attitudinal correlates of health care among Mexicans. *Journal of Health and Social Behavior, 14,* 205-213.

Woolhandler, S., Himmelstein, D., Silber, R., Bader, M., Harnly, M., & Jones, A. (1985). Medical care and mortality: Racial differences in preventable deaths. *International Journal of Health Services, 15*(1), 1-11.

Wright, A. L., Holberg, C., Taussig, L. M., & the Group Health Medical Associates Pediatricians. (1988). Infant feeding practices among middle-class Anglos and Hispanics (Part 2). *Pediatrics, 82*(3): 496-503.

6

Redefining Health
in the 21st Century

Marcia Bayne-Smith
Lorna Scott McBarnette

The compendium of chapters in this book is an effort to answer the question, What is the health and mental health status of African American, American Indian and Alaska Native, Asian/Pacific Islander American (A/PIA), and Latino women relative to other members of society? The authors identified those diseases that are the current leading causes of death for the women of their groups. Looking beyond diseases, they also provided discussions of the social, economic, cultural, and political conditions that affect health status. These conditions are shaped by the underlying forces of race, class, gender, and culture. The authors analyzed the ability of these forces to limit the intellectual growth and development of women of color, both of which were shown to negatively affect their health status.[1] Although they do not claim to have explored all the conditions and complexities that determine the health status of women of color, the authors do provide substantive discussions of biological and nonbiological issues specific to the current health and mental health status of their respective groups. They also make careful assessments of the future health-related needs of African American, American Indian and Alaska Native, Asian/Pacific Islander American (A/PIA), and Latino women in the United States.

As a result of the regular interaction of race, gender, class, and culture in U.S. society, the health and mental health status of women of color is now, at the close of the 20th century, about what it was at the beginning of the century, in relative terms. Health care is currently inaccessible and unavailable for many women who continue to die in disproportionate numbers, compared with white women, from cancer, heart disease, and diabetes. The health industry, an institution in U.S. society, continues to rest on the biomedical model, which is designed to recognize and treat only disease, not illness. It is also designed to allow access in various degrees and measures on the basis of one's ability to pay.

The authors expressed concern about the level of stress in women's lives. Much of that stress is generated by conditions of poverty and its effects on their family structure and on family relationships, both between men and women and between parents and children. For some women, cultural norms make it more difficult to deal with domestic violence and other abusive behaviors from the men in their lives. The intensity of these different kinds of stressors was seen to be a leading cause of depression, substance abuse, and for some women of color, suicide.

At this period in the evolution of health service delivery in the United States, it must be acknowledged that the biomedical model led the way to an impressive array of technological advancements that cure diseases and save lives. Given the nature of the ills that now plague humanity, however, another approach is needed that is suited to the more challenging tasks of teaching and helping the various segments of the population to engage in behaviors that will prevent the onset of life-threatening diseases. The biomedical model has proved incapable of changing behavior, which is the key to prevention and improved health status for all people. In fact, it is now apparent that behavioral change on the part of patients is inextricably bound up with the behavior of physicians. This dual behavioral change is central to prevention efforts and improvement in health status for women of color.

HEALTH REDEFINED

Significant and sustainable improvement in the health status of women of color requires the development of new paradigms that expand or redefine the concept of health in order to encompass many of the currently ignored essential elements of well-being. Good health status, as a product, is best defined as the result of various kinds of investments in the total person as part of a group or family. The preceding chapters clearly demonstrated that the health and mental health of women of color must be viewed as part of a larger system. The health status of women of color cannot be separated from their roles as wives, mothers, grandmothers, daughters, sisters, employees, and so on. Neither can their health status be separated from the larger systems of culture and social structures that exist in society, such as work, education, health care services, religion, family structure, the economy, and housing. It is fitting that the dominant culture call on women of color to take responsibility for changing their health status. It is also necessary that the dominant culture acknowledge and work to correct the social structural and psychological conditions that contribute to their poverty and the lack of access to health care, which is often the result of their race, gender, class, and culture.

The mainstream has made halting efforts to do that. In recent years, federal and state agencies have come to recognize violence, as well as occupational and environmental conditions of work and living, as health care issues. The result has been an acceptance of the idea that a variety of factors contribute to health status. It is important to note that when the dimensions of health are expanded, health status is seen as the sum of a whole, a complex system in which race, gender, class, and culture play very important parts. Poor people of color are much more likely than whites to (a) live in substandard housing or, if middle class, in segregated communities with a dearth of health care providers, (b) work in hazardous occupations, and (c) live in communities where the concerns about health issues are as diverse as the level of violence and the environmental quality. When discussions in the preceding chapters are placed within the context of an expanded framework of health, it would appear that social and cultural influences are equally as strong as genetic inheritance in determining health status. At the very least, these chapters suggest that the interaction of genetic inheritance, the social conditions under which people live, and the psychological and cultural influences in their lives determines health status.

The development of a more comprehensive definition of health is as crucial for women of color as it is for the health care industry. Beginning with the latter, the U.S. health care delivery system was originally designed by and for members of the dominant culture to address the large-scale acute epidemics present in the beginning of the 20th century. At this juncture in history, outbreaks of diseases once thought to be conquered continue to flare up sporadically. There is also no way of anticipating what other kinds of chemical, viral, or germ outbreaks could possibly occur in the future. As a result, only in the last decade has the industry begun to make what seems like a reasonably logical and necessary transition from delivering acute care to providing primary care services.

As with most transitions, the industry is now experiencing some difficulties. First, this transition dictates the need for the United States to produce more primary care physicians, but primary care is still not considered a preferred area of specialization by most medical students or by the professors who not only train them but steer them toward the more lucrative concentrations. Second, although the health care industry appears to be in the process of transforming itself from a predominantly acute care focus to a focus on primary care, it continues to rely on a biomedical model that is not well suited to delivering primary care services with an emphasis on prevention. Finally, the industry is experiencing a developmental lag in terms of promoting the use of other approaches. For example, the biopsychosocial model is used by some primary care physicians for delivering care. However, it is estimated that probably only 1% of physicians who did not specialize in primary care use this or any model other than the Western medical model.[2]

Expansion of the definition of health and the framework for delivering health services is as vital for women of color as it is for the health care industry. In each chapter, it is demonstrated that the culturally and psychologically conditioned perceptions of health and health-seeking behavior of the women being described are different from that of the mainstream, and so there is not always a "goodness of fit" between their needs and the Western medical model for various reasons. First, in many non-Western cultures in the United States, where other options of treatment exist, health-seeking behavior does not move in a linear way from symptoms of illness to consultation with a physician. In fact, after attempts to self-diagnose and self-treat are unsuccessful, discussions are held with family members and other trusted persons about where or from whom treatment should be sought, how long one remains in care, how health problems are communicated and symptoms are presented to different types of healers, and what criteria are used to evaluate the effectiveness of care.

Second, the technological success of Western medicine notwithstanding, the use of folk medicine and alternative healers is preferred by many cultures in the United States because of a deep-seated mistrust of Western medicine. This mistrust by people of color is not unfounded; indeed, it is justifiable behavior because to do otherwise would be to entertain the possibility of fatal results. A case in point is the longitudinal Tuskegee study in which black men in Tuskegee, Alabama, were diagnosed but left untreated with syphilis in order that medical science could observe the progression of the disease in human beings. The study subjects were provided with placebos and left untreated without their knowledge. They were not provided with accurate information and were not given any treatment (American Medical Association [AMA], 1994).

But prior to Tuskegee were the eugenicists, whose roots were in Darwinism. Eugenicists claimed scientific objectivity and used quantitative methodology to "prove" claims based on their racist and class biased thinking. With support from private foundations for their research, they claimed that society (read, white-educated-successful) needed to protect itself from the propagation of the inferior. Eugenics offered an alternative in the United States at the beginning of the 20th century to the costs of the incarceration, housing, feeding, or eventual execution of those considered to be expendable. The eugenicists slowly converted their beliefs into public policy during the legislative campaigns of the 1920s when compulsory sterilization became law in 32 states. The result was that, between 1907 and 1945, more than 45,000 persons in the United States were involuntarily sterilized. Compulsory sterilization laws are still part of the statutes of many states (Hartmann, 1987; Petchesky, 1990). Without question, the thrust of involuntary sterilization was an outright attack on the lives of poor, unskilled, unemployed Americans, many of whom were women of color. That attack continues and is very much in use, whether it takes the shape of mandatory sterilization, Norplant birth control implants, or other forms of controlling the reproduction of the poor, many of whom are women of color. Also of significant note is the fact that the work of eugenicists and the projects that carried out the sterilization of women of color were funded for decades by large sums of both public and private money in the United States.

Finally, it is important for mainstream providers to recognize that whenever health care services are delivered cross-culturally, sensitivity to race, gender, class, and culture is essential. Because most mainstream health delivery agencies and the professionals who staff them rarely know enough about the people they are serving, they are usually not in a position to deliver culturally sensitive and acceptable services. At the very least, Western-trained physicians must be aware that whether they accept or reject their patients' cultures, the likelihood is great that the patient and the family may already be actively involved in healing rituals and ceremonies with their own traditional healers, which exist in every non-Western community in the United States. To improve the health status of women of color, providers must also be willing to involve spouses, parents, and extended family members if necessary, because many cultures perceive individual poor health as a family problem requiring that health care decisions be made by a family network. These steps will bring the mainstream closer to reaching those patients considered to be "hard to reach" and to bridging the chasm or lack of fit between the health care needs of women of color and the service delivery system.

A majority of the health service delivery agencies are culturally incompetent to meet the needs of those members of the population who are different. And probably no other group embodies difference more than women of color, by virtue of not only their gender but also their race and, in many instances, their social and economic class. And, as they get older, ageism also becomes a factor. So, at every point along the continuum of the life span, women of color have had to deal with one form of health-related problem or another that directly flows from their race, class, and gender. At the same time, they have suffered psychological assaults on their self-image, self-esteem, and family structure. When taken together, all of these factors contribute to poor health and mental health status for women of color.

Therefore, it is time to begin expanding the definition of health. It is a necessary first step to moving away from the arrogant insistence that all creation fits into the biomedical model. The understanding that good health is the result of a whole system of well-being leads to another level of awareness—namely, that as with all systems, when difficulty arises in one component of the system, corresponding difficulties will arise in other parts of that system. With this understanding of what constitutes good health, it is strongly suggested that the approach to improving the health status of women of color in the United States have two foci: health reform and improved socioeconomic status for women in general.

HEALTH CARE REFORM AND THE HEALTH STATUS OF WOMEN OF COLOR

At the start of the Clinton administration, some serious intent was apparent in the struggle with the question of how best to reform the health care industry toward the goal of a government-operated, single-payor program with universal coverage and universal access. The outrageous maneuvers and opposition tactics mounted by the health care industry and their lobbyists successfully removed health care from the top of the nation's list of legislative priorities. During the heat of the health care debates of 1993-1994, the opposition argued that Medicaid as a public-sponsored health insurance program is available to meet the health care needs of the indigent and that therefore massive reform of the system was unnecessary.

The negative health status of poor women of color indicates that Medicaid has not accomplished this. Eligibility restrictions for Medicaid make it available only to those in deep poverty; this restriction limits a woman's participation in the workforce and at the same time leaves out all of the working poor. Even when eligibility requirements can be met, the current variation in the Medicaid reimbursement structure from state to state and the voluminous paperwork involved have created such an unattractive program in Medicaid that almost from its inception physicians and hospitals have refused to accept it as health coverage. So, although Medicaid did provide access to health care for some on the very bottom of the economic scale, often the access is to a level of care not of the same quality as that available for those who can afford to pay (Dutton, 1978).

An example of how some states provide inadequate services through Medicaid was demonstrated in the Oregon plan, which was severely criticized for establishing priorities that excluded from Medicaid coverage necessary services for women. Critics labeled the plan a form of rationing of health care that is disproportionately injurious to the state's poorest women and children, many of whom are nonwhite (Reingold, 1991). Since the Oregon plan was proposed, a new Congress has taken up residence in Washington, the mood of the country has changed, and now several other states—New York, Florida, and California, to name three—are well on their way to implementing cutbacks in their public-supported health care programs. A most flagrant example of unequal availability of health resources is found in the case brought before the courts by the Tennessee Medical Association against the state of Tennessee. The Tennessee Medical Association argued that the Tenn/Care Plan, effective since January 1994, set severe limits on the ability of the poor to access a quality of health care equal to that of the rest of Tennessee's population. It must be noted that the residents serviced by the Tenn/Care Plan are the 697,411 Medicaid patients in Tennessee, 230,861 of whom are black ("Tennessee Tragedy," 1994).

Probably, the more harmful problem is that eligibility for Medicaid limits a woman's participation in the workforce; this problem points to the need not only for health reform but also for social and economic reform. In both instances, the new members of Congress appear to have interpreted their election to office as a mandate to drastically and indiscriminately reduce or eliminate service programs that benefit the poor.

With regard to health care reform, serious questions have been raised about the type and amount of change that can be achieved by Capitol Hill (Blendon & Brodie, 1994). While the health care debate in Washington disintegrated into inaction, several states opted not to wait for federal intervention but began making major changes in their health systems, prompted by a combination of market forces, such as the concerns of providers, consumers, government, and corporate America. This process of transformation has been ongoing during the past 15 years and is unlikely to be interrupted by whatever incremental changes come out of Congress during the next few years. This transformation process has yielded a set of fundamental characteristics that appear to be part of the projected shape of the U.S. health care industry in the future.

Despite the existence of several definitions for the terms *managed care* and *managed competition*, their basic structure includes three dimensions:

1. A restructured relationship among physicians, hospitals, and insurance companies in which hospitals and physicians form a provider group, sometimes under a health plan
2. A free market approach based on three fundamental aspects:
   a. The establishment of networks or cooperatives that will purchase group insurance to pay for basic benefits provided by a health plan
   b. Networks that will use three streams of revenue to purchase group insurance:
      (1) Employer/employee premiums with perhaps an 80%/20% premium payment mix, respectively
      (2) Individual premiums
      (3) Government payment of premiums for the unemployed
   c. Health plan provider groups that will submit bids, from which networks will select the best price and quality of care in order to award a contract from an insurance company to the health plan; the health plan provider group will then offer health care to their subscribers
3. Government regulations that will
   a. Mandate every employer to provide a basic benefits package for his or her employees

    b. Require everyone to join a purchasing cooperative, network, or health
       plan
    c. Pay the premiums for the unemployed
    d. Mandate each state to set up an independent review board to determine:
       (1) Basic benefits packages that employers will have to provide
       (2) Costs of packages and limits on health care spending for different
           geographical regions within the state

Proponents of managed care extol its ability to effectively control costs, particularly through the concept of capitation. In awarding contracts to health plans, insurance companies will set a fixed fee per subscriber per month (capitation), payable to the health plan provider group in advance. Capitation offers providers a different kind of incentive from what existed under "fee for service," wherein physicians and hospitals receive fees for every service provided to patients. In that system, revenues are highest when service use is high. In contrast, the incentive of capitation is to provide fewer services because unused funds are distributed among the providers in the group. High use of health services under capitation will mean a loss of revenue for the provider group. When use is low, the group makes money.

A fundamental question must now be asked: How will managed care as the basis of current and proposed changes in the health industry affect women of color, especially poor women? It is not difficult to imagine that a reconfigured and consolidated health care industry may function efficiently in terms of holding costs down but still not produce any improvement in health status for women of color. Managed care or managed competition is projected to accomplish a redistribution of health care personnel into previously underserved communities because both public and private health insurers will service their clients through managed care plans with similar capitation rates. When people of color in the low or middle class have health insurance comparable to that of the mainstream population, that in itself will become a built-in incentive, along with other government mandates, to make it profitable for providers to service poor communities. The mere existence of providers in a community, however, is not synonymous with any guarantees of adequate health care, increased use of available services, greater cultural sensitivity in the delivery of services, increased availability of services, or improvements in the health status of women of color for various reasons.

First, the health industry is without equal in its historical unwillingness to provide gender-appropriate and culturally sensitive services. Second, every indication is that, without uncompromising intervention in medical education, the industry will continue to provide services in the Western tradition without training physicians and other providers to recognize and respect differences in race, class, and culturally conditioned health behaviors and beliefs, as well as issues of gender. Third, physicians of color have expressed concern about being excluded from joining networks and health provider plans. This exclusion is a problem for women of color because although physicians of color have also been trained in the Western tradition, they are sometimes more adept than mainstream health professionals at identifying the effects of race, gender, class, and culture on the health status of women of color. As a result, these physicians are better able to distinguish between the need for biomedical treatment and the need for a referral for social and or support services. Physicians of color are also important to the improved health status of women because they are in a position to influence the diagnosis and treatment decisions of their mainstream colleagues about women of color and therefore influence the quality and acceptability of care that women of color receive. Fourth, but probably most important, is the capitation structure of managed care, which provides incentives to deliver less service. This arrangement becomes extremely dangerous for women of color, whose disproportionately worse health status dictates the need for health services of higher quality than available in the past.

The greatest concern for women of color is the question of how issues such as race and class will play out in a managed care system. Networks servicing a predominantly nonwhite clientele will still be interested in making a profit. For groups with a disproportionately worse health status than whites, however, safeguards must be built in to ensure that access to services will not be limited by the new profit incentives in managed care. If the industry's past performance serves as a predictor, it will be necessary to build accountability and responsibility into managed care systems in order to prevent them from delivering unacceptable, culturally incompatible services of lesser quality to communities of color. Now more than ever, the inclusion of women of color in decision-making and policy positions is vital to the improvement of their health status.

The entire health care industry is at a unique juncture in its history. Some sections of the industry have almost completed the tasks of streamlining as part of the transition from a reliance on acute care to the delivery of primary care. These tasks included acquisitions and mergers between hospitals and joint ventures among health maintenance organizations, physicians, and insurance companies. Medical schools, however, have been slower in their response. Because of recruitment efforts, more women than ever before are in medical schools, but the same attention has not been paid to the recruitment of people of color or people from lower socioeconomic classes. Despite the increase in female medical students, women are still not well represented in the more lucrative specialties, as full professors at medical schools, or in the upper echelons of the administrative hierarchies of the health care industry. The curriculum in medical schools, though changing, is still not designed to influence positive, accepting, and respectful physician behavior toward people whose race, class, and culture are different from that of the physician.

IMPROVED SOCIOECONOMIC AND HEALTH STATUS OF WOMEN OF COLOR

The preceding chapters have discussed how the negative health status of women of color is tied to socioeconomic factors. To improve the health, mental health, and general well-being of women of color, a more meaningful reform would be "overarching" in scope. By this, we do not refer to the current proposals of the new Congress for the kind of welfare reform designed primarily to severely cut back financial assistance to women and children. Rather, what we call for is a national investment in women in general and in women of color in particular. This investment would defeminize the poverty conditions under which they overwhelmingly live. The need is to provide women heads of households with the resources they need to improve their personal, intellectual, and material development and that of their children.

For some time, elected officials, policymakers, and political pundits have been fully aware that many of the social, economic, and political policies of the United States do not help but in fact hurt some of its most vulnerable citizens, who in today's political and economic milieu are the single-parent families headed by women of color (National Commission on Children, 1991, p. 83). Policies such as the current methods by which income is transferred to people on welfare render the people at the bottom, who tend to be disproportionately women of color and their families, economically, socially, and politically dysfunctional.

Edin (1994) points out that the welfare system is based on myths about dependence and self-sufficiency. The dependency myth has led to Aid to Families with Dependent Children (AFDC) payments that are too low to support families; the self-sufficiency myth ignores the fact that many parents in low-wage jobs do not earn enough to support their families. In addition, penalties are built into the current AFDC system for work, marriage, and two-parent families. Infraction of any of these rules usually results in loss of income, security, food stamps, housing subsidies, and health benefits; such results make for a system that does not work. Thus the question we are forced to raise here is, What is the difference between (a) AFDC payments to families not earning enough to support themselves and (b) federal subsidies to major multinational corporations such as Chrysler and Grumman or to Mexico to bail these corporations and nations out of their fiscal crises of the moment? Is the difference purely that of different levels of economic potential and political power? In their book *Regulating the Poor,* Piven and Cloward (1971) cautioned that capitalism demands that there always be low-income laborers to meet the laws of supply and demand. Their point begs the question, Why is it that as structural adjustments took place in the U.S. economy, there was not an even distribution of joblessness, morbidity, mortality and incarceration across all people? Racism has undoubtedly played a role. Admittedly, structural changes in the U.S. economy have had deleterious effects on everyone. Nevertheless, the overwhelming burden of this situation has resulted in an aggressive assault on the family structure, male/female relationships, and the overall health, mental health, and general well-being of women of color. It is safe to assume that almost everyone in the United States concurs that the AFDC system is in need of reform. Welfare reform, however, is inextricably interwoven with other areas of social reform, such as health care reform, the development of low-cost housing, and guaranteed employment. A fundamental question must be how and why AFDC became a necessity for so many people, particularly people of color, in the United States.

A clear example of how the lives of politically impotent people are affected by bad policy is found in the teen pregnancy polemic. Elected officials, policymakers, and political pundits are fully aware, and have been for a while, that the pregnancy rate (pregnancies each year per 1,000 teenagers) is disproportionately high for black teenagers (186 per 1,000). In fact, the rate for white teenagers in the United States (93 per 1,000) is twice as high as that for teenagers in other parts of the world: England and Wales, 45 per 1,000; Canada, 44 per 1,000; France, 43 per 1,000; Sweden, 35 per 1,000; and the Netherlands, 14 per 1,000 (Hacker, 1992, p. 76). It must be noted, however, that governments, schools, and churches in some of those other countries have invested less energy in moral posturing and more effort in the development of social and economic policies that work.

Despite the statistics cited above on teen pregnancy in the United States, threats were made during health care debates by the nation's Roman Catholic bishops that they would flex the considerable political muscle of the Church through their ability to influence the voting habits of parishioners. It is not uncommon during election periods for churches of different denominations to provide their congregations with a suggested list of candidates who, if elected, are likely to vote for legislation in accord with the values and tenets of the church. This legislation, of course, would not include any health reform package that includes coverage for abortions (Steinfels, 1994, p. 1). Most rational minds would agree that abortion is not a solution to teen pregnancy. Most would also agree that the best kind of prevention is abstinence. The numbers previously cited, however, indicate that preaching abstention as an appropriate mechanism for handling teen pregnancy prevention is not effective in all cases; some young people, for a variety of reasons, do not readily hear that message. For those young men and women, other efforts have to be made in their behalf. Although the Church's position on abortion is morally and ethically acceptable to some, it is not acceptable to all young people.

Serious questions must be raised, however, about the Church's refusal to support sex education or contraception. These are much better alternatives than abortion. They provide preventive approaches for unwanted pregnancies and the spread of sexually transmitted diseases for those teens who are not able to hear messages about, or practice, abstinence. Instead, the Church's solution is that abortion be excluded from public health insurance programs, and that any individuals who want abortion coverage be allowed to purchase supplemental insurance policies. It is inconceivable that the Church and elected officials are not cognizant that the costs of this "solution" will be borne only by the poor, who are unable to purchase supplemental health insurance, who tend to have larger families than the middle or upper classes, and who are disproportionately composed of people of color. This kind of policy decision appears intended to deny all poor women, especially those of color, their reproductive rights, because Church officials know that the rich will always be able to buy whatever services they desire.

POLICY RECOMMENDATIONS

As the 21st century approaches, the larger concerns for poor families and families headed by women of color are twofold. First is the need for poor women of color to enhance their capacity for family planning. That must be combined with short-term job training, as well as long-term educational opportunities for initially obtaining and subsequently upgrading their marketable skills.

If poor women are to take advantage of education and job-training opportunities, however, they must have the incentive of equal pay for equal work, health coverage, child care, and welfare reform designed to enable rather than inhibit women. Undoubtedly, the major issue here, as it was at the population conference in Cairo, is the extent to which governments, churches, and societies the world over are willing to empower women in general and women of color in particular (Usdansky, 1994). If improvement in the health, mental health, and general well-being of women of color is a serious goal for the United States, then we offer the following suggestions as an initial outline for policy recommendations that would begin to address the problem.

Social Reform Versus
Welfare or Health Reform

Welfare reform that is not simultaneously accompanied by health and social reform will be ineffective. Cutting off welfare without building opportunities for growth and development will be analogous to the extinction of inner-city communities because they will be left, in some instances, with no other alternative but to implode. In those instances when they explode, however, everyone's life will be affected. Therefore, we suggest an overarching social reform program that will include health and welfare. This social reform must begin with AFDC and be based on a comprehensive set of services available to all families headed by single females, teenagers, and older women, white and nonwhite, especially in poor communities. This means the development of policies to establish community centers, job training, and after-school programs that open up opportunities for involvement, spark the interest of youth, and give them a career direction. Conservatives should note that what is being recommended is social reform that is not race specific or available only to the urban nonwhite poor or rural white poor, but that must be available to all who are living below poverty levels, who are attempting to raise children by themselves, and for whom life has become meaningless.

The social reform services in this program must be designed to provide the kinds of incentives and values that functional families provide for their members. Teenagers who believe that they have a sense of worth, self-respect, purpose, direction, a religious base, plans for the future, and goals to work toward tend to practice contraception if sexually active and are more likely to abstain much longer before becoming sexually active. Health policymakers, elected officials, and their king makers, from liberals to the religious right, would need to take bold steps by first dispensing with their moral and political posturing, racism, sexism, and hypocrisy. They need only consult the numerous scientific studies and other documentation that already exist, covering diverse topics from research studies on the causes of high teen birth rates in the United States to abortion rates, all of which refute any hypocritical posturing and moralizing about teen sexuality. Given the preceding discussions and all that is known about the lifelong negative effects of teen pregnancy, and given the state-of-the-art technology and distinctly American penchant for ingenuity, policymakers have the ability to develop not only socioeconomic but also psychological and emotional profiles of those children most likely to experience teen pregnancy. Anything short of active program planning, development, and implementation targeted toward these youngsters for the purpose of pregnancy prevention is tantamount to criminal activity on the part of government.

Tax Reform for the Poor

Conservatives and liberals alike have devised plans to provide the middle class with tax cuts. In contrast, plans targeting the poor tend to focus on cutting social programs. We propose that in two areas the tax code could be revised to benefit the poor. The first area is the dependent care tax credit, which is unfair because it is not a tax refund; rather, it can only be deducted from taxes owed. The poor do not earn enough money to owe taxes, so those who benefit are primarily middle- and upper-income Americans. For the poor to benefit, both parents must work, and documentation must be provided to show that money was paid for child care. The poor often do not have receipts for child care payments because they have arrangements with caregivers who do not report these payments as income and so are unable to generate receipts.

The second area is the personal exemption tax, which was created in 1948 to level the playing field by limiting the tax burden on families with children. However, it has not kept pace with wages or inflation. In 1948, the median family income was $3,182 and the personal exemption tax was $600 per person, which totaled $2,400 (National Commission on Children, 1991, p. 86) for a family of four and thus reduced their taxable income to $782. The personal exemption tax for 1993 was $2,350, which was increased in 1994 to $2,450.[3] In 1994 dollars, the 1948 personal exemption tax should be worth $9,700 per person and total $38,800 for a family of four. The 1994 median income for a family of four living in New York City is estimated to be approximately $29,879;[4] therefore, a family of four with an income of $30,000 or less would have no tax liability. It would certainly require political courage to propose legislation of this nature because it would represent costs in the billions of dollars in lower tax revenues for the federal government. Courage is needed because the only way to offset those costs would be to begin (and this is just in one area) by closing some of the loopholes in the complex tax laws so that taxes on estates of the wealthy, who currently enjoy a $600,000 tax-free limit that is well beyond the assets of most Americans (Inhaber & Carroll, 1992, p. 170), could be collected.

Work Reform

In a society that defines men primarily by the kind of work they do, the greatest test of manhood is a man's ability to financially provide for his family. Increasingly, women as heads of households who are unable to live up to the mythical societal expectations of gainful employment and self-sufficiency are being put to the same test. In the process, they have begun to experience tremendous stress and loss of self-esteem. We know that, for those who are capable and want to work but are unable to do so because of market forces that are in large measure based on race, their lives are made unhealthy by the very system that then condemns them for not working and for being unhealthy. This catch-22 places most people of color in the United States in a classic double bind.

Therefore, consensus must be achieved in the United States that if society agrees there is great human and personal benefit for mothers to work if they choose, then society must agree on the importance of implementing four pivotal goals:

1. *Provide the training and services needed,* such as health care and day care, for single female heads of households to use training in preparation for employment.

2. *Subsidize jobs* when the private market does not provide enough jobs despite the efforts of many city and state governments to privatize government services.

3. *Conduct studies on how corporate America can begin to transform itself into a more "family friendly" environment,* where the careers and professional advancement of men and women do not suffer because they also have families. This kind of research has become necessary because

Americans believe in the value of family as much as they believe in the value of work, and ways must be found for them to do both.

4. *Address the issue of equity, especially as it relates to race, gender, and economics in the United States.* For more than a decade, reports from the Women's Bureau of the U.S. Department of Labor have documented that the income of women has not kept pace with that of men and that the income of women of color is even farther behind (U.S. Department of Labor, 1993).

The last point requires greater elaboration because of the huge impact of socioeconomic status on the health status of women of color. A recent report (U.S. Department of Labor, 1993) points to a rise in the income of women in general as a percentage of men's income from 66.7% in 1983 to 75.4% in 1992. Talked about less frequently and certainly less loudly is the fact that the incomes of women of color have remained stable and consistently lower in the same 10-year period than everyone else's in the economy. To talk seriously about a male/female earnings gap is to look carefully at who is earning the least, why, and how best to correct that problem.

Statistics from the Women's Bureau indicate that women of color earn less, relative to others in the United States. Several explanations for this finding have been provided by the Department of Labor. Some explanations focus on women's choices of occupations, others on the human capital characteristics of women (educational levels and work experience), compared with those of men of the same race (U.S. Department of Labor, 1993, pp. 3-9).

Gender issues regarding nontraditional women's jobs are mentioned in these explanations, as is sex discrimination. The obvious omission is that of the effects of race or the combined effects of race and gender on income levels and career advancement opportunities.

The Department of Labor provides projections to the year 2005 of the overall labor force participation of women, which is expected to reach 47%, up from the 1990 level of 45%. The fastest growth among women from various ethnic groups entering the labor force is expected to occur among Hispanic, Asian and Pacific Islander, and American Indian and Alaska Native women. It is estimated that an 80% growth in the numbers of women from these ethnic groups in the labor force will occur by the year 2005. The growth rate for black women already in the labor force in large numbers, however, is projected to reach 34%, exceeding the rates for all other women. The Department of Labor's projections also indicate that most of the job growth is expected to be in the service-producing sector, where despite the rhetoric from Democrats and Republicans alike on "less government," governments at the federal, state, and local levels will be the major employers.

Although fewer skills are required for service jobs, earnings are also less. Earnings are usually highest in the top three occupational categories, which also require the highest educational investment: (a) executive, administrative, and managerial; (b) professional specialties; and (c) technicians and related support. Of the three categories, employment will grow fastest for technicians and related support occupations, such as paralegals, data processing equipment repairers, surgical technologists, respiratory therapists, registered nurses, and computer programmers. Many of these jobs do not require a college degree, but they do require some additional training after high school.

When these data projections from the Department of Labor are joined with the ample literature substantiated by sociological and psychological theories that support the benefits of work, U.S. policy directions for improving the health and mental health status of women of color become focused and clear. Some current ideas about reforming the welfare system, especially the focus on moving mothers off AFDC and into the world of work, are not entirely without merit. To those elected officials proposing very short time limits, however, it must be stressed that 2 years is insufficient for undergoing training and obtaining a job that will be adequate to support a family. It would be more realistic and logical for Americans to accept that, in a reconfigured economy, the only way to break the welfare cycle and what is often seen as "dependency" will be legislation that (a) builds in effective training and educational incentives that will equip people to participate in what is now a drastically new and different economy, (b) establishes a system of national day care as some European nations have already done, and (c) requires the government to subsidize workfare for those who would otherwise have to resort to AFDC when jobs are not available in the private sphere. Such legislation will enable marginalized people to participate in the labor force. After a person's job training and entry into the labor market, AFDC supplements should continue, with gradual, realistic reductions as the earned income of women becomes more in tune with their primary living expenses, with a cap of 5 years in the AFDC program. But even this more realistic time frame is too little too late for at least three generations of women of color in the United States whose existence on AFDC has crushed not only their spirits, hopes, and sense of meaning in their lives, but also that of their children and grandchildren.

A New Research Agenda

One last policy recommendation we would make is in the area of research. Any improvement in the health status of women of color should flow from a strong research agenda. To deliver effective preventive health care to all Americans and especially to women of color, the challenge facing the United States and the health industry is how best to bring about behavioral change. As far as women of color are concerned, some of the more pressing research questions facing mainstream providers and health policymakers are, Why do services fail to reach some nonwhite groups? What institutions and media best relate to these groups, and how do certain groups interpret the existing health care information available to them? Probably the most important question, however, is, given the ability of preventive behaviors to improve health status, how can biomedicine expand in order to change behavior? With a future research agenda focused on the questions posed above and on the needs of community, it is hoped that new information will be forthcoming on how best to help people modify their behaviors to prevent disease.

Research from the field of outcomes management provides some documentation that improvements in health status are connected to the roles of both the patient and the physician delivering the care. Some outcomes management research indicates that patient compliance with medical treatment is influenced by physician behavior and characteristics (DiMatteo et al., 1993). To be effective, outcomes research techniques must be incorporated and implemented in every branch and phase of the health care industry, from the board level on down.

We suggest a two-pronged approach to outcomes research in the health care industry. The first is continuous research at the local level for the purpose of making reimbursement contingent on outcomes. The second is ongoing outcomes research that professionally and fiscally holds physicians and health care organizations accountable and responsible for the health of a community. These approaches are expected to produce positive changes in the behaviors of physicians, the health industry, and as a result, the health status of women of color and their communities. A national health research agenda focused on health industry outcomes that are also linked to reimbursement may begin to address the disproportionately worse health status of women of color and their families.

WHERE DO WE GO FROM HERE?

Each of the contributing authors sounded a note of hope about the future and the possibilities for improving the health status of women of color. They discussed the strength and optimism shared by many women of color regarding the possibility of improving their health and mental health. The basis of this optimism is found in some very effective strategies that women of color are using to improve their health status.

African American, American Indian and Alaska Native, Asian/Pacific Islander American (A/PIA), and Latino women are attempting to join their health care needs to their available group knowledge and expertise about the functions of the political and economic structures of American society in an effort to secure better health care services for women of color. As a result, people of color at both the national and local levels are collaborating successfully to influence the industry. Through targeted efforts resulting from organized effort, women of color have begun to encourage their elected officials and health policymakers to be mindful of issues of race, gender, class, culture, and ethnicity. More of this kind of organizing is strongly recommended.

Some women of color have successfully created health care organizations in various parts of the country. Using their intelligence, skills, determination, and persistence, women of color have begun to negotiate with the mainstream to secure better health care. Women of color across the United States have rejected the notion that people who are economically and politically less powerful are unable to influence change in systems, structures, or industries. In a study of health service delivery by ethnic organizations to different immigrant groups in New York City, one author (Bayne-Smith) discussed alternatives to the biomedical model, as well as strategies used by several ethnic health care organizations to obtain economic and political support from the mainstream, a place for their organizations at the health care planning table in New York State, and improved quality and quantity of health services for their communities (Bayne-Smith, in press). Change is undoubtedly taking place, however incrementally, at both local and national levels, spearheaded by women and men of color who are attacking the poor health of their communities in various ways.

The goal of some community-based and national organizations of women of color is to educate people of color on ways to improve their health. Other groups have taken as their goal the challenge to humanize the Western medical model without stripping it of its technological capabilities. Yet, for others, the goal is to move more women of color into positions of policy input so that they can inform the decisions being made about the quality of health care that will be delivered to people of color. These efforts point to probably the most powerful recommendation for women of color about where to go from here, which is that women of color must begin to create connections, networks, and coalitions across social, economic, philosophical, and political lines as a means of securing the kind of health care they need from the health care industry.

As the previous chapters demonstrated, women of color are aware that improvement in their health and mental health status must focus not only on disease but also on a more comprehensive approach that speaks to the whole of their lives. Women of color also recognize that they have to spearhead much of the work that needs to be done. The significance of this recognition is that it signals the timeliness for a new focus of their energies in the next century. Significantly, some women plan to demedicalize some of their health issues and to assume greater responsibility for improving their health, mental health, and general well-being and that of their families. To that end, an initial dialogue has been ongoing among women of color in the United States about a national movement toward the professionalization of women and the defeminization of poverty, both of which will contribute to improving health status. Much of this dialogue is taking place primarily at the grassroots level. The small numbers of women elected to local, state, and national offices are also adding their voices to the discussions. As women talk about improving health care, awareness is growing that they must seize the power to change the system. And they can do so because employees at the lower levels of the health care industry tend to be 90% to 95% women, and a majority of those are women of color.

These various efforts by women on behalf of women, their families, and communities are grounded in the recognition that capitalist economies must create "surplus value." Any investment in improving the health and mental health status of women of color and in providing them with job training helps create a reliable source of labor that, in some instances, will continue to be low income. These people can also contribute to increasing the gross domestic product (GDP) and the accompanying economic profits of corporations in the United States. Therefore, governments, the health industry, and all of corporate America should be willing to share in this investment and to provide workfare and other subsidies, when there are no jobs, to the many families headed by women as a means of protecting the "surplus value" of the nation. It is time for the United States to follow recommendations made at the 1985 Conference on Women's Health:

As a group, minority women suffer disproportionately from socioeconomic disadvantages and discrimination that impact on their health. Many must also overcome ethnocultural barriers in gaining access to the health care system. In addition to sharing these common obstacles, each minority has its special problems and needs. Today, minority women bear a disproportionate share of diseases, homicides, and unintentional injuries. Their special health care needs present an important challenge to persons in all facets and at all levels of the health care system. Becoming aware of and sensitive to the plight of minority women is a crucial first step for policymakers and service providers. There should be a concerted effort to educate both health service providers and consumers about ways to break down ethnocultural barriers. . . . Lastly, there should also be a sincere effort to increase participation by women in all aspects of health care. (U.S. Public Health Service, 1985)

NOTES

1. For a discussion on how the culture, history, and intellect of black people have been altered, disfigured, and made meaningless by others, see Madhubuti (1990, pp. 3-15).

2. Estimate provided by Dr. Peter Frank, Associate Professor of Family Medicine at the University of Rochester.

3. Figures provided by Cynthia Brown Franklin, legal assistant and administrative secretary, law firm of Strook, Strook and Lavan, New York City, April, 1995.

4. Data are from Stafford (1994, Table I, p. 19); projected calculations by M. Bayne-Smith.

REFERENCES

American Medical Association (AMA). (1994). *Culturally competent health care for adolescents: A guide for primary care providers.* Chicago: Author.

Bayne-Smith, M. (in press). Ethnic organizations and the politics of multiculturalism. In J. Stanfield II (Ed.), *Research and social policy,* vol. 4. Greenwich, CN: JAI Press.

Blendon, R. J., & Brodie, M. (1994). *Transforming the system* (Future of the American Health Care Series, Vol. 4). New York: Faulkner & Gray.

Committee on Economic Development. (1987). *Children in need.* Washington, DC: Government Printing Office.

DiMatteo, M. R., Sherbourne, C. D., Hays, R. D., Ordway, L., Kravitz, R. L., McGlynn, E. A., Kaplan, S., & Rogers, W. H. (1993). Physicians' characteristics influence

Dutton, D. (1978). Explaining the low use of health services by the poor: Costs, attitudes, or delivery systems? *American Sociological Review, 43,* 348-367.

Edin, K. (1994). *The myths of dependence and self-sufficiency: Women, welfare, and low-wage work.* Unpublished manuscript. (Available from K. Edin, Department of Sociology, Center for Urban Policy Research, Rutgers University, New Brunswick, NJ 08903)

Hacker, A. (1992). *Two nations, black and white, separate, hostile, unequal.* New York: Ballantine.

Hartmann, B. (1987). *Reproductive rights and wrongs: The global politics of population control and contraceptive choice.* New York: Harper & Row.

Inhaber, H., & Carroll, S. (1992). *How rich is too rich: Income and wealth in America.* New York: Praeger.

Madhubuti, H. R. (1990). *Black men: Obsolete, single, dangerous? The Afrikan American family in transition.* Chicago: Third World Press.

National Commission on Children. (1991). *Beyond rhetoric, a new American agenda for children and families: Final report of the National Commission on Children.* Washington, DC: Government Printing Office.

Petchesky, R. P. (1990). *Abortion and woman's choice.* Boston: Northeastern University Press.

Piven, F. F., & Cloward, R. (1971). *Regulating the poor: The functions of public welfare.* New York: Vintage Books.

Reingold, E. M. (1991, November 25). Oregon's value judgement. *Time,* pp. 32-41.

Stafford, W. (1994). *New York City's black family.* New York: Office of the Borough President of Manhattan.

Steinfels, P. (1994, July 13). Bishops enter health battle with a warning on abortion. *New York Times,* p. 1.

Tennessee tragedy [Editorial]. (1994, July). *Medical Herald, 7,* p. 4.

Usdansky, M. L. (1994, August 31). Birth control, abortion are tough issues. *USA Today,* p. 1.

U.S. Department of Labor, Women's Bureau. (1993, December). *Facts on working women* (No. 93-5). Washington, DC: Author.

U.S. Department of Health and Human Services, U.S. Public Health Service. (1985, May). *Report of the Public Health Service task force on women's health issues: Vol. 2. Women's health.* Washington, DC: Government Printing Office.

Index

About the Editor

Marcia Bayne-Smith is Assistant Professor of Health Education in the Health and Physical Education Department at Queens College, City University of New York (CUNY). Previously, she was Director of Social Work at Parkway Hospital in Forest Hills and later at St. John's Episcopal Hospital in Far Rockaway, New York. She has been actively involved for the past 10 years with the Caribbean Women's Health Association (CWHA), a community-based agency that provides health, social support, and immigration services; she is currently Chair of the board of directors. In addition to her local activities, she consults and provides technical assistance on health policy concerns nationally and internationally, focusing on health and mental health issues of women of color.

About the Contributors

Aida L. Giachello, PhD, is Associate Professor at the Jane Addams College of Social Work, University of Illinois at Chicago. She is also Director of the Midwest Latino Health Research, Training, and Policy Center for Medical Treatment Effectiveness Program (MEDTEP) at the same institution. After her undergraduate work at the University of Puerto Rico, she earned a master's degree from the School of Social Services Administration and a doctorate in medical sociology with a specialty in health and ethnicity at the University of Chicago. As an educator, writer, and expert on Hispanic/Latino health care issues, most of her professional interest, research, and policy work centers on access to medical care, maternal and child health, HIV/AIDS, geriatrics, multicultural issues in health care, and women's health and social issues. Currently, she is initiating studies in the areas of asthma, diabetes, hypertension, and pregnancy outcomes.

Tessie Guillermo, MPH, is Executive Director of the Asian & Pacific Islander American Health Forum (APIAHF), a national health advocacy organization, based in San Francisco, that conducts policy analysis, information dissemination, and technical assistance on a broad range of health concerns for Asians and Pacific Islanders in the United States. Her background is in multicultural community health, including work for 8 years at a community health center in Oakland, California, serving indigent, monolingual Asians. She is active in a number of health organizations that she helped found, including the California Pan Ethnic Health Network, the Asian/Pacific Islander California Action Network, and the Filipino Task Force on AIDS. She also serves on the California

Department of Health Service Task Force on Multicultural Health, as well as on numerous health policy advisory boards on state and federal levels. She has presented and published on minority health policy issues, focusing on access to cultural and linguistically appropriate health care, Asian and Pacific Islander health status, and the lack of adequacy in data collection, analysis, and reporting of A/PI health and health-related data.

Yvette K. Joseph-Fox, MSW, is Executive Director of the National Indian Health Board (NIHB). She was a staff member on the U.S. Senate Committee on Indian Affairs for nearly 8 years. During her tenure, she authored legislation and appropriations affecting American Indian and Alaska Native tribal governments and communities and served on President Clinton's Task Force on Health Care Reform Working Group on Indian Health. Previously, she was an Associate with The Colorado Trust, a private grant-making foundation; an intern with the Colorado Children's Campaign, a statewide child advocate organization; and, for 5 years, Manager for the Colville Confederated Tribe's Alcoholism Program in Washington State. As a leading nonprofit organization to address tribal health issues, the NIHB advocates improved health care delivery among 550 tribal governments, the communities they serve, and the federal government. Its principal office is located in Denver, Colorado.

Jo Ann Kauffman, MPH, is President of her own consulting firm, Kauffman and Associates, Inc., headquartered on the Nez Perce Indian Reservation in Kamiah, Idaho. She moved her firm to the Nez Perce Reservation in 1994 from Washington, DC, where she had been a lobbyist and consultant to American Indian tribes, urban Indian health providers, and other groups nationally for 5 years. Prior to that time, she served for 7 years as Executive Director of the Seattle Indian Health Board, a comprehensive multiservice health program. She has been Executive Director of the Northern Idaho Indian Health Board and has administered both rural and urban health care delivery programs. She was the founding Board President for the National Association for Native American Children of Alcoholics and has served as a board member for organizations concerned with the health and welfare of American Indians.

Audrey F. Manley, MD, MPH, is a physician and health care administrator who has worked in the public health field since 1976. A native of Jackson, Mississippi, she graduated cum laude from Spelman College and earned her MD at from Meharry Medical College. She completed her residency in pediatrics at Cook County Children's Hospital in Chicago, and, in 1962, she became the first African American woman and the youngest person ever to be named Chief Resident of that hospital's 500-bed facility. She holds a Master of Public Health degree from the Johns Hopkins University School of Public Health and Hygiene. She has served on the faculty of the Abraham Lincoln School of Medicine at the University of Illinois, the Pritzker School of Medicine at the University of Chicago, and Emory University School of Medicine in Atlanta, Georgia. She holds honorary doctorate degrees from Spelman College, Tougaloo College, and Meharry Medical College.

Lorna Scott McBarnette, PhD, served on the board of directors of the Center for Women in Government at the State University of New York at Albany (SUNY), which advocates for and prepares women to serve in policy-making positions in government. She served as President of the Center from 1987 to 1990. In 1993, she became Dean of the School of Health Technology and Management at the State University of New York at Stony Brook and played a major role in establishing SUNY's only School of Public Health. She has served as Acting Commissioner of the Health Department of the State of New York and has provided leadership in designing the state's response to the AIDS, tuberculosis, and measles epidemics. She continues to be a vigorous advocate for the concerns of women in preventing infection with HIV. She has received numerous awards and honors from organizations such as the Caribbean Women's Health Association, 100 Black Delta Sigma Theta Sorority, Alpha Kappa Alpha Sorority, and People's Alliance of Community Organizations.

Reiko Homma True, PhD, is Assistant Professor at the University of California at San Francisco, in the Department of Psychiatry. She also serves as Director of Special Projects with San Francisco's Department of Public Health. Previously, she served as Director of Mental Health, Substance Abuse and Forensic Services, for the San Francisco Health Department. She has been active in initiating community-based health and mental health services for Asian American communities in the San Francisco Bay Area and is one of the founding sisters of Asian Community Mental Health Services in Oakland, California. She also has been involved in developing self-help groups for interracially married Asian women and has been instrumental in starting programs to serve Asian immigrants and women abused in domestic violence situations. Most recently, she has been involved in providing psychological disaster assistance to the victims of the Kobe earthquake in Japan.